The Bible
According to Eve

The Bible
According to Eve

The Naviim II: The Seers:
Eve Supplants Lilith

Hadassah Alderson

1603 Capitol Ave., Suite 310 Cheyenne, Wyoming USA 82001
1-888-980-6523 | admin@urlinkpublishing.com

URLink Print and Media is committed to excellence in the publishing industry.

Book design copyright © 2022 by URLink Print and Media. All rights reserved.

Published in the United States of America

Library of Congress Control Number: 2022905128
ISBN 978-1-68486-141-5 (Paperback)
ISBN 978-1-68486-142-2 (Hardback)
ISBN 978-1-68486-143-9 (Digital)

18.11.21

Eve in the Darkness with Lilith
Thorns shall grow up
Nettles and briers in its strongholds
It shall be a home of jackals,
An abode of ostriches.
Wildcats shall meet hyenas,
Goat-demons shall greet each other;
There too the Lilith shall repose
And find herself a resting place.
Isaiah 34:13-34:14

i

Eve faces her man's first love Lilith in
Eve's Spirit Rival forever in Love
for her man loved Lilith before Eve;
for man has loved her spirit; not Eve's flesh.
Yes, Eve and Lilith remain opposed for
They have both become opposites in this:
Eve is the gentle, loving one who yearns
for the man who rules her as chattel slaves
to become different than Master to
his wife among the women he does know.
her ishi rather than her baali as
God promised Israel to become, too.

ii

For God loves Israel but remains Lord;
is there no better way to pray than this?
Is God not better known as "Friend" than "Lord"?
Is it not possible that instead to
call our God "Friend of Abraham," and say
"we elect for God" in our worshipping?
Why is it impossible, as it's said,
to worship without an abasement of
the self in relation to Holiness
or masculinity of womankind.

iii

For surely Holiness is Beloved;
and yet to love God can be done in ways
that express democratic ideals, too.

iv

The ideals of equality of all men
and of all women to all men in rights;
that love does require freedom between two.
As God says "I will Be what I will Be,"
so humankind gives in the freedom of
Love, creating a Tabernacle for
the Modern Jew which replaces the lost;
for Babylonians the first such one
from God's own Temple where it belonged in.

v

Yes, like God, individual humans live
in Becoming, for Goodness or for Ill.

vi

Yet we have Lilith in the corners of
our minds—the evil one who dominates.
She causes men to think ill of their wives;
yet she has power the wives cannot have.
In that last women envy Lilith, too.
She inspires amulets of fear made to
place on the necks of babies protecting
them in their mother's minds from early Death—
brought on by Lilith in the Dark of Night.
She inspires lust in men, who believe she
will tempt men from their mortal wives to clutch
their souls and drag them into Gehenna.

vii

Oh, the cruel torments and the pleasures of
sins creating those ceaseless torments, too!
Yet Lilith plagued the minds of Judaism.
The Dark Wood of the Medieval Jews kept
the mind of humans chained to terrors which
in Modern Times are largely forgotten.

viii

Yet God has promised us in Darkness that
our demons shall be someday exorcised.
For human beings shall reach out to God;
and God will answer them as Father who
loves without sharpness in His rebuke towards
the human supplicant who loves God back.
Our world would not be complete without us.
Our God has whispered this in our ears since
the days He befriended His children both:

priests Abraham and Sarah's followers
and Man and his Eve, and their children, too.

ix

Then Lilith finally will repose, retiring
from her days spent in wicked deeds done towards
the race of men in particular acts
which injure males in legends told by all
by zaydies and by bubbes in the dark.
Yes, Lilith will have a black cat to keep;
a guardian among animals for
the wicked spirit, no mere mortal, whom
Eve could not tame in side of womankind.
She would come out... and did come out... in those
who were deemed monstrous in their desire for
equality among their mortal kin.

x

So "In a Dark Woods" in the Netherworld
the unconscious of wishes deferred is
the wicked Lilith who among her kin
is feared by mortal men and women, too.
Here there be dragons, too; and carpets fly—
yet the depths of the tales will never die.

ISAIAH

The Widow's Lament

I

Uphold the rights of the orphan
Defend the cause of the widow.
Isaiah 1:17

II

I was poor in the land of Egypt
but poorer still in Israel when
the famine of the Lord plagued me and
soon after when my husband had died,
I went to my rich neighbor for food.

III

He told me it was the will of God
that I should suffer starvation with
my children in the promised land while
he and his family ate off plates
carved out of ivory and silver.

IV

I prayed to the Lord YHWH for help
as this rich man gave nothing to me.
One of my sons died because there was
no food in the house for him to eat.

V

When the draught passed I gave my prayers
to Israel's Lord, begging him that
I should not starve with my children
as years passed new moons followed new moons;
while I and my sons and my daughters
will follow men who harvest wheat fields
for wealthy landowners in my land.

A City on a Hill

I

Alas, she has become a harlot,
The faithful city
That was filled with justice,
Where righteous dwelt—
But now murderers...
Your rulers are rogues
And cronies are thieves...
They do not judge the case of the orphan,
And the widow's cause never reaches them.
Isaiah 1:21-23

II

O Lord we have sinned grievously and
yet we find ourselves wondering why
if you love widows and their children
why they are allotted to suffer
and if we give to some poor widow
will the coins we give her last the day?

III

When widows starve why does do you let
the rich man prosper who gives no aid
to her in her state of her starving?
The wealthy man says, 'If I gave than
how would I live with my own children?'
but secretly he counts more money
than he could ever spend by himself—
he is a miser, he twists the arms
of debtors whom he could have spared for
a few more shekels of pure silver.

IV

This man steals when no one is looking;
he takes what does not belong to him.
Your city becomes decadent and
yet if we received punishment would
it not be the case that your chosen—
for surely the Lord's beloved are
those impoverished by His own hand—
will feel the brunt of your wrath first hand.

V

O Lord, do not purge those who love you
for there are wicked people by the hundreds;
we rather would wish that you would spare
the widow while you punish robbers
who have stripped her bare for sale in gold.
Lord forgive us our negligence as
we soften our hearts towards orphans.

The Jerusalem Women

I

The LORD Said
"Because the daughters of Zion
Are so vain
And walk with heads thrown back
With roving eyes,
And with mincing gait,
Making a tinkling with their feet"—
My Lord will bare the pates
Of the daughters of Zion,
The LORD will uncover their heads.
Isaiah 3:16-7

II

Now Jerusalem's wealthy women
dressed brazenly as Egyptian wives
for they were beautiful as bodies;
their lascivious forms which shined in
the rays of sunlight in the noontime.

II

These women's outlines glowed in their gold
the cannibals of the white beams of
the light that came down to the earth from
the heavens reaching far above earth;
they were like Egypt's castaway that
dressed like they wanted to be wives of
the Pharaoh in the land of Egypt.

III

These wives pinched shekels so that they could
have their hair dressed to perfection and
their physical maid's work at home
their lives were those of pleasure—not work.

IV

Their immaculately kept houses
were tended by their servants who could
not read or enjoy their parties with them—
who instead watched them breaking Kosher
in order to eat foods the maids that
would still feel pious scruples despite
those which were delicacies which came
from overseas in places far off
like Egypt or Greek Philistia.

V

So it was that the worshipers of
the luxuries they enjoyed like gods,
kept the Law slovenly at their best.
For these wives, bitter draughts of
sour vinegar now awaited them.

The Finery of Jerusalem's Women

I

In that day, my LORD will strip off the finery of the anklets, the fillets, and the crescents; of the eardrops , the bracelets, and the veils; the turbans, the armlets, and the sashes of the talismans and the amulets: the signet rings and the nose rings; of the festive robes, the mantles and the shawls; the purses, the lace gowns, and the linen verses; and the kerchiefs and the capes.
Isaiah 3:18-24

II

The Jerusalem women of wealth,
the well-to-do wives who wore clothes that
were glamorous, styled with bright gemstones
and jewels to be stripped bare to bones
that, lying naked beneath the flesh,
were dissected as medical schools
cut open cadavers on tables;
for their forms were that encased
in bejeweled and golden nose rings
and festive robes the colors
of peacock's tails as gaily they strut
in multicolored glorious hues.

III

The Lord now proclaimed his wrath at these
bright, spectacular birds with plumage
that exceeded birds of the jungle;
He suggested that this was excess
in luxury for Zion's women
who were to be as decorous in
their attitudes, as serious as they
were modest in their bearings as well.

IV

These women were like ornaments to
their husband's money, expensive though
they were to keep as beautiful wives.
They were like decorated carpets
from Turkey before a great sultan.

V

They vied for men's eyes although married;
just as rugs vied for the great king's eyes.
Lord YHWH was the sultan before
whom these rugs were shown and he judged them
as wanting and as needing to be
thrown on the fires of his wrath because
they had not behaved seemly at all
as Israel's own daughters should have.

The Burning of the Jerusalem Women

I

And then—
Instead of perfume, there shall be rot;
And instead of an apron, a rope;
Instead of a diadem of beaten-work,
A shorn head;
Instead of a rich robe.
A girding of sackcloth
A burn instead of beauty.
Isaiah 3:24

II

The women of the city fell to
the rot of their own destroyed Temple.
Lord YHWH's Temple suffered neglect—
the Temple of God neglected so
the temples of their bodies could be
as worshipped as the Pharaoh was by
the Egyptians whom Israel served
like idolaters serving their gods.

III

Now instead of the Pharaoh, it was
the sin of luxury that enslaved
the women along with the gods of
the Canaanites with whom they were not
to worship as ones espoused to God.
Yet these rich women were stripped of gods
and of their luxuries that they served

and reduced to pulp by Lord YHWH.

IV

Their desires for their fleshly pleasures
was replaced by the death's fear and pain
as the Lord's reckoning came to them
like Moses' burning bush, a wrath that
did consume without leaving a trace
on the bush burning within its midst.

V

These women were like burning bushes;
their souls were on fire although their forms
were wilting with their bodies to ash.
This divine retribution belonged
to them as if they had been chosen
for luxury is abhorrent to
the Lord when it is matched by a lack
of compassion for the poor who lived
around them without food and water.

VI

Their previous grace in their bodies
meant to match their clothes gilded in gold
now burned as sinners they met their fate.

The Sword Falls on Jacob

I

Her men shall fall by the sword,
Her fighting manhood in battle;
And her gates shall lament and mourn
And she shall be emptied,
Shall sit on the ground.
Isaiah 3:25-26

II

On the Eve of the battle God spoke,
"I shall leave you to the fate given
to stoned adulteresses, that is who
in public with the gods you served as
if they were lovers thirsted after
like fine wines saved for festivals which
dealt with the harvests in spring and fall.

III

"The lives of Israel's men shall be
cut short in battle because they fought
on the side of gods besides YHWH—
the Canaanite gods, Asherah and
the Baalim who promised good crops
while YHWH is a great 'Man of War'—
and, angered at this treachery, God
now unsheathed his wrath on the country.

IV

"She—Israel—sinned too long against
her Lord and Abraham's God worshipped
as faithfully by Abraham as
prayed to with hypocrisy by her—
as she lived on the virtue that was
an inheritance of the Fathers,
that included both son and grandson
of Abraham, that's Isaac and his Jacob.

V

Now bleeding from the head she called out,
"My fathers! Protect me from my sins!"
but the wrath of God moved on its way,
for the Lord's hand is steady when it
moves across the land of his people
and Israel mourned her sins towards
the Lord of Israel and Isaac.

Seven Women

I

In that day seven women shall take hold of one man, saying
"We will eat our own food
And wear our own clothes;
Only let us be called your name—
Take away our disgrace!"
Isaiah 4:1

II

In the days following the Lord's wrath
the hand of seven women shall graspped
the altar of the bedroom they share:
Come marry us and save us seven
from the great infamy of harlots,
of women loose in virtue because
they were no virgins when first married
to other men killed in the Lord's war.

III

Yet to save their own reputations
they grasped the remaining men firmly
to regain standing in the country;
to grant sons legitimacy in
the suspicious eyes of their own peers
and themselves—for they doubted themselves
the goodness they were supposed to have.
So they were willing to be married
one man to seven women a piece.

IV

They demanded no money or clothes;
they provided their own homes to
the men who married them for reasons
that hardly mattered to the sevens
of women desperate to preserve
their reputations as women
who were then faithful to God and to
their husbands, living and dead as well.

V

This fulfilled prophecy of
the war brought on by unfaithfulness
of Israel to its Lord YHWH.

The Suffering for the Lord

I

When my Lord has washed away
The filth of the daughters of Zion,
And from Jerusalem's midst
Has rinsed out her infamy—
In a spirit of judgment
And in a spirit of purging—

II

The LORD will create over the whole shine and meeting
place of Mt. Zion clouds by day and smoke with a glow of
flaming fire by night. Indeed, over all the glory shall hang a
canop, which shall serve as a pavilion shade from heat by day
and as a shelter for protection against drenching rain.
Isaiah 4:4-6

III

In cleansing Jerusalem YHWH
would clear the sinners male and female
away from the Earth where they all lived.
These sinful children of Lord YHWH
had committed acts idolatrous
and lustful with their bodies
acts infamous to their Lord YHWH—
and so they have been washed away clean
in their salty tears in death's grip.

IV

The people begged God asking YHWH,
have you not gone too far and destroyed
not just our Temple but our sons and
our daughters, robbing us of sinners—
but also of saints who chose to keep
the cause of the Lord close to their hearts.

V

For indeed, Zion's children stayed firm
and suffered as though for the whole world—
yet cruel death overtook God's children—
they did not deserve such harsh treatment
nor did their ancestors years ago
for their sins were those of most peoples
who lived in their part of the world, too.

VI

Why do you torment your own people?
It is as if you spare least those who
love your name the most while they're living
are tortured with a special grief from
Lord YHWH, a grief hornet's sting with—
the evil spirit sent to King Saul
who groped in the dark for Lord YHWH.

VII

Lord, you should regard Your own people
as faithfully as any people.
For dipped deep in their hearts with love is
a pouring out of pious love to
the Lord of golden promises of
the land of milk and honey combined
with recompense for suffering for
the name of Israel's Lord YHWH—
Lord remember us with your kindness.

The Wild Vineyard

I

Let me sing for my beloved
A song of my lover about his vineyard
My beloved had a vineyard
On a fruitful hill.
He broke the ground, cleared it of stones,
And planted it with choice vines.
He built a watchtower inside it,
He even hewed a wine press in it;
For he hoped it would yield grapes.
Instead it yielded wild grapes.
Isaiah 5:1-4

II

The Lord made Israel his vineyard,
and cared with it as with choice grape vines.
He expected it to love Him back—
'But is this love?' the vines would wonder,
and so they began to fight the Lord
and wild vines outnumbered the tame ones
and cost the Lord grief beyond measure.

III

Soon the whole vineyard revolted and
so the Lord found that He cursed His work—
yet He would not give up his vineyard—
for secretly he loved his vineyard
more than the pliant others outside.

IV

So loved were these vines that they still took
for granted their Lord trying hard to
prune the vines in their vineyard itself—
and they fought back relentlessly.

V

The vineyard was in revolt against
the planter, Israel's Lord YHWH.
Yet there was a spark of love inside
the Vineyard hiding from Lord YHWH.

The Bleeding of the Vineyard

I

"Now, then,
Dwellers of Jerusalem
And men of Judah
You be the judges
Between Me and My vineyard
Why when I hoped yield grapes,
Did it yield wild grapes?"
Isaiah 5:3-4

II

"When can tell what the fruits of our deeds
were when our punishment has increased
and it has been so long since our sins
were committed that only a few
still remember what they were and what
harm was done towards You, Israel's Lord.

III

Yes, instead the Lord's vineyard suffers
far beyond the crimes of its monarchs
and Jerusalem's people as well—
at least those we recorded by
our ancestors those ages ago.

IV

The vineyard within contains ourselves
the Jewish people's essence itself
shrinks under brutal pruning that cuts
through branches slicing us till we bleed.
So damp is our red surface that we
feel polluted as though our women
were perpetually menstruating as
this form of uncleanliness was once
not to come near the scrolls as God's word—
that word which encapsulates YHWH,
as a god speaks through his own scriptures
the words the clothing of the godhead.

V

Yet Jerusalem's blood is said to
cleanse the Lord's vineyard like a body
that's prepared for new life in the womb.
For like the great red heifer women
the Woman is a Holy Vessel
the blood makes menstruating as impure
as the blood renders herself unclean.

VI

Why, O Lord, is the bleeding profuse
and process painful to give birth to
the Vineyard that should have been those years
long ago when forgotten sins were made?

VII

For surely Eve's sin was not so large
it must be passed down generation
to generation as a sentence
too harsh on her poor daughters because
it's Adam's duty to work the fields—
but work is a joy while Eve's burden
is mankind's misogyny itself.

VIII

It is as forgotten why we give
the painful birth from affliction as
our birthing process continues to
take centuries for God to produce
our Messianic Age you promised
in scrolls long ago written because
we as your vineyard strayed from Your law.

IX

This punishment is harsh and more than
we as your bleeding Vineyard can bear.

The Ravished Vines

I

"Now I am going tell you
What I will do to My vineyard
I will remove its hedge
That it may be ravaged;
I will make it desolation;
It shall not be pruned or hoed,
And it shall be overgrown with briers and thistles.
And I will command the clouds
To drop no rain on it.
Isaiah 5:5-6

II

O Lord, why have you done this to us?
Why have you not spared your own people?
Why have you not spared your vineyard?
Are we not called your beloved vines
of whom like gemstone, carved with care we,
bring forth the beauty of the night sky.

III

Do our sins merit punishments that
are as great beyond endurance as
ours has been from the destruction of
the Temple to Spain's expelling Jews
to the cruel Holocaust's great horrors—
a death by which we claim the Lord's Name.

IV

Did your poor Vineyard sin that greatly?
Did she so warrant affliction that
these wretched woes should prune her into
a bonsai tree with pieces lying
on the ground having fallen dead or
clean from the jagged tree's roots and stem?

V

Your vineyard, O Lord, contains only
a few trees left where there were once more;
why have you afflicted us so much?
Why have you become wrathful to clean
out beloved vines leaving the rest
as desolate as funeral trains?

VI

Bring back to life your vines, O YHWH,
for you are beloved of the vines
who long for fulfilled promises that
you made to us when we were young vines.

The Howl of the New Nation

I

Howl!
For the day of the LORD is near;
It shall come like havoc from Shaddai.
Therefore all hands shall grow limp,
And, overcome by terror,
They shall be seized by pangs and throes,
Writhe like a woman in travail.
They shall gaze at each other in horror,
Their faces livid with fright.
Isaiah 13:6-8

II

The day of the LORD has not yet come
as though the pangs of birthing produced
a stillborn in the pain of childbirth;
the unjust pain of womankind in
the case of Israel's young women.

III

The nations pains from birthing have been,
the limited good coming from them
as though a stillborn was born thereof,
thus causing its new mother to weep.

IV

O Lord, when will you grant us that we
shall not be barren anymore or
we'll experience no agony for
our child shall finally have been born,
one squalling with pain and life, grabbing
the new day with hands like red roses,
that are hot like coals in hellfire.

V

Lord YHWH agony comes to us,
and out of agony the nation
gives birth to the great coming age of
the Jewish peace a thousand years long.
Then a great infant's howl will be heard
for the new day in Israel to
start, beginning a reign of Heaven.

The Woman Israel

I

Therefore my loins
Are seized with trembling;
I am gripped by pangs
Like a woman in travail,
Too anguished to hear,
Too frightened to see.
Isaiah 21:3

II

Gripped by pangs, Israel in travail
gives birth to a great unknown something
far in the future wracking the soul
of Israel and causing it pain
as the birth of an age takes place from
years of toil, sorrow and sweat throughout
the persecution of those outside
the faith of the Jews towards the Jews.

III

So it was Israel is herself
a Woman through whom YHWH gives birth
in labor to that great day wherein
Lord YHWH's human plan is realized
for YHWH fulfills plan for us
through us as his sons and daughters.

IV

For Israel and YHWH join to
be parents to all humanity
who still wait for the coming age of
the promised peace and prosperity
of the Lord's Messianic Age when
a baby shall play over the hole
like the one Eve had encountered in
the primal humanity's Garden.
The great wolf will dwell with the small lamb
and a child shall lead them to heaven.

V

So it shall be that Israel shall
be called the beloved of nations
known for the fruits of her own labors.

Tyr Plays the Harlot

I

In that day, Tyre shall remain forgotten for seventy years,
equaling the lifetime of one king. After a lapse of seventy
years, it shall go with Tyre as with the harlot in the ditty:
Take a lyre, go about the town
Harlot long forgotten;
Sweetly play, make much music,
To bring you back to mind.
Isaiah 23: 15-16

II

There's no whore like an old whore, dancing
in the street to be remembered by
the Jews in retrospect as Tyre is.

III

Now Tyre sang itself the old harlot,
to rejoice in her punishment by
Lord YHWH, Israel's lone friend who
loved Israel when no one else did.

IV

For wicked people sometimes rejoice
In receiving their due from YHWH.
For YHWH's absence cuts far deeper
than the lone person without YHWH.
Is it not better, says all children
to receive punishment from the ones
on whom they rely as their parents
than to be left alone by themselves—
with nobody to forgive in love.

The knowledge of Lord YHWH heals all.

Untitled

I

Behold,
The LORD will strip the earth bare,
And lay it waste,
And twist its surface,
And scatter its inhabitants.
Layman and priest shall fare alike;…
Handmaid and mistress…
The earth shall be bare, bare;
It shall be plundered, plundered;
For it is the LORD who spoke the word.
Isaiah 24:1-3

II

My Lord, your decrees come down as harsh
as whips on our backs cutting us up
like ribbons whose flesh is laced with pain.
We are stripped bare by our Lord's decree
and we no longer understand why;
why have you closed your eyes to the pain
of your once beloved, the children
you gave birth to in Israel when
the world seemed new to both You and us?

III

Lord we have come with circumcised hearts
and you have left us with fresh bruises,
with the six million corpses inside
the camps of Treblinka and Aushwitz.
How could you let this happen, YHWH?

IV

We sacrificed for generations
for the sake of your holy name and
yet you left us to die as victims
in tens of thousands in cold ditches.

V

For knowledge of Lord YHWH's love is
That which if it's embraced heals the heart.
Yet besides YHWH's revelation
there is more proof of YHWH love for
the humanity created by
Lord YHWH, universally proved God.
It is not philosophical proof, true.
Yet it speaks the heart in beauty.

VI

Yet, Lord, in the depths of our hearts we
feel a crest of love strong as rivers
like the great Mississippi, flowing
and soothing our pain to read your words.

VII

Let us now recall nature as though
we could see your eyes in hills that slope
as gently as above the blue skies
grant us a bounty of fresh air to
breath just as the fish in the water
are granted life from the deep oceans.

VI

Yet nature itself is a mirror
of You, Lord, peaking down on us here
and we wait for you as young babies
play hide-and-seek with loving mothers
who tend them and give them food to eat.

VII

So You peek down on us and we smile.
Not personally at the death camps
I do not know if there were laughter
but in its wake we cannot just cry
but also pray to our Lord YHWH.

VIII

Yes, Lord, if time heals we shall forgive
the God of justice and the heavens
and our dead shall be returned to us.
but before disappearing it was vile.

The Repentance of Tyr

I

For after a lapse of seventy years, the LORD will take note of Tyre, and she shall resume her "fee-taking" and "play the harlot" with all the kingdoms of the world, on the face of the earth. But her profits and "hire" shall be consecrated to the LORD. They shall not be treasured or stored; rather shall her profits go to those who abide before the LORD, that they might eat their fill and clothe themselves eloquently.
Isaiah 24:17-24:19

II

O YHWH, the sins Tyre are great
and yet their playing harlotry has
cost them more, for their indiscretions
less overflowing than their reward
for sinning the way Israel had.

III

Yet at the same time their name has been
as blotted out of history as
we Jews were remembered by their foes—
the foes of the Jews persecuting
their victims to death as though vampires
who drink blood oozing out of the Jews.
Yet memories were saved for Jews
while for Tyr they formed forgotten days.

IV

To be so forgotten, as decayed
as fossils in the earth long ago,
bones rotting in the ground—that is Tyr.
Tyr's descendents would forget her tears
while Jews have sacred ancestors to
keep remembered lest their death become
accusation of towards those who live.

V

Lord, if there be some hidden scholar
who still loves Tyr as their own country;
grant him or her the blessing of Jews.
Lord, let the Jews be citizens of
the city of Tyr in our caring
let us still remember Tyr in prayers
with Jerusalem on Yom Kippur.

VI

Let us cry for their sins and pray for
the children to have our own portion
in sacred scrolls not written yet by
the Israelite's or Judah's children.

VII

Lord commute the harsh punishment of
Tyr with that of your children the Jews
bring back the memory in the world
of the great civilization of
King Hiram, Solomon's friend who bought
wood for the Temple from King Hiram.

Keep Your Promises, O Lord

I

Approaching childbirth,
Writhing and screaming in her pangs,
So are we become because of You, O LORD.
We were with child, we writhed—
It is as though we had given birth to wind;
We have no victory on earth;
The inhabitants of the world have not come to life!
Isaiah 26:17-18

II

In labor with the world you create
we find that we, Your children wail with
the pain of unknown progeny whose
fate cannot be known to us because
the future is a distant fleck in
the Lord's eye, vanishing as we search
for any hopeful signs that lie in
the looming future descending on
us rapidly from time's far reaches.

III

Time vanishes like a hand unseen
that moves us through the blankets
our space's curving dimensions
in times of happiness—and sadness.

IX

For moments ripping in that pain we
see our souls stretched across the walls
of prison in the past years when men
cast us out of Queen Isabel's Spain
or in the Gestapo hauled us off
to concentration camps in Poland.

X

The Romans came and went and we shall
still outlast them all to our last breaths,
with *Sh'ma* on our lips to declare,
"Hear Israel, Lord YHWH is God
the Lord is One;" and we're his children.

XI

Yet there was a great promise made us
the hope of Isaac written years past,
a birthing of a nation's newborn.
The newborn shall be peace by itself
and contentment shall overflow Jews
and spread to non-Jews in love given
in exchange for the nations' cruelty.

XII

The nations' persecution shall end
and they shall repent previous wrongs.

Untitled

I

Oh, let your dead revive!
Let corpse arise!
Awake and shout for joy,
You who dwell in the dust!—
For Your dew is like the dew on fresh growth;
You make the land of the shades come to life.
Isaiah 26:19

II

At last your promises are realized.
From Ariel, City of David
"Ah, Ariel, Ariel,
City where David camped!
Add year to year,
Let festivals come in their cycles!
And I will harass Ariel,
And there shall be sorrow and sighing.
She shall be to me like Ariel.
Isaiah 29:1-2

III

Why harass your own beloved, Lord?
For Ariel, you say, was David's city—
not quite a Bethlehem yet a home
for the young David hospitable
when David escaped persecution
as Saul chased David through the country.

IV

For Israel is David's land with
the rolling deserts that are Zion.
Yet as Saul persecuted David
so You, O Lord, have persecuted
Your children, Israel, to our death.

V

You've been our tormentor O YHWH
as both our lover and our mother
our enemy and dearest friend, too.
Your passion has so consumed us, Lord;
in yearning we reach out for Your grace.
Be tender towards us, O YHWH.
Your city Ariel that you loved
that's mostly forgotten to the world.

VI

Lord spare not only Israel as
a whole but remember the city
of Ariel, the beloved of
King David, recall after his death
that Ariel housed David who was
as beloved as the Jews almost.

VII

O YHWH remember King David;
bless Ariel as it blessed him first.

The Repentance of Ariel

I

She shall be remembered of the LORD of Hosts
With roaring, and shaking, and deafening noise,
Storm, and tempest, and blaze of consuming fire.
Then, like a dream, a vision of the night,
Shall be the multitude of nations
That war upon Ariel,
And all her besiegers, and the siegeworks against her,
And those who harass her.
Isaiah 29:6-7

II

Lord, shall you remember us only
in wrath and not in love as well when
you recall David's Ariel in
the countryside where David rested
while King Saul pursued him through the land
of desert wilderness, or will you
send a vast tempest of the nations
at war with Israel while blazing
with rage like a fire harassing us.

III

Your earthquakes shake the ground that's beneath
our feet placed gingerly on the earth.
O Lord, your armies are cruel against
the children of the Israelites, too.

IV

The besiegers of our stone walls will
be successful as Joshua was
at Jericho years before when we
had arrived triumphant in the land
you promised to our father Abram.

V

How can a vision at night turn to
a battle of the nation's soldiers
who come from nations angered by You
but spiteful in their aggression that's
aimed towards us from without and has
no reason regarding us to fight.
Why must poor Ariel be destroyed?

VI

We're but one city of the many.
So tell us at last why you can't grant
us amnesty from the foul clutches
of the great nations like the ones at
the tower created at Babel?

VII

Your servants, O Lord, descend from those
who sheltered David ages ago—
so forgive Ariel's sins, YHWH.

Menstruation

I

And you will treat as unclean the silver overlay of your images
and golden plating of your idols. You will cast them away
like a menstrous woman. "Out!" you will call to them.
Isaiah 30:22

II

When women menstruate they are cast out
of their homes by their husbands, cursing
the bleeding as a used and foul thing.
A woman is as unclean, men think,
as in the desert blood's hard to rinse—
and they like idols are cast off and
in every way castigated
by men who consider them evil
the silver melted down from statutes.

III

This impurity was said to be
an idolatry, like the worship
of goddesses of Asherah or
the consort Anat of the Baal.

IV

What troubled Israelite men so when
it came to women's bleeding if not
its resemblance to sacrifice done
to Canaan's own gods before YHWH?

V

This blood gave life in providing wombs
for babies to rest within women
and be fed until grown enough to
have lived on in the world of children
till they're allowed adult lives which
in some past ages women still weren't.

VI

Birth represented sacrifice that
was very painful to have endured.

VIII

So it was not hard to see how when
to men a woman's bleeding would come
to resemble the sacrifice of
the 'pagan' idolaters who burned
the flesh of their own children to gods
like Molech of the Moabite tribes.

IX

The blood like tears flows when women
aren't fertile giving birth to children—
so it was said by Hebrew males who
were afraid that there would be no sons.
So it was that men feared their own wives.

Carefree, Young Women

I

You carefree women,
Attend, hear my words!
You confident ladies,
Give ear to my speech!
In little more than a year
You shall be troubled, O confident ones,
When the vintage is over
And no ingathering takes place.
Isaiah 32:9-10

II

Ah, you men vainglorious and proud
who impinge on the freedom which we
have stolen from you through the constraints
through chains forged of the ivory that
you bought to provide decorations
to your wives, decorations themselves.

III

We flaunt our servitude through these things
these purchases made with the money
our husbands provided in order
to beautify both we wives ourselves
and our homes, liberating we slaves
to passions forbidden by the Laws.

IV

We don't care of these protestations
made by the angry and old prophet—
we're young and vibrant today only—
leave tears of repentance to old age.

V

So spoke the richest women within
the land of Israel to the man
abused as YHWH's prophet himself.
Their insouciance provoked him and
he cursed these 'modern women' who broke
the tradition of who came before.

Untitled

I

We believe youth and money were meant
in order to be enjoyed today!
Tremble, you carefree ones!
Strip yourselves naked,
Put the cloth about your loins.
Isaiah 32:11

II

Strip us stark naked if you dare to!
we'll lie in the sun, baking and yet
as lascivious as before we were!

III

For youth has its own fleeting resilience,
while young a man can survive daggers
and youthful women satiate lusts
that grow dull and sad for old whores who
now do for habit what was once done
for love or money decadently.

IV

Ah! We are not shamed; rich young women
are the ones life was granted for now!
Why trouble ourselves with an old age
that may not come to our own heaven!
Lament upon the breasts,
For the pleasant fields,
For the spreading grave vines...
Isaiah 32:12

V

Lord, your own punishments come on us
like youth which fleets like the sun setting.
Zion Speaks to the Assyrians
From the Lord YHWH of Israel to the invading Assyrians:
Fair Maiden Zion despises you,
She mocks at you;
Fair Jerusalem shakes
Her head at you...
Isaiah 37:22

VI

The maiden Israel bares herself
with hauteur, dancing the death knew of
the Assyrian invaders bent
on destroying the fierce young flower
which blossoms in the desert's raw heat.

VII

She deports herself as one with pride
that can't be humbled by mere mortals
and whose own ancestor gained the name
of Israel by wrestling with God—
and prevailing, by his own account.
Now Jacob's daughter Israel mocks
the invaders from Assyria;
they shall not conquer Israel's land
and deport Judah's population.

VIII

The maiden Israel will mock them
when their cruel soldiers attempt conquest:
we Israelites will outlast conquests
and remain faithful to our YHWH.
Our Lord speaks to you of our vengeance,
Because you have raged against Me,
And your tumult has reached My ears
I will place My hook in your nose
And My bit between your jaws;
And I will make you go back by the road
By which you came.
Isaiah 37:29

IX

So our Lord rebukes those who attack
the maiden Israel in their land.

The Dove

I

Speak tenderly to Jerusalem,
And declare to her
That her term of service is over,
That her iniquity is expiated;
For she has received at the hand of the LORD
Double for all her sins.
Isaiah 40:2

II

Your maiden Jerusalem has loved
the tender words of the Lord towards
his maiden Jerusalem, blameless
through persecution unjust and cruel
but never despite these things
to dislodge love of YHWH from Jews
whose hearts are directed to their Lord.

III

For the love of God runs deep in us
to the core of the Jewish psyche.
Lord, grant us your love as we suffer;
for if we suffer for you we are
as blessed as if we gained riches—
and deserving praise beyond that wealth—
your words coax us like a bride should be
on her first night with her new husband.

IV

For Israel is YHWH's own bride
as lovely as the graceful dove in
the Lord's sight, even as She's pursued
by enemies like lustful foxes
who chase Her in to slay her through the heart
the entrapment of predators on
the path to the land promised by God—
a graceful bride who sprouts wings to fly!

Maidens of War

I

I will say to the North, "Give back!"
And to the South, "Do not withhold!
Bring my sons from afar,
And My daughters from the end of the earth—
All who are linked to my name,
Whom I have created,
Formed, and made for My glory—"
Isaiah 43:6-7

II

Your daughters, O Lord YHWH, gather
to dance from the earth's edges far off
from Jerusalem towards whom we,
the daughters of the Israelites pray.
We dance from North and South, East and West,
we dance to proclaim Lord YHWH is Great.

III

Like Miriam the prophetess when
the Israelites crossed the vast Red Sea
we sing the victory of the Jews—
the survival which defies the odds.

IV

Our Lord is a Man of War and we—
we're soldiers loyal to His Cause—
we worship at the tables serving
as altars upon which food has been
used as a sacrifice and displayed
like menorahs at Chanukah time.

V

Then after sacrifice we go forth
to the good fight of being Jews when
there are still anti-Semites watching—
if we could survive expulsions we
will survive this day's apathy, too,
and be the stronger in our stiff spines
than the Jews met by pogroms and wars—
for you may kill a Jewish body
but a Jew's soul can survive because
Lord YHWH is in the Jew's Spirit.

V

The women of the Israelites will
dance together on the street when we
are acknowledged as a great Phoenix
arising praises to Lord YHWH.

The Craftsman and His Work

I

Shame on him who argues with his Maker,
Though naught but a potsherd of earth!
Shall the clay say to the potter,"What are you doing?
Your work has no handles"?
Shame on him who asks his father, "What are you begetting?"
or a woman, "What are you bearing?"
Isaiah 45:9-10

II

Lord, has a person no right to say
what they will become, even as they
still love their redeemer and maker?
Do we not shape you as you shape us?

III

For in our hearts you are our Mother
who learns from us as we learn from you—
for mothers although wise learn during
the time they raise young children into
adults who love their children and who
will create independence within
their sons and daughters—so they will live.

IV

Lord undying we nourish you in
our hearts when we age after childhood—
for a Jew's greatest sacrifice is
the heart we're given by you at birth—
the sacrifice of the heart transforms
the people into loving children
as pure as Adam and Eve once were
in the time before their fall from grace.

V

At that point the Lord will live in us
and we will live in the Lord as well
and yet we and the Lord shall still be
as separate as golden coins made
from the same mettle but that also
will exist apart from each other,
and can lose their own goodness when spent.

VI

For the Lord is the soul's own craftsman;
and the good soul comes back to the Lord
as one that's purified by good deeds.
Your clay bends better when your hands are
as sensitive and gentle as Love.

The Rape of Babylon

I

Get down, sit in the dust,
Fair Maiden Babylon;
Sit, dethroned, on the ground,
O Fair Chaldea;
Nevermore shall they call you
The tender and dainty one.
Isaiah 47:1

II

Lord, forgive Babylonian for despite
her sinning both against You and us
we cry for her as she is tortured,
a writhing animal that's injured
on the ground, bleating its tears to God.

III

Don't torture our old nemesis so,
for crimes dead however cruel living.
She bleats as she is dead or dying.
Grasp the hand mill and grind meal.

IV

Remove your veil,
Strip off your train, bare your leg,
Wade through the rivers
Your nakedness shall be uncovered
And shame shall be exposed.
I will take vengeance,
And let no man intercede.
Isaiah 47:2-3

V

I intercede as one who is female
and therefore not a man but instead
a woman, able to give solace
to those who despite their guilt are now
as afflicted as we, the Jews, are.

VI

Do not rape Babylon, O YHWH,
for she's already dead and buried
a corpse in the earth below the stones
which mark both the graves of the wicked
or of the righteous—foreordained to
alike end in death before Judgment.
Ah—YHWH's Judgment redeems our deaths
but it can't erase them from the earth.
To brave death then is everman's goal.

VII

Sit silent; retire into darkness,
O Fair Chaldea;
Nevermore shall they call you
Mistress of Kingdoms
Isaiah 47:5

VIII

Lord forgive Chaldea as she is
dust like the bones of skeletons that
are long since digested by the worms.
The kings of Babylonia now
no longer are the nation breakers
who worshipped Marduk, king of their gods.

IX

Let the dead rest, and so grant peace to
the living as well, O Lord YHWH.
O Lord allow your mercy to trump
your justice regarding your people
and all the nations living on earth;
for it is compassion in which You
are revealed in Your Own great Splender.

The Twin Punishments of
Israel and Babylon

I

I was angry at My people,
I defiled My heritage;
I put them into your hands,
But you showed them no mercy.
Even upon the aged you made
You thought, "I shall be
The mistress still."
You did not take these things to heart,
You gave no thought to the end of it."
Isaiah 47:6-7

II

Show Babylonia more mercy,
O Lord, than You have shown Your Own Bride.
For You, Lord, have sent armies to us
in order that You subjugate us
the Beloved You picked while I was young.

III

You used the Babylonians as
Your tool in order that You chastise
Your virgin bride named Israel who
was naughty after our vows to You
yet did not mean her transgressions when
You punished Your bride severely as
though she were a brute animal that
pulls Your cart on the dusty back roads.

IV

You treated us as though we were beasts,
as human chattel with no rights left.
How could Lord YHWH have abused one
as the wife dedicated to You
or—frankly—disobediently
a wife whose wantonly like Gomer
the prostitute Lord YHWH ordered
the prophet Hosea to marry?
Is your love really made so shallow?

V

Poor Babylonia was Your pawn
so forgive her past cruelties towards
Your bride the Israelites who love You,
if only You could also forgive
the fresh young bride who waits for You still.

You have Abused Us, O Lord

I

These two things, O pampered ones—
Who dwell in security,
Who think to yourself,
"I am, there is none but me;
I shall not know a widow
Or know loss of children"—
Isaiah 47:8

II

Lord, we have not been pampered by you—
you instead have abused us as when
a jealous husband does his poor wife
when brought jealous passion because
of zealous ardor rather than proof
not an Eve's 'faithlessness' to YHWH
but the 'love' of wives subjugated.

III

We feel your battery and yet weep
for like that wife we still love the man
who violated our trust so much—
yet Lord it would break our heart to have
a bill of divorcement placed within
our hands with fingers stretched out with love
and adoration to our hearts' Lord.

IV

Do not leave your once beloved, Lord,
but return to the early state of
our marriage to you those years ago
when we fell in love in the mountains
of Zion when we were young and proud—
still loved by You, our mighty YHWH.

Mother Babylon

I

And now hear this, O pampered one—
Who dwell in security,
Who think to yourself,
"I am, and there is none but me;
I shall not become a widow
Or know the loss of children"—
These two things shall come upon you,
Suddenly, in one day:
Loss of children and widowhood
Shall come upon you in full measure,
Despite your many enchantments
And all your countless spells.
Isaiah 47:8-9

II

The loss of children weighs as greatly
on Mother Babylon that she will
cease to be as a living nation.
She, instead, is so tormented that
she only remembers the good times
in nostalgic tears during the bad—
and this is protested by the one
who was once Babylon's own victim.

III

Lord, forgive she who You spurred on to
do battle, gaining victory, with
the Bride You chose but abandoned next.
Your cruelty exceeds Babylon's as
the Babylonians have acted
as ones that will act without knowledge
of their sins towards Your Bride who loves
You still and without measure as One.

IV

You made Your promises to Your bride
while she was young and even callous
to her Lord who was Husband to her.
We love our tormentor, O YHWH;
we love You with the passion of youth,
of a youth which does not age with time.

V

We beg You to let Babylon rest
for despite being wicked she has
left this earth for the dead in sheol.

God As Mother

I

Zion says
"The Lord has forsaken me,
My Lord has forgotten me."
Can a woman forget her baby,
Or disown the child of her womb?
Though she might forget,
I never could forget you
See I have engraved you
On the palms of My hands,
Your hands are ever before Me.
Isaiah 49:14-16

II

O to be your child once more, YHWH,
to experience love overflowing
from Israel's own Divine Mother
for the Lord is our mother as well
as father to His children brought up
an arduous plague within the womb,
the opening womb that gives forth life.

III

O Lord in birth we have caused You pain
and You have born us loyally through
the centuries, as mothers will bless
their infants believing their children
are beloved in justice as well
as plain, bare fact, both loved and loving.

IV

The love of the Lord is deep and full
like the great Mississippi the Lord
will continue to support much life—
the surface and the bottom both teem
with breathing plants and animals that
form ecosystems that exist within
Lord YHWH also the great Mother.

V

Both masculine and feminine is
the Rock in Whom there's nothing wrong towards
the humanity She gave birth to.

VII

The Israelites are God's own firstborn
Her beloved whom She clings to deep
in Her heart, saying, "I shall love you,
my son, as though I have no other;
this despite having many children
whom I love because also human
made in my own image life genomes
the inherent stamp Holiness is
in each and every last human
which never can be leniency lost.

VIII

"As I gave birth to you so I will
not leave you in your death throws if they
come, unaware or expected by
the Israelites who live by My love.
For when you are stripped bare by humans
you shall be bejeweled by your Lord."

VIII

Lord, when we were stripped bare to the bone
faith in You carried us to across
the pains of death like Israel through
the Red Sea out of Egypt to shore.
Through various cruel expulsions and
the Holocaust, our fellow men have
been cruel but Your voice carried us through.

IX

Lord, Your love is a mother's and we
ask You to grant us breath one more day.

The Bride of God

I

Look up all around and see [your children]
They are assembled, are come to you!
As I live
—declares the Lord—
You shall don them all like jewels,
Deck yourself with them like a bride.
As for your ruins and desolate places
And your land laid waste—
You shall soon be crowded with settlers,
While destroyers stay from you.
Isaiah 49:18-19

II

We are both soldier and bride to God;
the Israelites of Joshua when
we conquered Canaan in the Lord's name.
O YHWH the land is yours—and ours.

III

Our girdles are made of hard iron,
thin, straight bars like sticks to stoke hot fires,
used instead of whale bones to mold as
once corsets were by women to look
as pretty, petite and small waisted
as they could during maidenhood to
do what they could to entrance young men.

IV

So Israel is despite her sex
a warrior for God fierce and agile
an Achilles whose heel is that she
will sometimes become lazy when times
are good and yet is strengthened in times
of unendurable adversity.

V

Yet we are the Lord's gentle bride, too,
we are the young bride beloved of
the wedding canopy when youthful
and mother of Lord YHWH's children.

VI

For Israel is more than enraptured bride;
she is a mother to sons as well—
the sons and daughters who are the Jews.
As such she wears stones emblazoning
the virtues she must possess to be
God's beloved in marriage itself.

VII

O Israel has vomited out
all sinfulness that perverted her;
she's reclaimed the Lord's divine mission
for her from birth till the end of time.
Her children will now gather circling
their beloved who is their mother—
for mothers are the beloved that
their sons hold near to them in their hearts.

VIII

So Israel is emblazoned on
her sons' hearts just as God claims daughters
when they are small and innocent still.
O bride of God, light unto nations,
you are the delight of the old age
of all those who read Lord YHWH's Word.

The Bride's Redemption

I

Fear not, you shall not be shamed;
Do not cringe, you shall not be disgraced.
For you shall forget
The reproach of your youth,
And remember no more
The shame of your widowhood.
For He who made you will espouse you—
His name is "Lord of Hosts."
The Holy One of Israel will redeem you—
He is called, "God of the Earth."
Isaiah 54:4-5

II

Lord we wait for the day when we shall
be redeemed as the age old dream comes
to pass, when the world shall be One and
shall worship You, our Divine Father,
one Universal God who is named
Peace, filling the earth with our prayers
which waft up into the skies filling
the Universe with Godly concern
which is One inspired by the Divine
in each and every one of us.

III

O Lord, we long for the day when You
shall fill the earth with glory because
on that day nations will take their swords
and beat them into ploughshares so that
there will be war no more on earth.
We shall embrace all of Your kindness—
for besides Peace Your name is Love and
so besides bringing peace You bring us.

IV

Your redemption is what we've waited
for millennia, suffering, Lord,
for You and the great Realization
Your promises were given to us—
the promise which is YHWH fulfilled
as YHWH empties Himself into
our history while remaining Real
in recesses of universes
including our own which we can't touch.

V

And humanity's inner voice will
come reunite with YHWH Itself
and forever be in the future
a part of the great Transcendent God.

The Return to Zion

I

The Lord has called you back
As a wife forlorn and forsaken.
Can one cast off the wife of his youth?
said your God.
Isaiah 54:6

II

Our Lord and Husband, YHWH whom we
still await patiently and with love,
You are the Husband who has been gone
for too long on a journey to lands
far from us in the ancient cities—
of Nineveh, Tyr, Jericho, Ur—
which we have visited years ago
and revisited recently in
imagination till we moved back
to Middle Eastern Jerusalem
when we were on our honeymoon with
our Lord and husband those years ago.

III

O husband return to the home of
our youth as ones who are those espoused
by their Lord in the beginning by
our father Abraham with his wife,
the lovely Sarah, admired by kings.
They were told "Sacrifice all for God"
and without knowing YHWH's name, did.
They wandered where the Spirit led them.

IV

We love You, O Lord and we wait for
the coming of the promised age called
the messiah's by Orthodox Jews
but by the other Jews an age with
no mortal save for the Truth Herself
Lord YHWH's other name which remains
a hidden one till the Age of Peace.

V

And at last the world shall be as one;
then the age old dream shall come true as
we finally are united to
the others who have recognized You
as God, the redeemer of mankind.

VI

In that day God and humankind shall
then unite as One, just as before
the couple Adam and Eve were one—
but Adam and Eve were flesh whereas
the Lord is a pure spirit and we
bend our souls to our god Lord YHWH
of ancient Israelites and the Jews.

VII

In modern times, since the great nightmare
done to us in the Holocaust to
be followed by the miracle of
a home state for the Jews at last in
the country Israel, our old home
there are those disillusioned by life
the cruelties of the Nazi regime.

VIII

O tragic human mistake on earth!
O unanswered 'Why?' from Lord YHWH
whom was called 'Abraham's friend' willing
to sacrifice all for this friendship.
Yet there is Hope to strive for in God.
So at last we shall rejoin YHWH.

The Divine Husband

I

For a little while I forsook you,
but with vast love I bring you back.
In slight anger, for a moment,
I his my face from you;
But with kindness everlasting
I will take you back in love.
-- said the Lord your Redeemer.
Isaiah 54:7-8

II

O YHWH, I long to embrace You
with open arms which you greet each Jew,
as the dear friend I've known since my birth,
the one who overflows with love for
his people Israel both at once
as individual person like me
and also collectively in groups.

III

We are Your beloved, Lord YHWH.
Jews pray as a group to Lord YHWH;
Yet I still long to pour out my heart
to You, Lord, personally praying
You speak to me as one who's espoused
with passion by the beloved spouce.

IV

For love hides faults that are seen plainly
by dispassionate observers who see
the bare facts only regards people.
So Lord let me drink from cups of love;
that divine vine that ties You to us.

Untitled

I

My Husband it is You that I love.
The Coming Temple of the Lord
Unhappy, storm-tossed one, uncomforted!
I will lay carbuncles as your foundations of sapphires.
I will make your battlements of rubies,
Your gates of precious stones,
The whole encircling wall of gems.
Isaiah 54:11-12

II

Lord, we are desperate for Your love.
For with Your love we are then redeemed;
more than that, we are resplendent, as
the Temple shall be covered in stones
of green-blue sapphires and red rubies
that, inlaid with gold carvings display
the glory of the Lord who loves us.

III

These gems shall be like concrete making
the buildings resemble the marble
of banks whose inside is smooth, polished
and beautifully waxed on each day.

IV

Yet instead of mere money, this is
the Temple dedicated to God
with seven candelabra branches
as decoration in the walls with
the lining openings of those limbs
filled with the olive oil of past times.

IV

In the days coming we shall receive
our consolation and our reward,
the promises of our holy prophets.

All God's Children

I

And all your children shall be disciples of the LORD,
And great shall be the happiness of your children…
Isaiah 54:13

II

What's it mean to have happy children?
It must mean many things—for children
come unprepared to the world so that
they meet a world not concerned with them.

III

Their mothers try to protect them and
yet sometimes they fall through cracks—or worse—
all children need food—yet some do starve—
all children need some shelter as well—
yet we know there are children without
a home, on Rio's streets or on those
of Calcutta's, young Oliver Twist
still lives in the world's darkness asking
the indifference of those with wealth
for "more" food, water and warm clothing.

IV

A child needs love and yet in Brazil
a stepfather will doctor the wounds
that he had himself inflicted on
the child with salt, and add to pain
more pain from a man devoid of care
till then the boy runs into to streets
which, although kinder, will kill the boy
and other children before they see
their own adulthood come like children's.

V

This surely was not the Lord's intent,
when the Lord called His creation "Good."
No, this is what the beasts would call "Bad,"
they would not permit these abuses.
They would ask why the race of humans
so betray their own off-spring this way.

VI

Now governments can act and sometimes
they will on behalf of starved children,
but the plight of poor children requires
more care than a state alone can give.

VI

If nothing better money at least,
but adoption or spending a year
in charitable work done elsewhere
than your home country would be ideal—
these deeds will stack high before YHWH
and they may be a life's great work that
will follow like a prayer through jobs
that may mean less by comparison.

VII

For living is not getting by with
what life gives you if you are lucky,
about their giving until it hurts
to give and then the admittance that
you did what you could not just for you
but also for your fellows in life—
and especially for our children.

The Struggle

I

But as for you, come closer,
You sons of a sorceress
You offspring of an adulterer and a harlot!
With whom do you act so familiarly
At whom do you open your mouth
And stick out your tongue?
Why, you are children of iniquity
Offspring of treachery—
Isaiah 57:3-4

II

O YHWH, we're your children even
if we are recalcitrant, stubborn
and outright disobedient when
You ask of us the docility
of lambs in the fields of green grasslands;
the only similarity to
those lambs is our keen desire to play
and frolic in the fields of their mothers.

III

You who inflame yourselves
Among the terebinths,
Under every verdant tree;
Who slaughter children in the wadis
Among the clefts of the rocks.
Isaiah 57:5

IV

O Lord, You surely exaggerate
our treachery; is it not the case
that You gave Abraham the demand
to sacrifice young Isaac to You?
Did You stop Jephthah from the act of
the same thing towards his own daughter?
Is it such a grave act to follow
their examples when one was stopped and
the other acted out God's judgment,
the punishment for oaths made with haste.

V

With such are your share and portion,
They, they are your allotment;
To them you have poured out libations,
Presented offerings.
Should I relent in the face of this?
Isaiah 57:6

VI

O Lord have mercy on Your people,
for however we may not deserve
the love You promised us in our youth
we still claim it as our hold on You,
our prize and possession that won't fail.

VII

Through centuries we will not let go
of our Lord YHWH who is our core.
Yes, YHWH lives in every Jew.
You may still regret but you will
not forget us—no matter how hard
You struggle attempting to elude
our grasp like Jacob's wrestling YHWH.

The Lord's Dancers

I

Raise your eyes and look about:
They have all gathered and come to you.
Your sons shall be brought from afar,
Your daughters like babes on shoulders.
As you behold, you will glow;
Your heart will throb and thrill—
For the wealth of the sea shall pass on to you,
The riches of nations shall flow to you.
Isaiah 60:4-5

II

Your daughters, O Lord, will dance for You,
with thrilling hearts they will dance, circling
in the Lord's Divine Presence as though
they were made for no other purpose
than embracing the spirit of God.
For the sea of love surrounding them
shall deliver their spirits into
an ecstatic form of their praying
to their Lord and their Divine Husband.

III

These daughters of the Lord shall be young
as Miriam when she watched Moses,
a baby hidden in the Nile of
the Egyptians yet also vibrant
as the same Miriam when she led
the Israelites in singing later
at the Red Sea where she crossed with God.

IV

So these girls from four years to twenty
shall dance as virgin daughters for God.
They shall laugh and sing and wail to Him,
proud of their figures and their spirits—
the child brides of Lord YHWH in dance.
They champion the day of the Lord.

Israel's Mother

I

You shall suck the milk of the nations,
Suckle at royal breasts.
And you shall know
That I the Lord am your Savior,
I, the Mighty One of Jacob, am your Redeemer.
Isaiah 60:16

II

Lord, we have never been cared for by
a Parent besides You and we wish
for none but You to be our Mother
save Your own Divine Spirit who is
the feminine part of Your Godhead—
and indeed if the Lord's mind is male
the soul of the Lord which breaths upon
the earth is female and both of them
are spirit, for God has no body.

III

So wean our spirits at Your own breasts—
the divine form which nourishes souls—
for if a sometimes wrathful father
the Lord is a life-giving mother
a loving Goddess as well even
as She will lash out at the wicked.

IV

For our God is He and She and yet
our Lord and Lady YHWH is not
an "it" at anytime for the Jews.
God of the Israelites grant Your care
to us that's better than that of Queens,
for royalty is not as good to
its children as is Israel's God.

A Journey

I

I greatly rejoice in the LORD,
My whole being exults in my God.
For He has clothed me with garments of triumph,
Wrapped me in a robe of victory,
Like a bridegroom and adorned with a turban,
Like a bride bedecked with her finery.
Isaiah 61:10

II

Yes, I am like a new bride before
my God and sacred Husband to whom
I deliver my prayers in love,
I rejoice knowing You'll accept me
as both a wife and daughter of sorts—
for Jews are more than YHWH's children,
they're married to their Lord as they are
part of the nation Israel, too.

III

As Rabbi Akiba has named it,
the erotic 'Song of Songs' is called
'the Holy of the Holies,' that is
an allegory of the Lord and
his sacred people, Israel which
still mysteriously lacks God's name—
and this makes each girl YHWH's true bride.

IV

It also made each man the husband
to the pure Shekinah the Spirit
of YHWH, our Lord's Feminine Soul.
This protected, chaste beloved is
one intending to return in love
I offer up my devotion, Lord,
for You have always proven a strength,
and when small even a child's heart can
beat with the rhythm of faith within.

V

O Lord, I believe I knew You when
I was a child, that I could touch You
and smell you like a cedar table.
When I was older my path was blocked
yet at rare moments You still visit
a presence permeating the night.

VI

When my eyes dim the last time I hope
to rejoin You with the soul you gave
pure as the water raining on days
in early spring when the sun flows through
to the ground parched in order to give
birth to an assortment of green plants
to enliven the animal world.

VII

Like rainwater the Soul is still pure
when a Jew keeps out pollutants and
the Soul like water is life's first source
no life can exist without water.
When I die I hope my Soul is pure,
So I can rejoin YHWH who loves,
decked out like a bride I would be then,
and ready for the rejoicing of
the pious Jew for his or her God.

The Flowers of God

I

For as the earth brings forth her growth
And a garden makes the seed shoot up,
So the Lord God will make
Victory and reknown shoot up
In the presence of all the nations.
Isaiah 61:11

II

From the earth come forth gardens of plants,
the blooms of which color spring days
or wild, hot summer afternoons with
golds glowing in the purples and reds
mixed together in flowerbeds with
a gentle glow that blossoms in light
that bends down from the sun above us.

III

Like roses, the Lord will cause to sprout
not just the Victory of the Jews
but that of humankind years ahead
with evil subverted to good by
the transformation undergone of
mere suffering to love, of torment
to trust as unfortunates realize
how others like them in pain must feel.

IV

For wickedness their sins were purged to
the white hot fires of gehenna[1] from
which most of them pass on to heaven
but from which a few never leave as
once their bad deeds are purged, they are left
clean without deeds left to speak for them.

V

In final conquest over evil
the Lord will lift the fallen and bind
their wounds with mercy's fresh swabs and casts
to heal them till their injuries are
though like pearls to the Lord, are painless
to those who are found constant to God.

VI

They bloom like a rose bush planted over
a grave, to explain Victory of
life over death by our Lord YHWH
the symbiosis of rose and thorn.

---

[1] Gehenna is the Jewish version of hell, mentioned in the Talmud and in
Jewish folklore.

The Lord's Child Bride

I

Nevermore shall you be called "Forsaken,"
Nor shall your land be called "Desolate";
But you shall be called "I delight in her,"
And your land "Espoused."
For your land shall be espoused.
Isaiah 62:4

II

Lord, we Your Divine Wife and Consort
long for the glorification of
Your Name to be made manifest to
all of the nations of the earth through
your Child-Bride Israel who waits on
the Lord as though He were Her Father
and She His Daughter serving Him tea,
a special tea of a five-year-old Girl.

III

A tea that's flavored strawberry to
the Child-Bride playing with cups made of
the modern plastics toys are made of—
this Bride is cherished as a Daughter,
for when a Father is good He shows
a reverence for Children beyond
the merits of Their deeds and in keeping
with their worth, nourishing hearts
as well as stomachs with food they need.

IV

In giving YHWH's message to Jews
Your Spirit emanates from outside
the Universe to the Souls within;
for inside of us we find You, Lord,
for though You are more than mere mortals
the Divine Sparks still exist within
the human creature Jewish or not.

V

We long to realize those sparks throughout
a transformation of our hearts to
the divine likeness shared by the pair
of our first parents, Adam and Eve.

The Young Loves of Israel

I

As a youth espouses a maiden,
Your sons shall espouse you;
And as a bridegroom rejoices over you.
Isaiah 64:5

II

As maiden Israel waits for her sons,
her collective male adolescence that
is too young to be married and yet
old enough to pine for the pleasures
adulthood brings, not knowing that they
bring sorrow just as often as joy.
In Israel they find the bliss of
a wedding without dangerous lust
the sweetness of a young bride in love.

III

These sons of Israel shall hold her
near to their beating hearts while dreaming
and chastely imagine that she has
not known men, despite evidence to
the contrary and despite her age.

IV

"O Israel," they cry our, "You are
our beloved for whom we received
each one of us his own bar-mitzvah."

V

For young men who love gently find that
their love is reciprocated by
the wife who's always young and fertile,
as when they're older they will produce
more sons for Israel, their first love.

Israel's Birth Pangs

I

Before she labored, she was delivered;
Before her pangs came, she bore a son.
Isaiah 66:7
Who is she, Lord? Who is mother
to the child You formed within her womb?
Who has heard the like?
Who ever witnessed such events?
Isaiah 66:7:1-2

II

Lord, although a birth's marvelous to
a bride, it seems a miracle that
if miraculous happens daily.

III

Can a land pass through travail
In a single day?
Or is a nation born
All at once?
Isaiah 66:7:3-7

IV

Do nations give birth at all, our Lord?
Do even royal nations give birth
to specific young children, O Lord?
If so what do they resemble, Lord?
Do they come out with royal bloodlines?

V

Are they as beautiful as lilies,
as peaceful as doves or as humble
as the sad donkey, traveling on
the road from heaven to the city
of Jerusalem, walled yet holy,
and perhaps able to be holy
just because it is walled up.

VI

For Jews to survive remain a group
apart among the nations so that
they survive onslaughts from the outside.
Yet all the while we survive we pray
for those who persecute us, so that
they may see that their ways are wicked—
and thus end their cruel persecutions.

VII

Yet Zion travailed
And at once bore children!
Isaiah 66:8:8-9

VIII

Yes, Lord, through You all's possible and
we pray to be made whole once again.
More we pray for the child in our womb.
Shall I who bring on labor not bring about birth?
—says the Lord.
Isaiah 66:9:1

IX

Lord, if You can bring about a life
of a child You can create nations.
Shall I who cause birth shut the womb?
—said your God.
Isaiah 66:9:2

X

Lord as sure as our women give birth
so we as Israel shall give birth.
For You are our dear Divine Husband
and we trust in You more than in men;
we know that You shall deliver us
and Our own progeny—Yours and ours—
in the due course of the time coming.

In Defense of the Jews

I

Rejoice with Jerusalem and be glad for her,
All you who love her!
Join in her jubilation,
All you who mourned over her—
That you may suck from her breast
Consolation to the full,
That you may draw from her bosom
Glory to your delight.
Isaiah 66:10-11

II

O Nations be kind to Jews for we
are the bride the Lord's claimed
by Christianity and Islam;
you claim to be our heirs and you know
that with the widow he will judge us.

III

For centuries we have been captive
to your whims, persecutions and praise—
'the conversion of the Jews' has been
as proverbial as true love's sweetness—
if praise is mostly unintended
for anti-Semites assume Jews are
tough crabgrass compared to the masses.

IV

The murdering of infants lingered
on pious priests' lips throughout the days
when Europe's Church ruled the roost and it
would describe communion type rituals
in which the matzo was soaked in blood.

V

This language was picked up by
the racial anti-Semites later
and used in grotesque language as well.
It tantalized its perpetrators.

VI

Now that we've escaped Christians and gone
to Islam's Middle East we pray to
our Lord in regards what we've witnessed,
'Bring peace for Your bride who waits, O Lord,
that nations recognize You as God.'

The Eternal Sabbath

I

And new moon after new moon,
And Sabbath after Sabbath,
All flesh shall come to worship Me
—said the LORD.
Isaiah 66:23

II

On Saturday the Sabbath Bride comes
but in the World to Come our Queen shall
come to her spouses so that we may
then gather her embraced as tightly
as beloved brides will hold their grooms
on nightly wedding night's eve.

III

This fervid held embrace joins us to
Lord YHWH judging all of mankind,
and witness to our every deed.
God's love shall permeate the ages
that follow the times that we live in.
Our Sabbath Bride will become our wives
the Beloved who our souls desire.

JEREMIAH

The Pride of Israel

I

Go proclaim to Jerusalem: Thus said the LORD:
I accounted to your favor
The devotion of your youth,
Your love as a bride—
How you followed Me in the wilderness,
In a land not sown.
Jeremiah 2:2

II

You nurtured us while we were young, Lord,
but then You demanded that we pay
You obeisance ill-fitting a wife;
for a real wife is tall, strong and proud
as nurtured saplings become great oaks
not bending to the wind's harsh beating.

III

How can You condemn us when You raised
Your children Yourself, spoiling us and
then blaming us for sins we commit
as if they were not merely products
of indiscretions on Your own part—
for children's faults are often results
of their own parents' sins; as mirrors
in dressing rooms at the mall will reflect
the original copies into
a view of eternity showing
a reality imagined starkly.

IV

We are like dominoes to You, Lord—
or at least would had You not restrained
us and yet also made us free to
be, to live our own choices in life.
For human pride is cherished by all—
by You most in Your nurturing us—
the soul that flees like a bird to You.

Our 'Rebellion'

I

For long ago you broke your yoke,
Tore off your yoke-bands,
And said, "I will not work!"
On every high hill and under every verdant tree,
You recline as a whore.
Jeremiah 2:20

II

Why do You make accusations of
slack, lazy, indifferent and in
a perpetually idle state, Lord?
Jews are known even those who
are faithless to work too hard, too long—
when anti-Semites pretend that they
feel pity instead of mere envy,
they say our lives are nothing at all
save useless labor warring with God.

III

They never doubt we work harder than they—
hence taking perverse pride in being
as lazy as our ancestors held
those to eat ham as being to God.
How can You call Your bride a harlot?

IV

This is abuse which we have been spared
by the hand of our Lord and Husband,
our protector who caressed us while
we were, still fresh and naïve, pampered
by You to believe You would coddle children
that Your young bride would bring forth for You.

V

To this sweet idyll You brought to us
a brutality that we had not
yet experienced as Your innocent bride.
Your decrees as unbearable
to us as holocausts and cruel wars.
We cry for Your love only to be
those ejected out of the Temple.
Give us back our fresh Eden of Youth.

O Faithless Lord

I

How can you say, "I am not defiled,
I have not gone after the Baalim"?
Look at your deeds in the Valley,
Consider what you have done!
Like a lustful she-camel,
Restlessly running about,
Or like a wild ass used to the dessert,
Snuffling the wind in her eagerness,
Whose passion none can restrain,
None that seek her need grow weary—
In her season, they'll find her!
Jeremiah 2:23-24

II

Lord, You've accused us of our playing
the harlot, acting as a dog in
heat towards many Baalim who
we commit their adultery towards
You, our Lord, with the very beasts,
as faithful as You demand us to
be towards You, with reverence in
our hearts in regards You, Lord YHWH.

III

You, YHWH gave us to Nazis
and the pain festers when we recall
the cruelty with which we were treated
to the point where some of us are Jews
for the sake of the victims therein
but not Yours any longer because
their relatives who died in that place
have mattered more than their cause itself.

IV

Yet they still continue to mourn that
which was lost: their faith in You, O Lord.
We all miss the One for Whom they died.
Lord, wee accuse You, yet we do it
with love both for our ancestors and
for You, Lord YHWH, redeemer of
the Israelites, dear God of our faith.
No other God could understand us.

V

For true love forgives and the wounds that
we've suffered will heal despite how cruel
the perpetrators have been to Jews;
once more we will love our Lord as though
we'd received honey and warm milk from
our Lord and not the harshness of men.
Come back to us, our beloved Lord.
Do not say 'goodbye' to Your people.

The Blame of Love

I

How skillfully you plan your way
To seek out love
Why, you have even taught
The worst of women your ways.
Jeremiah 2:33

II

The 'worst of women' receive more blame
than is their due while the worst of men
are blamed on womankind's lack of care.
For Freud blamed careless mothers themselves
for mishaps done by wicked children—
'To seek out love' is now the dictum
of what young children desire at birth
and perhaps it is true that the child
who's unloved is most likely to stray
from the path of the righteous when grown.

III

Did Freud have his own Oedipal traits
the wish to kill his Divine Father?
And yet to regress into the state
of infancy's sweet gratifications?

IV

Were these the reasons why Freud while he
wished liberation sexually for
his women patients denied their needs
for liberation separate from
their bodies physically only?

V

Was it the case that Freud like most men
of that time preferred subjugation
for women when it conflicted with
with men's own desires, especially
when sex with them was involved in them?

Repent, Our God

I

*[The word of the LORD came to me] as follows: If a man divorces
his wife, and she leaves him and marries another man, can he
go back to her? Would not such a love be defiled? Now you have
whored with many lovers: can you return to Me?—says the LORD.*
Jeremiah 3:1

II

Lord YHWH, You who promised us we
would be Your wife no matter what came
and now we've survived fifty years since
the greatest pogrom conceivable,
the Holocaust in Europe, where Jews were gassed.

III

What 'lover' could be as great a cause
to feel a sense of betrayal as
the murder of a third of all Jews?
The crimes of Israel were like those of
a loose wife; we failed to see what we
had, failing appreciation of
our Lord whom we loved and who loved us.

IV

The crushing blow we received in turn
was beyond those small misdemeanors
and ritual infractions we had done.

IV

Our frailties were just that: we were frail,
we loved You despite character flaws—
the petty, undisciplined crimes of
youth, those left behind and blamed by those
who have left youthfulness far behind
in their flawed memories of themselves.

V

Is it not the case that we loved You
When our crimes were at their most hurtful?
We still love You in remembrance of
Your tenderness in Israel's land,
long before we were expelled from there—
the Holocaust left a bruise on us,
but Lord we wait for You to repent—
as You did in the age of Noah—
for we still believe in Your goodness.

Unfaithful

I

And you defiled the land
With your whoring and your debauchery
And when showers were withheld
And the late rains did not come,
You had the brazenness of a street woman,
You refused to be ashamed.
Jeremiah 3:2:4-3:3

II

Your words are scalding to us, O Lord,
like boiling water they burn the flesh.
For to call Your bride a street walker
abuses her like Balaam's donkey
when YHWH's angel stopped him short in
the road to curse the Israelite tribes.

III

The nations unconsciously see us
decked in Your Royal Splendor Itself.
Your bride is recognized as one who's
apart from mighty earthly nations
and yet we're at their mercy, helpless.
They say God abandoned us to them.

IV

Let's unsheathe our lust upon the Jews.
Your beloved was murdered within
the concentration camp of Auschwitz
out of pure jealous hatred because
in his heart Hitler envied the Jews.
He knew You loved the Jews above all.

V

So in Your neglect of us it looks
as if You lack true compassion for
Your young bride, Israel whose son were
those murdered in the concentration camps
of creation which fell away from
from Your kind intentions for the race
of men and women, meant to love You.

VI

To trust in God now is hard and yet
we are told that in death's great valley
Lord YHWH is both needed most and
waits for us on death's other side where
our loved ones generations back wait
for us to join them in embraces.

VII

Death is not punishment for the Jews—
it releases us from life's shackles
the pain of being tortured by foes
who also are held in the thrall of
the wickedness which humans can do.

VIII

To willfully do evil was what
our modernity brought to the Jew—
as modernity's heirs leave to us
the isolation of our new state
for the heirs of the Holocaust's plague
on Jewish people murdered by men.

IX

The poor souls whose death pursued them in
the Holocaust will receive portions
that will be double their pains on earth;
the Lord will not check their deeds or faith;
they will at least be given their due.

X

Yes Lord, we doubt You still; we still think
'Was it poor Israel who had played
the harlot, acting out the great guilt?'

A Cry to Our Father

I

Just now you called to Me, "Father!
You are the Companion of my youth.
Does one rage forever?"
That is how you spoke.
You did wrong and had your way.
Jeremiah 3:4-3:5

II

We say once again, "Father! We long
for mercy's cup of kindness towards
Your child-bride Israel, the one who
has loved You from our beginning days.
Why do You, instead, rant and rail at
Your offspring and wife Israel as
though we were murderers and thieves and
known for our wicked deeds to nations
as far from us as China and Guam?

III

Do we so deserve be known for
our sins that when we call You "Father!"
Your rebuke us with harsh wrath raining
down upon us like a storm in March.
Will our cruel punishments have no end,
and our faith in You finally be
as fulfilled as Your promises were
meant to be in the Garden of Eve?

IV

We've waited centuries for You, Lord,
yet villains have robbed us and raped us;
they've "unsheathed their lust upon" the Jews.
They claim to be our heirs while they rob
our children of food and drink which they
need to live, swallowing down the gall
of bitterness and of need instead.

V

Bring forth Your redemption, Lord YHWH.
We do not fear Your Judgment because
we know it's tempered with Your Mercy.
We can wait no more and yet we long
for intimacy with You, O Lord.
We cry out for You in night's darkness
and yet we recoil from harsh words.

VI

We long for You, Lord, to come to us as
once in the wilderness You were ours.
True to You after our fashion
The LORD said to me in the days of Josiah:—
Jeremiah 3:6:1

VII

O YHWH, Jeremiah spoke well,
"Do not ask for the Day of the Lord,"
but Jews always have prayed for that day.

VIII

Ah, Lord, that was so many ages
in the past; what's the good of dwelling
on unpleasant days remembered now?

IX

Have you seen what Rebel Israel did, going to every mountain
and under every leafy tree, and whoring there?
Jeremiah 3:6:2

X

Ah, but Lord, the tall leafy trees are
as beautiful to look at as if
they were the pillars holding the sky
up with their trunks, leaves spreading across
them as if green stars were above us.
Why are trees unworthy of worship?

XI

I thought: After she has done all these things, she will come back to me.
Jeremiah 3:7:1-2

XII

Ah, Lord, the lush green grass that's woven
On the ground underneath the tall trees
is heavenly as it gets on earth.

XIII

Lord, surely it is not such a sin
to linger here on the ground where trees
are planted in Your honor and ours—
this despite prohibitions by You
on idolatry and tree worship.

XIV

But she did not come back; and her sister, Faithless Judah,
saw it. I noted: Because Rebel Israel had committed adultery,
I cast her off and handed her a bill of divorce; yet her sister,
Faithless Judah was not afraid—she too went and whored.
Jeremiah 3:7:3-3:8

XV

O Lord, we sisters may be faithless
but lying comfortably on grass
we cannot help but worship the trees
which rise up us to greet above clouds,
the white and fluffy leaves of the skies
which mirror the tree leaves that hang on
the trees which hold up the great blue skies.

XVI

In our poor idolatress eyes when
we look up, herself wondering 'Why?'
the reasons of our existence as
a whole on our earth below the skies.

XVII

*Indeed the land was defiled by her casual immorality, as
she committed adultery with stone and with wood.*
Jeremiah 3:9

XVIII

Too true, Lord, Israel and Judah
lie worshipping in forests praying
to idols devised of wood and stone—
as though we were carved out of tree trunks.
It is as though wood animates us
and not the breath You ensouled us with.

XIX

*And after all that, her sister, Faithless Judah, did not return to
Me wholeheartedly, but insincerely—declares the LORD.*
Jeremiah 3:10

XX

Ah, Lord, we sincerely love our trees;
Is it not enough for our Father
who created us that we're happy?
Lord, forgive infidelities on
our part, for we're true to You after
our fashion—as Cole Porter would write—
and know that You will outlast the trees.

The Two Daughters

I

And the Lord said to me: Rebel Israel has shown
herself more in the right than Faithless Judah.
Jeremiah 3:11

II

Lord, it is Jews who continue on
among the living despite the fact
You blessed Your daughter Israel blessed.
Blessed, O Lord, but save a few hundred
who continue in calling themselves
the Samaritans, largely they're dead;
for ordinary life like Aushwitz
would not seem apt to favor the good.

III

It is an act of faith to believe
that virtue's rewarded yet it is
still shocking that the faithless daughter
was chosen accordingly by God,
whose will is unfathomable as
the ocean appears from the seashore.
Lord, where does 'Faithless' Israel lay
in hiding in Mt. Zion's mountains?

IV

Is she poor Samaria, that is
as persecuted as we and yet
a smaller nation now in numbers?

How could it be that Samaria
was much less resilient than we were
when she seemed virtuous when compared
to her own smaller sister Judah?

V

O Lord, Your faith in us must have been
as impenetrable as space is
when its spread across universes and
then begs us to try to go across
it to the other side to find life.
It may be impossible travel,
for the fact is that the star nearest
to us is light years from us on earth.

VI

Yet we ask why You have dealt us blows
that are so brutal compared to those
that others endure for their faith's sake.

Your Love Cleanses Us

I

Since I have espoused you, I will take you, one from a town and two
from a clan, and bring you to Zion. And I will give you shepherds
after My own heart, who will pasture you with knowledge and skill.
Jeremiah 3:14:2-3:15

II

Lord, will You forgive us for our sins,
for when we receive promises from
You we find that our stony hearts melt
back into flesh which responds to You
with tenderness and penance for sins
we did with youth's cruel indifference.

III

For Lord, if we saw You cry we would
then respond in kind for Your own sake.
Love, we would say, we offer You love,
in exchange for the anguish we caused
You, our Lord with whom salvation rests.

IV

For if a child must be spanked while young
adulthood's moved towards compassion and
and pity—most especially when
it's dealing with her aged parents,
the revisited caretakers of
her youth on whom she relied while young.

V

A woman becomes her own mother
to her own mother now in childhood—
the woman herself far from her years
in pristine infancy when she was
a little girl and vulnerable.
This love is like the feminine love
of and by God, who gives of Herself
and Himself to his and her children.

VI

For just as male and female are made
Lord YHWH's divine likeness, so God
has traits of the two kinds of humans—
and such is the Lord's love for us that
it washes from us hardness of heart
in us and gives us hidden power.
Your love thus cleanses us of our sins.

The Love of the Lord

I

I have resolved to adopt you as My child, and I gave you a desirable land—the fairest heritage of all the nations; and I thought you would surely call Me "Father," and never cease to be loyal to Me. Instead, you have broken faith with Me, as a woman breaks faith with a paramour, O House of Israel—declares the Lord.
Jeremiah 3:19-20

II

Lord, why do You blend promises with
cruel accusations towards Your wife
and children, Israel whom You love.

III

You are a jealous God of the Heart,
and vindictive in angry judgment
of Israel, your child-wife, who waits
for Judgment to be washed away with
the Mercy promised to Your people
and the Bride yearning for her Husband
are in fact interconnected with
each other instinctually because
they resemble us and Lord YHWH.

IV

We've waited millennia for You
to fulfill the warm promises to
the children whom You loved so well in
the wilderness when we left Egypt.
Oh, we still remember the promise
of milk and honey in the desert.

V

We remember You loving Zion
as though we were Your missing soul mate—
the twin at birth that's also our spouse
as though the Freudian knot were tied
so the child's yearning for its Mother.

VI

We love Your unfathomable depths
yet we wish You would grant us respite,
we give You pious prayers in hopes
that You won't abandon us, that You
will give us back the love we gave You.

VII

Lord, You are beautiful far beyond
mere mortal women to men in love
and as such humans were made to be
One being whose soul is yours espoused,
Your companion in the love from You,
a deity whose loneliness caused
Him His third act of creation, us.

VIII

The first, the Torah and the second
the universe that looms as below
its Creator a testimony
to the Lord who made it's great wisdom.

IX

Yet despite Your great wisdom You were
One, alone, and so lonely for us—
just as a human without a God
is One who is One lonely for You.
For You gave us Your breath and granted
us Your own spirit for our own souls.

X

Yet we are treasured because we have
been proven loyal to You, O Lord.

Repentance

I

But the Shameful Thing has consumed
The possessions of our fathers ever since our youth—
Their flocks and herds,
Their sons and daughters.
Jeremiah 3:24

II

It is hard to start anew, O Lord,
and hard accepting failure for us
just as for Americans the war
in Vietnam was regrettably
a protracted war when our leaders
could not or would not admit defeat.

III

To say 'I was wrong' is for many the phrase
from which their penance begins so that
they can move, healing festering wounds—
yet others never make this leap and
so become embittered people—
a tragic defeat costlier than
the problem itself for most people.

IV

To move on—to say, finally, that
the past can't be and maybe shouldn't
be recovered, that instead we can
make ourselves anew each day and yet
no person can make the past vanish—
its remembered but that is all that
is possible as unflinching as
a gaze must be to still gain from it.

V

God asks us to move on, to forget
the "good old days" when David was king
and yet to remember the bad with
the good, for to change requires penance.
While we should remember our past yet
we should not live as ones trapped by it,
for living the past again will cut
a people off from its own future
by strangling itself in the process.

VI

Do not try to live David's life for
he is dead and his life can't be lived
for better or worse, again (by us).
True faith lies with the future, with hope,
which, informed by the past, is not bound
in its cruel tentacles to the dead.

Spare Us for Your Own Sake

I

Tell the nations: Here they are!
Announce concerning Jerusalem:
Watchers are coming from a distant land,
They raise their voices against the towns of Judah.
Like guards of fields, they surround her on every side.
For she has rebelled against Me
—Declares the Lord
Jeremiah 4:16-4:17

II

O Lord, why treat us perversely when
we are the people serving You while
the nations gathering like jackals
are the ones indifferent to You,
not knowing Your name or much caring.

III

O Lord, if You love Your name You should
then remember that it shall be lost
to human beings if You slay us—
for Israel's foes will not recall
the name of the Lord, instead they will
think of the ease of victory and
so assume that You're powerless to
fight for or against them, so that You
will not be worshipped again either
by foreign nations or those dead at
the Israelite home of Your worship.

IV

So Lord, for the sake of Your own name
will You now recall Your own people
and forgive her for mercy's sake as
You shall prove Yourself merciful and
a worthy God of any people?

V

For YHWH shall You fail to live up
to principles You Yourself set down:
six hundred thirteen commandments with
the expectation that we will live
so our deeds reflect the oath that we
swore to Lord YHWH at Mt. Sinai?

VI

Your principles, Lord, are what make You
a just and compassionate God in
both the eyes of men and in Your own.
If You fail to live up to them men
will not be alone in their blaming
their Lord, the very angels will fight
in rebellion grouped together as
one against You like Satan himself
and finally Your conscience will take
Your throne and topple it to the earth.

VII

Lord, who will believe in a God who
allowed the death of his poor people?
Lord, You must spare us for Your own sake.

VIII

Preparing for God
And you, who are doomed to ruin,
What do you accomplish by wearing crimson,
By decking yourself in jewels of gold,
By enlarging your eyes with kohl?
You beautify yourself in vain:
Lovers despise you,
They seek your life!
Jeremiah 4:30

IX

In vain, Lord? How can our Lord deny
our beauty, nurtured carefully on
soap made of flower petals sweetened
by bitter, desert roots in the sand.
For our trunks are like daffodils grown
high in the summers' grasses out West—
we are like flowers blooming in grounds
that are hard, gravelly and pebbled.

III

O Lord, why do You chastise us so?
When we are beautiful it adds to
Your glory, causing envy inside
the nations of Your chosen people.
When we are ugly it makes us doubt,
and with us other nations on earth,
for they say that their gods are the ones
who've benefitted them throughout success.

IV

They will say, "We are beautiful through
the strength of our gods, gracious and good."
They will say, "Israel is ruined through
a god who's powerless or faithless."

V

Lord YHWH, don't allow this to be
please instead remember Your Bride who
longs to be beautiful as our youth,
not just to other nations but to
You God of Israel and Judah.

VI

For while God is far beyond the wiles
of women, even David was loved
for being handsome to Lord YHWH,
and Israel should herself should be
one beloved by her dear husband,
loved for her physical as much as
for moral beauty, and so therefore
not opposed to her decorations
that she wears on her youthful body.

VII

Do not tear her down limb for limb for
she wears her jewelry out of love
and jealous pride for her own husband.
You Lord should realize that we wait for
Your coming with love's anticipation
and cannot help our preparing for
our wedding day and Divine Husband.

White Tigers

I

I hear a voice as of one in travail,
Anguish as of a woman bearing her first child,
The voice of Fair Zion
Panting, stretching out her hands:
"Alas for me! I faint
Before the killers!"
Jeremiah 4:31

II

You have made us worse than if we were
a persecuted people only.
We instead, alas, have now become
as small in number as white tigers
have become due to encroachment on
their lands where outright poaching occurs
to further reduce the small numbers
of these cruel and yet beautiful beasts.

III

So persecution has made Jews one
of the earth's endangered list of men,
as if they were as hunted down as
white tigers from cold Siberia, too.

IV

Lord, You have inflicted abuse on
we Jews just as we are in labor
thus preventing our giving birth to
Your child, the newborn Moses born to
the people Israel who love You.

V

Lord, it is our love for You that we
give birth to in the messiah's age.
For God, You promised Abraham that
his nation would be numberless as
the stars in the night sky above us.

VI

We instead are the tigers, that is
they are cats nearly extinct despite
their awesome beauty to those who go
to special places where they are kept
in hopes that human beings will let
them live wild and free again once more.

VII

Lord, recovering our lost numbers
will require marriage to those outside
of the faith, thus we're required to be
as gorgeous as their white fur with stripes.

VIII

But it will also require us to
have time to recuperate as if
we were in hospital beds after
a catastrophe, one as great as
the disasters of Treblinka and
of Buchenwald and Auschwitz as well.

IX

For You have acted falsely and so
it's the case that we ourselves doubt You.
The tigers themselves now no longer
have faith in their own ability
to survive without outside help from
the race of human beings who they must know
once hated tigers beyond reason itself.

X

Yet even now we have not given
You, YHWH, up, for it is through You
that we shall live another proud day
and with whom we shall cry tears despite
our sense of what was lost—through You Lord.

XI

For we know that You are first of all
our Comforter and next that you are
our Redeemer and only after
that our Judge; Judaism still affirms
that Charity and Judgment are two
sides of the same coin, expressing in
two different ways, the Love of God.

XII

Allow us to give birth and grant us
that the worst is past and done with now,
so that we shall be redeemed at last.
Your tigers' survival is certain
as long as even one roams the earth.

XIII

We, Jews, are that breed solitary;
the great White Tigers of Lord YHWH.

The Women of Jerusalem

I

Roam the streets of Jerusalem,
Search its squares,
Look about and take note:
You will not find a man,
There is none who acts justly
Who seeks integrity—
That I should pardon her.
Jeremiah 5:1

II

O Father! Surely if You looked for
Your justice is that the young women,
Your virgins waiting to be married,
You would find a more fervent love
of God than men are capable of.

III

For young men are boisterous as dogs
and superficial to the eyes of
the discerning, in need of teaching
by some sage to be good in God's eyes,
while it is women learn our lessons
from the earth, an old second scroll of law
that men failed to draw learning from and
that women plucked foods and herbs both from.

IV

While men would always educate sons
young daughters learned at home to be wives,
but women would pray to You as maids
to put their frivolities aside
and house the Lord in their hearts, teaching
their younger siblings to pray as well.

V

Their hearts have overflowed with passion
for their Lord even as they search out
men so they can get married while young,
this even as they wished to pray with
the men their fathers educated.

VI

They helped their mothers prepare houses
for Shabbat and rest sleepily on
the day God chose for Himself to rest;
they waited alone for their fathers
to return home to tell them stories.

VII

It was the women who kept Kosher,
while the men merely relied on them,
the sorting and the cooking of foods
for Shabbat itself, one day a week.

VIII

Our Lord is also a good blessing
for women in times ancient and new.
We, the young women, declare ourselves
in sacred devotion to our Lord!
We declare if he lacks good men he
should go in search of some good women!

Israel's Defense

I

When I fed them their fill,
They committed adultery
And went trooping to the harlot's house.
They were well-fed lusty stallions,
Each neighing at another's wife.
Shall I not punish such deeds?
Jeremiah 5:7:4-5:9:1

II

Lord, we have sworn "As-the-Lord-Lives" for
more than two thousand years since we spoke
and we've grown weary of the rebuke
that Jewish men chase harlots, thinking
that they are remorseless studs chasing
each his best friend's wife as though she were
a mare in heat for "lusty stallions"
the horses passionate far beyond
the wild beasts themselves covered with sweat.

III

Lord, it is not quite animal lust
for which Jews themselves are known
to even the worst anti-Semites.
The Jews know better than to believe
the reverse; Jews are not more virile
than other men and aren't more in love with
the baser passions men fall prey to
than Catholics or Protestants are.

IV

It's instead the case that Jews are less
prone to be committing those crimes which
are violent and are well known for
their honesty in business, too.

V

Why, then, would Jews be lecherous to
Lord YHWH, when it has been eons
since You made promises to us which
have not been kept to us as of yet?

VI

If even wicked people will not
doubt the Jew's chastity, why does God?
Why have You not seen us wait on You
for centuries with faith and with hope?

VII

You've made us acquire Israel by
the secular means we had abhorred,
won't You help us find lasting peace with
Your guiding hand reached out and holding
us up like children with their parents
the first time walking across the streets.

VIII

You are our Divine Father and we
wait despite our own irritation
for the day when Your will reign on earth
and not just in the far off heavens.

Untitled

I

It is an enduring nation,
It is an ancient nation;...
Their quivers are like a yawning grave—
They are all mighty men
They will devour harvest and food
They will devour sons and daughters...
Jeremiah 5:15:3-4; 5:16; 5:17:1-2

II

Our prayers have been soldiers for us
the troops through time who fight for us like
great armies for their generals when
the actual battlefield is not clear.

III

O Lord, please listen to us and call
back Your cruel armies against the land.
The nations gather against us, Lord,
and we know that it is Your who spurs
them on to punish us for the crimes
You say we commit both against You
and You are remorseless in pursuit
of us, our enemy and husband,
who sends the armies of the earth to
go conquer his own errant people
and punish them for crimes against God.

IV

Yet we shall overcome You using
Your sacred name of YHWH towards You.
In the vast battlefields where pray would
seem to be the one hope we have left.
We shall pour our wrath upon You, God.

V

Lord, You are angry but so are we—
You've inflicted pain upon the land
and used the hands of warlords to act
and You have taken from us land with
the intention of vindictiveness.

VI

Lord, why is it that it is always
You who has the right to be angry,
when we have suffered so much for You
and You have taken Your own time to
send peace to humankind, so that we
have become the pawn of the nations,
a 'no-thing' worshipping a 'no-god'
in the eyes of those who don't believe
as we do, Christians and now Muslims.

VII

We grow more indignant at chiding,
for time and again we've fought for good,
fought because there's been nothing to do
save fight for our lives and faith in You—
Lord we have fought the good fight for years,
when will You return listening to prayers
that have come down through ages through us.

VIII

Yes, we shall fight the nations along
with the Lord of all nations as well.
We shall watch them from hilltops, praying,
and demanding our recompense from
our YHWH whose been recalcitrant
in listening to Israel pray.

The Lord Puts Down a Revolt

I

Fair Zion, the lovely and delicate, I will destroy.
Jeremiah 6:2

II

We shall not be a flower destroyed!
We are a lily of our Lord YHWH!
Lord YHWH's One who would not destroy
his chosen people Israel if
we immolated children to Him.

III

We shall not cave in to God's demands,
Not until the Lord admits that we
shall never be forced into a state
of submission or leveraged out
of rebellion by You, drums beating
of nations from great faraway lands.

IV

Against her come shepherds with their flocks,
They pitch tents all around her;
Each grazes the sheep under his care.
Jeremiah 6:3

V

"Ah!" cry the Israelites to their God,
"Tent dwellers like the Arabs come to

us in Your name, yet we don't believe
these turbaned travelers who tell us
in honeyed words that "YHWH sent us."

VI

For in our rebellion we refuse
the word of the Lord itself if it
will prophesy much evil against
the people Israel, his servants.
Prepare for battle against her:
"Up! We will attack at noon."

VII

"Alas for us! For day is declining,
The shadows of evening grow long."
Jeremiah 6:4

VIII

We shall be ready by the daybreak!
It is our only hope left to us!
We'll succeed or fight stubbornly till
we are killed by God's angry weapon.
[God whispers into enemy ears,
in the voice of her generals lisps,]
"Up! Let us attack by night
And wreak her fortresses."
Jeremiah 6:5

IX

It is too late! The Lord strikes at last.
For Israel is laid waste by God.

The Rape of Israel

I

For thus said the LORD of Hosts:
Hew down her trees,
And raise a siegemound against Jerusalem.
She is the city destined for punishment;
Only fraud is found in her midst.
Jeremiah 6:6

II

Our virginity is lost, O Lord;
poor Israel is beaten down by
the Lord she expected to tend her;
she is like a young girl who is raped—
and by her first love and her father.

III

So recovery from this loss of
her 'chastity' as prized by men is
like the torn limb that's grabbed a hold of
by a man of an animal so
that the jerk of pain causes them to
think, wondering, once, 'Will I die now?'
for it is forbidden to do so
to a mere animal by our Lord,
yet the Lord inflicts this on his wife,
poor Israel must be more loyal
then she is capable of being.

IV

We cry for both our suffering and
for Israel's limbs as they bleed, too,
both now and in the past, for we see
that grieving helps us admit the past.

V

In our tears of blood, we will recall
that our Lord loved us once, and once more
will scoop his little Israel up
in His arm, 'Forgive me, child, I wronged
you and was delinquent as Father.'

VI

Ah, was it truly YHWH who let
the sufferings of His poor people?
Lord, we still suffer, waiting for You.

The Leopards of the Lord

I

As a well flows with water
So she flows with wickedness
Lawlessness and rapine are heard in her;
Before Me constantly are sickness and wounds.
Jeremiah 6:7

II

Lord, if our sinfulness is so great
tell us the secret of how our spine
was hardened so that we could withstand
the onslaught of abuse that's received
from the hands of the nations whose hearts
like Pharaohs were so hardened against
us that they would not let go of us—
they were like leopards who had just caught
their prey and proceeded to play with
it because leopards are cruel as are
the human beings who hunt down Jews.

III

The only difference is leopards
are unintentionally cruel while
the human race has relished cruelty.
For leopards unlike men are
still blameless in their savagery.

IV

The leopard is a naïve creature
while humans understand what they do.
Just so, You have let hunters of Jews
through the ages to kill us—yet without
their cutting us from the roots of faith
for its faith on which Jews have relied.

V

For however we're angry we know
that our faith is what strengthens the Jews.
For through our faith we become vessels
of love that overflow and creates pure spine
as loyal to God as the leopard
to its cubs, caring constantly for
the promises of the Lord given
in trust to the Jews who cling to You.

VI

Why did You pick us if not to be
as stubborn with You as with peoples
from places unimagined by us
when You had rebuked us as sinful.
Lord, we are leopards, too, the creatures
who You love as rare survivors who
are part of the great environment
You created for us years ago.

VII

They're beloved as humans despite
their lack of human introspection
but tenacious like we Jews ourselves.

VIII

The leopards are Your precious jewels,
how much more so are the Jews scattered
through nations, waiting for You, YHWH,
to forgive us and bring us back home.

Israel's Demands of Her God

I

Don't put your trust in illusion and say, "The Temple of the LORD,
the Temple of the LORD, The Temple of the LORD are these
[buildings]." No, if your ways and your actions; if you ways and your
actions; if you execute justice between one man and another; if you
do not oppress the stranger, the orphan, and the widow; if you do
not follow other gods, to your own hurt—then only will I let you dwell
in this place, in the land that I gave to your fathers for all time.
Jeremiah 7:4-7

II

Your demands, O Lord, are strict and yet
these solid dictates inspire us to
give our own list of demands to You.

III

We ask of You that You will rebuild
our Temple as in the days of old,
that silver and gold will lace the grounds
that it will stand on many cubits
in height like a tall skyscraper which
for us is a great palace for us
to say our prayers inside of while
our high priest prepares inside of it.

IV

Let justice will be done on earth as
it's proclaimed in the far off heavens.
You comfort widows and their children
in grieving over the loss of those
who left them behind under duress,
yet in the future could You spare them
the loss of their loved ones dead before
their time to unwarranted causes.

V

Let justice wash through the great plains like
the waters during a great flood would—
You say it and we agree but we
are feeble creatures and need aid to
give rewards to the good and punish
the wicked here on earth to cure us
of wickedness at a state level.

VI

Make goodness pragmatic and we'll both
go do and obey your good commands
to create a more perfect in which
we shall live, bearing in mind that its
most of the wicked who still believe
they would be good if they could be good.

VII

Grant us these things and we will practice
all the six hundred thirteen commandments that
You've set up as our holy portion
of Your law granted us by Moses
in seeing You thus we pray to you
for day to day grinds like hard gravel
on the wheels of our faith and we need
more consolation than cruel shaming.

VIII

Thus modern preachers need preach more of
the reasons people have faith and not
preach against those who have their own flaws
in believing each Biblical tale.

The Sacrifice of the Children

I

And they have built the shrines of Topheth or the Valley of
Ben-hinnon to burn their sons and their daughters in fire—
which I never commanded, which never came to my mind.
Jeremiah 7:31

II

To sacrifice our best to our God—
is this not the Lord's very command?
And what could be more sacred to us
than children to whom we gave birth to?
To sacrifice our infants to You
proves You our beloved Lord YHWH.

III

Why do you protest violently
on these young children's behalf, O Lord?
Lord, perhaps it is all too true that
we sacrificed our children to gods
as distant from you as the Aztecs.

IV

Lord, if we grant You our best when
it is not commanded, is that not
a merit beyond even these two?

V

Assuredly, a time is coming—declares the Lord—when men shall not speak of Topheth or the Valley of Ben-hinnom, but the Valley of Slaughter; they shall bury in Topheth until no room is left.
Jeremiah 7:32

God Cuts Down Brides and Bridegrooms

I

The carcasses of this people shall be food for the birds of the
sky and the beasts of the earth, with none to frighten them
off. And I will silence in the towns of Judah and the streets
of Jerusalem the sound of mirth and gladness, the voice of
bridegroom and bride. For the whole land shall fall to ruin.
Jeremiah 7:33-34

II

Brides are not marrying in the land
that's promised to us by Lord YHWH
they'll instead remain virgins for God
one won't allow the suffering of
their infants by pangs hunger inflicts
exchanged for pleasure's longings fulfilled.

III

The relentless Lord YHWH cuts down
while cutting part for vultures these who
are delicate and pretty as brides.
They inherited sinfulness from
their parents sins of passion and lust.
To repay YHWH they adopted
a formidable chastity which
a Catholic nun would have admired.
They were warriors of chasteness.

IV

They fought the wickeness of the flesh
with the extreme of celibacy.
They became YHWH's sacrifice by
the opposing sin in all it's forms—
and in God's slaying the girls bercame
a Lord against as satisfied with
Lord YHWH's people as once before.

V

Now because these girls suffer they pray
to their Lord—with what result, who knows.
Their bridegrooms also pray for the Lord
to relent against Israel's young.

The Birds of Israel

I

Even the stork in the sky knows her seasons
And the turtledove, swift, and crane
Keep the time of their coming;
But My people pay no heed
To the law of the LORD.
Jeremiah 8:7

II

O Lord, train us as you trained the birds.
Mark us each season flying through skies
as if the air's own feathered bipeds.
Our hearts are meant to be as gentle
as a man would have to be to train
a stork or cane or turtle dove with
his hands and a bit of food for them.

III

Do Your laws come so naturally
as resembling the birds that migrate
in season towards the land promised
by their God as a home to flee to
when the cold weather beats down upon
their outstretched wings as they fly southwards?

IV

Lord, we need training just as the birds
were taught by maternal love to fly.
For our laws like the baby birds flight
is equally found branded onto
our hearts like tattoos branded onto
the leather hides of luckless cattle.
We love Your laws as a part of us
as circumcised hearts made of soft flesh.

V

You should use gentleness to woo us,
O YHWH of the Israelites for
if You use harsher means You may find
that we go extinct like some birds do.

The Carrying off of the Wives

I

Assuredly, I will give their wives to others,
And their fields to disposers;
For from the smallest to greatest,
They are all greedy for gain;
Priest and prophet alike,
They all act falsely.
Jeremiah 8:10

II

Would you take our wives from us, O Lord?
They are faithful towards their men
as though they are still youthful, tender
and fiercely carefree as young lovers
we recite of them that their virtues
are to be more prized than fine rubies.
They are Eves to our Adams without
whom we'd be lost as newborn kittens
when separated from their mothers.

III

Men rely on their mothers and wives
as though babes remaining in their cribs;
so widowers always look saddened
and dejected with spouses beneath
the bare earth, knowing her loss is one
which renders his life unlivable.

IV

She cooked for herself when her spouse lived.
She is a soldier in the battle
of life who waits for time mourn was.
A widow's upper lip is stronger
was living with her tenderness and
if desolate asks, "Whom do I care
for now that my spouse has gone to rest?"

V

Would it be possible that instead
the separation would be soldiers
who, conscienceless, would carry them far
from us and force them to live lives that
are separate from the lives we live.

VI

Yet it is tragic separating
at the grave, leaving one to wait for
the death person normally fears.
The one left behind patiently waits
to cross the river of life to go
to their friend's destination at last.

VII

Lord, would you carry beloved wives,
to women who look after us when
we're tired or unwell generally?
O Lord, our beloved, would You take
our comforters in sickness from us?

Dirges Turned into Victory Song

I

Thus said the LORD of Hosts:
Listen!
Summon the dirge singers, let them come;
Send for the skilled women, let them come.
Let them quickly start a wailing for us,
That our eyes may run with tears,
Our pupils flow with water.
Jeremiah 9:16-17

II

"The Lord is our King," they will declare.
"When all else fails we appeal to God!"
The women weep as they have uttered
these words to their Lord YHWH on high.
For it is women's pious wailing
that moves the Lord to tears; God is
as fond of people who are deemed as
the 'insignificant' as the great.

III

Thus rising both against kings and fools,
of orphans and of widows who are
the impoverished people whose hearts
will both embrace God as their lover
and their own beloved in their hearts
when needing friends they rely on Him.

IV

For the sound of wailing
Is heard from Zion:
How we are despoiled!
How greatly are they shamed!
Ah, we must leave our land,
Abandon our dwellings!
Jeremiah 9:19

V

"The Lord is our King," they will declare.
"When all else fails we appeal to Him."
The female timbres travel with us
to Babylon, far from our homeland—
the sopranos of Israel sing
out of the loss of their heart's desire—
for Israel's lost people desire
her to be their own again once more.

VI

O Israel, the sopranos cry,
we long to be your children again!
Let us come from the earth's four corners
to return to pray in the land that
our Lord has promised to us as we
have waited centuries for our songs
to be sung once more, not just dirges
but melodies with instruments that
will not be played for ages until
the Temple's also restored by You
and women gather to sing praises.

VII

Hear, O women, the word of the LORD,
Let your ears receive the word of His mouth,
And teach your daughters wailing,
And one another lamentations.
Jeremiah 9:19

VIII

"The Lord is our King," they will declare.
"When all else fails we appeal to God."

IX

Sing dirges that one day we will sing
The praise to the Lord for which we were
formed as a chosen people sung by
our women and men in the manner
of Miriam the prophetess who
led the song of the multitude when
the red sea parted for her brother.

X

the prophet Moses of whom none can
match, "Never again did there arise"
a second Moses nor will there be
an equal prophet until the end
of ages brings the messiah to
the children of the promised nation.

XI

Till then we will sing dirges yet not
not just with bitterness but with joy.
"The Lord is our King," we will declare.
"When all else fails we appeal to Him."

XII

And when we finally have appealed
to YHWH, finally God replies
with a kiss; we are rewarded for
our faith in YHWH who breathed our lives
in to our humanity at birth.

The Sacred Faun

I

Why should My beloved be in my House
Who executes so vile designs?
The sacral flesh will pass away from you,
For you exult while performing your evil deeds.
Jeremiah 11:15

II

Lord, if we weren't in your house with You
we would be cavorting with the gods
of Canaan, rivals without mercy
to our Lord, jealous, ignored, angry.
Yet in Your house, aren't we safe from?
All too fast these flash floods of passion
seem able to come overflowing
the YHWH overcome God's Spirit.

III

Lord YHWH making YHWH like those
the Greeks call "furies" who are bent on
the destruction of sinful humans.
Lord YHWH's fury makes God like them.
Yet whatever image is Your best.

IV

This untamed humanity is one
which shares in common the Lord's Fury
that vengeful justice we feel when wronged
and yet we know our YHWH is filled
with Divine mercy for Her children
like mother tigers have for their young.

V

Yet this is one side of our YHWH
another is the tenderness of
a beloved embracing us in
the arms which offer milk and honey.

VI

Another way of seeing YHWH
of a great Father watching over
his earthly sons and daughters below.
Another is the Mother Herself
who gave Birth to our Humanity.

VII

We long for You in Your house where we
pray hoping You will bring about more—
our redemption and Yours through prayer.
We wish You'd forgive us for frailties—
it is as though the forbidden foods
were inviting like lust for women
and Canaan's gods make promises that
are golden as the honeyed manna
we ate from Egypt to our good land.

IX

We hope You forgive us our frailties—
no, we know as Mother, You do—
but we have trouble believing this
as You are terrifying in the Form
of Lord Above us who wait for You.

X

We have been taught to fear You because
it was thought that the mitzvoth we kept
would require a God with teeth to keep.
Yet fear is detrimental to Faith
it causes pain in those who would Love
and Fear of YHWH is a falsehood
if practiced without the Love of God.

XI

O Lord we sometimes forget to think
of You yet You are constantly loved;
why isn't faulty love still better
than quaking fear of a God as stark
as a stag by the desert moonlight
a beloved glimpsed by a few men
who remembered to tell us the tale?

XII

The moon is beautiful as a veil
but how can it be loved or give love?
Is it not better to love something
as warm as the faun the stag sired with
it suckling love of its own mother?

The People Struggle with Jeremiah

I

Assuredly, thus said the LORD of Hosts concerning the men of
Anathoth who seek your life as they say, "You must not prophesy any
more in the name of the LORD, or you will die by our hand"—
Jeremiah 11:21

II

O Prophet desist! We can't take more!
We're troubled by your presence beyond compare!
Lord, why did you send us this dour prophet,
when all he has to foretell is gloom
and every last judgment becomes
fresh condemnation of Your people?

III

The prophet is sour milk past the point
of drinking safely or for the taste.
He predicts despair for us, wishing,
for appearances sake, death for us.

IV

He curses us and blesses those who
are enemies to Your own people.
We ourselves curse this nagging pest who
speaks in the name of the Lord Himself.
Just as he frightens us he annoys
his people, causing us to cry out,
"Take this false prophet far away! Go!
We want no more of him, he is not
a patriot or optimist and
we have grown weary of him! O Lord,
spare us this dreary, wretched 'prophet.'"

V

For we wish that this prophet of gloom
would take his prophecies and stuff them—
they're the least helpful advice on earth.
Who places down their arms in battle?
No, truly this will come to no good.

VI

*Assuredly, thus said the LORD of Hosts: "I am going
to deal with them: the young men will die by the
sword, their boys and girls will die by famine."*
Jeremiah 11:22

VII

"Let us stone him!" we cry out en masse.

Lemons of the Divine Mother

I

I have abandoned My House,
I have deserted My possession,
I have given over My dearly beloved
Into the hands of her enemies.
Jeremiah 12:7

II

You are a terrifying Mother.
You frighten as a Female Tiger—
a Mother Goddess is part of You
an idol prayed to in fear of You.
This terror ripples within us as
ones worshipping in understanding
which remains partial with eyes lowered
lest Your Image strike down the looker.
And yet our desire remains for You.
the Divine Shrew who cannot be pleased.

III

Lord, come back to us; for we miss You
as a lone husband misses his wife.
O Lord, the love You have for us is
a mother's love which overflows for
her offspring born of the pains of birth.

IV

You nourish us like mother tigers
will nourish their young save the fact You
will never leave us to the great wild
when our time to be an adult comes.

V

Yet You are a harsh mother sometimes
who rebukes leaving bruises on us
and rather than the milk and honey
that we were promised gives us sour grapes
that put our teeth on edge like lemons.

VI

Why do You punish us so much with
Your tartness which makes lemons taste sweet?
Our Divine Mother—for You're Mother
as well as Father to Your children—
seems all too anxious, punishing us,
to force us to give up the hope of
our achieving the perfection You
wish from us as Your devout children.

VII

O Mother and O Father as One!
Yet never 'Parent' only to us.
Will you embrace us tenderly and
with gentleness like mother sheep do
their lambs in suckling milk at their teats.

The Lions and the Gazelles

I

My own people acted toward Me
Like a lion in the forest;
She raised her voice against Me—
Therefore I have rejected her.
Jeremiah 12:8

II

Lord, do not reject beloved sons
and daughters however like lions.
For You have mistaken our intent.
They care of their Lord watching Him stalk
their Prey in the fields, tending their needs
by providing food for the lions.
The people merely worship their prey
they could not kill Him if they so willed.
Yet like the lion they live by Him.

III

It is a mystery for the Jews
why God trades the life of the gazelle
for the life of the lion because
this formula of Nature's being
as cruel as lions are in killing
and injured as the murdered gazelle
is beautiful and sad to love as
the feeling creatures that Great Cats are.

IV

Don't reject us, Lord, our love for You
still does not rebuke You and yet loves
both of them: lion and yet gazelle.
The animals sing praises to You,
and without knowing Your Name display
Your glory unconsciously because
few observing them doubt their beauty.

V

They suckle their young as God cares for
us and still understands we lions.
For human beings combine the traits
of lions and yet also gazelles.

Hunters of the Lord

I

My own people acts toward Me
Like a bird of prey [or] a hyena...
Jeremiah 12:9:1-2

II

Like animals we devour YHWH,
we tear God into pieces to eat
we feed the Divine Substance of God
to infants, nourishing the children
while sustaining them in adulthood.

III

Just as Greeks worshiped Bacchus so we
feed on our poor Lord's injuries, too.
Of course, with Bacchus the god reveled
in sinfulness while our Lord forbade
such licentious rites, like the mixing
of blood and wine in toxic mixture.

IV

Lord YHWH demands worship be chaste
while practices fit between two ways
a personified by lust itself
and by extreme aestheticism, too,
and the aesthetic being ritual
like sacrificing children to God.

V

Lust being Bacchanalian worship
amongst the lawlessness of pagans
the worshipers of YHWH feed on
the scars once inflicted on our Lord
like wolves who feast on a deer hunted
and brought down in the forest clearing.

VI

It is as though God was the hunted
and we were the cruel hunters of Him—
this despite the fierce dangers of such
a tantalizing game of hunting
a Lord the sight of whom kills the one
who sees the God of Israel's face.

VII

Will hunters of god survive the chase?
Let the birds of prey surround her!
Go, gather all the wild beasts,
Bring them to devour!
Jeremiah 12:9:3-5

VIII

While we lay with the souls dead, we still
have never seen the face of the Lord.

Crying the Lord's Tears

I

"They have made her a desolation;
Desolate, she pours out grief to Me..."
Jeremiah 13:11:1-2

II

O YHWH were made desolate You
beg you hear our tears and our pleadings;
it is Your compassion for our tears
for which we give prayers to You, O Lord
not just rain during the dry season
for the crops we need for food and drink.
You are more than food for your children.

III

Your Spirit transforms caterpillars
to butterflies as humans souls go.
The Spirit with You learns how to Love.
Pain because healing through You, YHWH.
For Lord, Your Spirit is in us all
if we will open our hearts to You.

IV

Your comfort nourishes us when we
have recalled prayerfully that You
are What has always existed and
will always exist beyond time's end
Yet You exist, in the heart itself
of human beings physically
and spiritually pass in form right
back to the Lord through souls in return
to the source and the author of ALL.

V

Lord YHWH, I trust my soul to You
as You and I are extensions of
each other, me with a small drop of
You within me, You incorporate
that drop called "I" in the "You" large and
in which the universe is stretched out.
When we cry out to YHWH, we are
embraced with the love of Lord YHWH.

Words of the Queen Mother

I

Say to the king and the queen mother,
"Sit in a lowly spot;
For your diadems are abased,
Your glorious crowns."
Jeremiah 13:18

II

"What's this?" the mother of the king asked.
"Am I to bend my will when I am
the queen of Israel, land of God?
Cast out this prophet and find one who
will prophecy more pleasing things
from the Lord YHWH's people themselves!
Cast him out because of his insults!

III

"You Jeremiah, speak cruel falsehoods
that deeply wound the people of God.
Why would the Lord choose a mere madman
if the Lord had a message that he
wished us to consider as monarchs—
than surely he would have picked a prince
or other distinguished king or queen?
Why should we hear this lunatic when
sane men will assure us 'all is well'?"

IV

This gloomy prophet foretells our doom,
and sanity is itself threatened
by Jeremiah's prophecies which
preach against worldly wisdom itself,
the wisdom acquiring such allies
as Syria and Egypt, countries
with whom we're forbidden to contract
our treaties with, the pagan nations.

VI

So it was Israel's blood was spilled
and the queen's last words were these "Madness!
O Madness for Lord YHWH on high.

VII

"For you are mad, O Jeremiah!
You have fits you call 'inspiration'
and bleak spells of gloom you call 'despair,'
and times of euphoria which you
know are not very often yet claim
'are worth my suffering for they bring
my spirit to the holiest springs
of the heart's Temple for Lord YHWH.
It is the Holy of which you speak?
You say so, but your sense is madness."

Israel Giving Birth

I

Shall not pangs seize you
Like a woman in childbirth?
And when you ask yourself,
"Why have these things befallen me?"
It is because of your great iniquity
That your skirts are lifted up,
Your limbs exposed.
Jeremiah 13:21:3-4; 13:22

II

In the fields surrounding the city
of Jerusalem, women work with
their husbands in the fields of Zion
and occasionally lie down to
give birth to a child in the dry heat.

III

A woman lies down gasping for breath
and pushes out an infant, while she
cries softly as the tinkling wind chimes
that play in the breeze like a flute's song.
The infant wails as pitifully
as though it fears that its birth will go
as unnoticed and unheralded
as the king's firstborn received notice
from Israel and foreign nations.
The baby squalls; the mother moans and out
comes an heir of a small one room house.

IV

So it is that when Israel is
a ravaged woman in her travail
we know the Lord forms squalling infants—
as Israel brings forth the treasure
that womankind in pain brings forth, too—
new generations of our people
in order that our salvation comes
and punishment be extracted from
the chosen people, brutally and
like birth pains inflicted on women.

Grant us Justice, Our Lord

I

Judah is in mourning,
Her settlements languish.
Men are bowed to the ground,
And the outcry of Jerusalem rises.
Jeremiah 14:2

II

Your decrees are harsh, O Lord YHWH,
for You have wiped out Judah's people.
Poor Judah, she cries, I am lost to
the Lord of all the Israelite tribes
the last ones recognizable as
the chosen descendents of Abram.

III

How pitiful we appear to God.
Our lives are desolate as the moon.
Still, our shrill outcry must shock the Lord,
for although he formed us he could not
have predicted the anger of Jews
more than their anguish over our loss.

IV

For Judah howls those truths in her heart,
how betrayed she was by her Lord YHWH.
She wants her revenge on her Husband.
Yet revenge on You cannot be had;
who can judge between You and Judah?

V

True justice cannot be had save through
Your will by Itself, O Lord YHWH.
Grant us our justice, YHWH, so that
we recover from our sad losses;
give vindication to the righteous.

Forebodings of Woe

I

And the people to whom they [the false prophets] prophesy shall
be left lying in the streets of Jerusalem because of the famine and
sword, with none to bury them—they, their wives, their sons and their
daughters. I will pour out upon them [the requital of] their wickedness.
Jeremiah 14:16

II

We prophets see the glass half full which
the prophet Jeremiah declares
is fully empty. In his dour sense
he sees no goodness where God isn't.
He remains constant to his vision.
He won't be moved to optimism in
the regard of a time that's sinful.
The good times only last, so he says,
if virtue remains in tact in us.

III

Don't doubt Lord YHWH's Truth must be kept.
A step away and Vengeance will come—
for YHWH insists individuals
embrace their Lord with all their hearts.

IV

He claims time is now running out for
the people of the tribes of Judah.
We prophets predict prosperity
with buoyant optimism that believes
a people despite their flaws and crimes
has hope of redemption when they've sinned.

V

It is the name of "Jew" which saves us;
the deeds are better done by others.
We preach as the dour Jeremiah
comes representing melancholy;
our saddened YHWH Judah abhors
to Judah's kings and people.

VI

For sadness is entailed in the fall
of humanity to Lord YHWH
God's bludgeoning is not meant to heal
God's warning to men indiscretions.
No joy comes from Lord YHWH's coming;
it's coming vengeance YHWH brings us
not answered prayers of those who've suffered.

VII

Although she loves Lord YHWH Judah
longs for glad tidings, happy news and
so deserves better than the wrath spent
by the Lord towards Judah's people.

VIII

You, Jeremiah, are the cause of
our misfortunes! It is you bringing
about them and not the Lord YHWH.
You frighten people and so cause harm
with your dire warnings, forebodings of
things that need not be until you cause
the pessimistic thinking to bring
bad tidings to God's people Judah!

Pearls

I

Their widows shall be more numerous
Than the sands of the seas.
Jeremiah 15:8:1-2

II

Our widows are like oysters who
hold pearls formed of the harsh sands within
their hard shells, the shells they need as Jews—
for a Jew eating oysters might
be cannibalistic in her heart;
for persecution causes Jews to
form hard shells and pearls within themselves.

III

I will bring against them—
Young men and mothers together—
A destroyer at noonday.
Jeremiah 15:8:3-5

IV

While widows produce single pearls its
the mothers who will create many,
in order to treat affliction caused
by the pain of lost sons who died young
or daughters with a similar plight.

V

It's mothers who will suffer in war
in throws of agony for children
who're crippled or killed by methods
as implacable as Lord YHWH.

VI

I will bring down suddenly upon them
but firstly the great alarm and terror
that unnaturally attend death.

VII

The Lord's an implacable foe who
slays women with the men as they are
left behind to grieve over the dead.
The pearls left by Him in the hearts of
the living are the sacred relics
of the dead, however they had died.

The Woman of Judah

I

She who bore seven is forelorn,
Utterly disconsolate;
Her sun has set while it is still day,
She is shamed and humiliated.
The remnant of them I will deliver of the sword,
To the power of their enemies.
—declares the LORD.
Jeremiah 15:9

II

"A woman who has seven children
will have no children left to care for
her in her old age," these are the words
of Jeremiah, prophesying
the gloomy doom of Judah's kingdom.

III

"This woman will watch as her children
meet the sword sent by our Lord," he says.
On these words, Judah's mothers cried out,
"A curse on prophecy and prophets;
in particular Jeremiah;
they've only bad things to say to us—
they predict our lives of ease will end
and instead we will suffer the loss
of sons and daughters, claiming that God
will chasten us with violent blows
and rip our beloveds clean from us."

IV

These burly matrons formed a pack to
face off the prophet Jeremiah
and, nearly killing him, had their day.
Poor Jeremiah sobbed in hiding;
he fully expected to meet death.

Mother of the Prophet

I

Woe is me, my mother, that you ever bore me—
A man of conflict and strife with all land!
I have not lent,
And I have not borrowed;
Yet everyone curses me.
Jeremiah 15:10

II

"O Jeremiah!" cries his mother,
for Jeremiah's mother spoke out,
one of the few not incensed by him.
"It's not enough that I accept you
are YHWH's prophet beloved of
a neglected God who loves us allegiance
and yet inexplicably wants
God's children to fear God as a King.

III

"In my womb he was gentle as though
a lamb which grazes Israel's fields.
Lord YHWH though his people the Jews
would butcher Jeremiah himself—
they will read his work reverently.
As for Lord YHWH's people—love, love
is what Lord YHWH insists from them
from Abraham's time onwards until
the monarchy and beyond till now.
Lord YHWH waits on us til;l we come
to realize YHWH's mercy ourselves.

IV

"My little prince! I knew you were born
a special boy entered the world.
I knew the Lord had picked my son's task
to be a blessing to God's people—
yet unacknowledged as one during
his lifetime because his news was bad—
for indeed warning catastrophe
is necessary and yet invites
the wrath of denial by people
who are as afraid of the future
for reason of a guilty conscience.

V

"In melancholic moments he comes
to me to revive his faith in God.
In ecstatic ones he will visit
in regards to his seldom joys.
Sad Jeremiah was picked by God;
he told me so when he was quite young;
an adolescent boy in tears.

VI

"I asked him what was so sad because
the sun that shined through the clouds that day.
He told me, 'I'm a prophet who will
be misunderstood by my people.'

VII

"My darling son spoke effusively
his burden fallen down on him from
the far off heavens like the teardrops
as it rained down on us as we stood.
I never count him a curse from God."

The Burden of Jeremiah

I

You are not to marry and not to have sons and daughters in
this place. For thus said the LORD concerning any sons and
daughters that may be born in this place, and concerning the
mothers who bear them, and concerning the fathers who beget
them in this place: They shall die gruesome deaths...
Jeremiah 16:2-16:4:1

II

O merciless Lord, why are we doomed
to childlessness in Judah's two tribes
We'll be too old to have children
and thus be numbered like the eunuch
bruised reeds who cannot continue on—
for we Jews believe it's a blessing
to be one remembered by offspring
in paternity's blessing: children.

III

What good is prudence at such a cost?
Why prepare for the worst of cases,
when we can't know the distant future
or even future times near at hand?
Why should the Lord send us this burden,
this meddler bringing us bad fortune?
Did the Lord not once declare that we
were to be fruitful, multiplying
in numbers beyond the above stars?

IV

Send this pest back to our Lord YHWH.
Flay the live Jeremiah for us
allow us our great happiness with
our children's children without an end
to Judah in an apocalypse.

The Mourners' Lament

I

They shall not break bread for a mourner
To comfort him for a bereavement,
Nor offer one a cup of consolation
For the loss of his father or mother.
Jeremiah 16:7

II

Lord, let us weep for beloved dead;
for Nature demands our grief for them.
Tear droplets beg to flow from our eyes,
for mothers, fathers, daughters and sons.
Why deny us our only relief?

III

Your cruelty consists of this failing:
You don't allow us to mourn for them
the losses which You have brought to us—
we could stand our great bereavement if
we were allowed our profuse teardrops.

IV

The consolation fated to us
ought to be bewailing what's happened.
It is the consolation of souls
in gehenna for sins on this earth
to cry tears without reserve hoping
that sincere remorse lightens burdens
of even those souls underneath us.

V

O Lord, why rob us of these tears sobbed?
It is like stealing from graves with
its restless solemnity granting
if not peace its own sense of closure.

VI

Weep with us, O Lord, for your children
long for some reconciliation.
Weep and let us weep so that we may
still turn back to Your arms that
are circled in a wide embrace of
those orphaned because of Death itself.

The Banished Bride

I

*For thus said the Lord of Hosts, the God of Israel: I am going to
banish from this place, in your days and before your eyes, the
sound of mirth and gladness, the voice of bridegroom and mirth.*
Jeremiah 16:9

II

When Jephtha's daughter met her fate she
was permitted to bewail, mourning
her tragic virginity before
he sacrificed his daughter to God.

III

Yet our brides when so deprived in life
aren't permitted to express their grief—
that womanhood be denied to them.
Their longings shall be frustrated with
the unexpressed grief choking them off.

IV

Their gentle yearning for young husbands
are blocked by bitter convulsions,
the grief God forbade them to express;
He demanded our stoic firmness
for repentance, the Lord said, requires
a docility in the face of
our being punished by Lord YHWH.

V

Yes, when stabbed by the pains of hunger,
we are to fall on our knees before
Lord YHWH, and accept his curses.

VI

Why, Lord, must we accept the rage of
the rambling Jeremiah coming
forth from your Israel's grim prophet?
For brides and bridegrooms to die before
the possibility of life lived
is surely worthy of our mourning.

More on the Burden of Jeremiah

I

Assured, thus said the LORD:
Inquire among the nations:
Who has heard anything like this
Maiden Israel has done
A most horrible thing.
Jeremiah 18:13

II

Lord, Maiden Israel has tired of
your prophet Jeremiah's complaints
we long for him to leave us alone
for distances more great than Egypt.
For Jeremiah has grown tiresome,
a burdensome old busybody
who trails to people's houses pouring
doom, plaintively said, into their ears.

III

Please take this man far from us
so harm won't come to Jeremiah—
from YHWH's chosen who are Judah,
for we are thoroughly tired of him.
Please grant us respite from his ranting
his doom-and-gloom ways prophesying.
Spar us the ugly picture which he
gives us as the cruel mirror of us.

IV

We find him irritating at best
and demoralizing, at his worst—
most particularly in war times.
If we could 'give' this prophet of doom
to Babylon our enemy we
might win the war as Babylon falls
in despair born of pessimism's gloom.

The Plot

I

They said, "Come let us devise a plot against Jeremiah—for instruction
shall not fail from the priest, nor counsel from the wise, nor oracle from
the wise, nor oracle from the prophet. Come, let us strike him with the
tongue, and we shall no longer have to listen to all those words of his."
Jeremiah 18:18

II

O! indeed let's rid ourselves of him,
this pest of whom there is no equal.
For years he's predicted our demise,
that the worst will come about towards
the people of Lord YHWH Himself.

III

All of these years he has plagued Judah.
He demoralizes the people;
his works are treasonous to Judah
for when war comes he predicts defeat.
This 'prophet' grumbles of our leaders
and of our common people to us
with nothing good to say of either.

IV

Should good be repaid with evil?
Yet they have dug a pit for me.
Remember how I stood before You
To plead in their behalf,
To turn Your anger away from them.
Jeremiah 18:20

V

Oh! Jeremiah rises early
to stand on the great mountains before
he declares to the people God's wrath.

VI

We see him pray for hours to then come
to pour forth gall and bitterness from
deep within him on Judah's people
so inspiring them with dread they flee.
Why will he not let us be happy?
Stone Jeremiah, this wild madman!

VII

Oh, give their children over to famine,
Mow them down by the sword.
Let their wives be bereaved
Of children and husbands,
Let their men be struck down by the plague,
And their young men be struck down by the sword!
Jeremiah 18:21

VIII

Stone Jeremiah! We've heard the last
of this pest irksome and filled with hate!

The Sacrifice of the Children

I

*And I will cause them to eat the flesh of their sons and the
flesh of their daughters, and they shall devour one another's
flesh—because of the desperate straits to which they will
be reduced by their enemies, who seek their life.*
Jeremiah 19:9

II

O Lord, the gruesome day that you've sent
is hardest on the children's mothers.
For You've taught us to treasure children—
by forbidding their sacrifice You
made them dear to us beyond measure.

IV

Why then would You tear open our hearts
by causing survival to be based
on sacrificing infants for food?

V

Why send this desperation to us,
Your people battered bloody with spears?
Among the punishments this is worst.

VI

Dead children laid out like a buffet,
their grieving mothers crying over
their meals, with trickling teardrops forming
their salty rivers of grieved remorse
at having done the unthinkable—
and sacrificed their children for selves.

VII

Lord, how could You send a fate so cruel?
Our children were Your children as well.

The Birth of Jeremiah

I

Accursed be the man
Who brought my father the news
And said "A boy
Is born to you,"
And gave him such joy!...
Because he [the man] did not kill me before my birth
So that my mother might be my grave,
And her womb big [with me] for all time.
Why did I ever issue from the womb
To see misery and woe,
To spend all my days in shame.
Jeremiah 20:14-15; Jeremiah 20:17-18

II

O Jeremiah, you bring to us
your misery on yourselves as one
whose devoted to principled gloom.

III

For fortunate you were once announced
on the day You were born a son to
your father joyous over his luck.
You remembered the burden you brought
to your once happy father who'd beamed
on baby Jeremiah in words
of declaration, "This is my son!"

IV

Know that you've brought him no such joy since
for you have not ceased bewailing us
for sinning against Jeremiah—
as continually you come harass
us with the bad news we've no desire
to listen to in dangerous times
when we need encouragement from God.

V

Would God choose Jeremiah to speak
for YHWH delivering God's word,
when Jeremiah's irascible
and was so even when a young man;
while youthful declaring the hour of
poor Judah's catastrophe's coming
he assured Judah, like the night's dark?

VI

Now your own father would be ashamed
to know you; he would crave the news of
the death of his son Jeremiah
as one who's outraged patriotism
found shame in his son's declarations
of the Lord's vengeance on poor Judah.

VII

It is you and not your birth to blame
the sun shined happily on that day
and your proud parents displayed you to
friends with the utmost cheerfulness, too.

VIII

It is a lack of reverence to
your parents you show today, speaking
words contrary to the Lord's teachings
the fifth of the ten commandments made
at Sinai by the Israelites with
the Lord you try to claim now loathes us.
Do not preach, Jeremiah, we will
not listen to your arrogant words.

The Faith of Righteous

I

Thus said the LORD: Do what is just and right; rescue the
defrauder him who is robbed; do not wrong the stranger,
the fatherless, and the widow; commit no lawless act, and
do not shed the blood of the innocent in this place.
Jeremiah 22:3

II

Don't oppress impoverished widows
You tell us, without explaining how
they became poor and stricken with grief.
It's as though You should repent with us.

III

I was told of a legend a Jew—
a pious Jew who prayed thrice daily
and all the prayers the Orthodox do
when they are devout and pray to God.
on the day of Yom Kippur on year,
"Lord, You tell us to pray in order
to obtain forgiveness for the sin
of creating poor widows, orphans
and casting out the strangers within
the tribe of Judah, what's left of it.

IV

"But Lord, I have done none of these things—
there are no orphans because of me
nor widows, impoverished or not—
and you have created so many
of such as these they can't be counted.
So this year I ask that You repent
with us, that You will also come to
Your children begging forgiveness for
the times You have hurt us—for You have."

V

So on Yom Kippur the Lord repents
the injuries he's done his children.
So Lord we ask for a day when there
are no more widows, orphans or poor.
We ask Your blessing for that day,
as it is through Your blessing that good
comes into fruition in this world.

The Late King

I

Assuredly, thus said the LORD concerning
Jehoiakim son of Josiah, king of Judah:
They shall not mourn for him,
"Ah brother! Ah sister!"
They shall not mourn for him,
"Ah, lord! Ah, his majesty!"
He shall have the burial of an ass,
Dragged out and left lying
Outside the gates of Jerusalem.
Jeremiah 22:18-19

II

When poor King Jehoiakim died
his sisters neglected his grave while
the new king rejoiced at the death of
his father, the late king of Judah,
so that his death was an old donkey's—
hence creating a state where his son
in unnatural jubilance cries,
"My day has come; I'm Israel's king!"

III

Of course, for Jehoiakim when
His reign had begun, overjoyed is
how the young Jehoiakim was.
Now the old king watched revelers who
looked forward to his own near demise
and for the first time mourned his father.

IV

Yes, prophets decried his reign as he
cried for his coming death, its clutches
like ice on the king's aged stomach.
King Jehoiakim's own mother
if she had lived would have showed concern
more for the festivities than for
her undistinguished son and lord king.

Letter from Jeremiah

I

Thus said the LORD of Hosts, the God of Israel, to the whole community which I exiled from Jerusalem to Babylon: Build houses and live in them, plant gardens and eat their fruit. Take wives and beget sons and daughters; and take wives for your sons, and give your daughters to husbands, that they may bear sons and daughters. Multiply there, do not decrease. And seek the welfare of the city to which I have exiled you and pray to the LORD min its behalf; for in its prosperity you shall prosper.
Jeremiah 29:4-7

II

The prophet promises us return
to the land where our nation was born—
but in the meantime how shall we live?
The prophet bids us that we live as
though the land we live in was our land,
a land where milk and honey will fill
the land from porous openings like
gates flooded with their immigrants who
are searching for a homeland with life
in a new country, continuing
yet unbroken with the change of place.

III

Men find wives so the race won't die off.
Wives marry them to produce offspring,
for male and female God made you both,
with matrimony as an end of
God's creation with tradition as
a binding force of generations
so granting Abraham and Sarah—
their immortality in children.

IV

Life must go on in exile itself—
with offspring as an example of
the destruction of the Lord's Temple
not ending every day events.

V

So Jeremiah bids us recall
that ordinary events don't cease
when tragedies or joyous events
break through the monotony of life—
and besides children reinforce that
if there is death there's also new life.

Men in Labor

I

As and see:
Surely males do not bare young!
Why then do I see every man
With his hands on his loins
Like a woman in labor?
Why have all faces turned pale?
Jeremiah 30:6

II

Do only women give birth in pain
or do men also bring forth children?
For perhaps convulsions of them both
are needed to give birth to nations,
hands spread out like flat foam on the waves
of the vast ocean's water which pours
when labor signals the way to
the hospital room where the baby
is born with its head floating outside
on the great surface of the body.

III

The sea will produce nations with laws
just as the women have pangs to give
a culture its own people without
whom it can't live for even a day.
For cultures can't live without people—
just as a people is stripped bare if
its denied its right to "be," is gone
in accordance with timeless precepts—
those located deep within its soul.

IV

So travail shared with men by women
gives rise to peoples and their cultures.

V

Ah, that day is awesome;
There is none like it!
It is a time of trouble for Jacob,
But he shall be delivered from it.
Jeremiah 30:7

Rachel Cries to the Lord

I

Thus said the Lord:
A cry is heard in Ramah—
Wailing, bitter weeping—
Rachel weeping for her children
She refuses to be comforted
For her children, who are gone.
Jeremiah 31:15

II

"My children though few in their number
are irreplaceable as gemstones
ground into familial heirlooms."
So one of Israel's wives spoke while
she regarded her children, the Jews.

III

The favorite wife of her husband
was the most beautiful when they met
where Jacob found her as he traveled
while on the road to find his uncle.

IV

Then Leah spoke, "Why is it your tears
and only your tears remembered by
the multitude of children born to
the four of us that include you, me,
and my maid Zilpah and your Bilhah.

V

Although our life is discordant it
seems indecorous to feud over
which wife comes first in the grave itself.
So Rachel rebuked, invited three,
her sister and their maids to lament
the fate of Israel's lost children,
the innocents who are too young to
raise voices to protest acts of
their parents disobeying YHWH.

VI

"O Lord," they cried, "Spare us our children,"
in mingled commiseration they
then recalled their own covenant with
the God of Jacob, beloved of
the women praying to God as One.

VII

Although they resent their own husband
they each loved their children by him.
More, Leah had cried out to the Lord—
when she wished for a firstborn she cried.
And Bilhah confessed her sins towards
her husband as she left the world in
death regarding his son, poor Reuben.
Although her husband knew she feared God
and asked for forgiveness for incest.

VIII

They'd all cried to the Lord in birth pangs
and during times of stress which revealed
that their own prayers constituted
a separate-made covenant with
Lord YHWH, Israel's God Itself—
no they cried out to their Lord, YHWH.

IX

"Lord preserve our dear little children,
they are deemed special to four co-wives
who bore them as their holy mothers.
For there's no greater tragedy than
the loss of children to their mothers';
the pain of pushing out the child through
their bodies carrying weight like
the undignified elephants when
they give birth to their elephant cubs
mass is not undignified only.

X

We, Israel's wives spiritually,
gave birth to all God's chosen so that
the death of just one crucifies us.
Thus the red strings from Rachel's tomb is
a thing that's especially good for babies.

XI

Lord spare our children beloved to
their four great mothers, wives to Jacob."
Thus said the LORD:
Restrain your voice from weeping,
Your eyes from shedding tears;
For there is a reward for your labor
--declares the LORD:
They shall return from the enemy's land.
Jeremiah 31:16

XII

God Courts Israel
Return, Maiden Israel!
Return to these towns of yours!
Jeremiah 31:21:5-6

XII

The Lord is exiled from the land,
a bridegroom awaiting his fair bride
with everlasting virginity
which continues on despite
the consummation brought by marriage,
the wedding canopy which the bride comes
to enter to be revealed to Him
in secret far from our eyes besides
the irreverence of the vulgar.

XIV

This togetherness between God and soul—
as Israel births humanity's
a new kind of the human being
in breathing the Lord's spirit like air
through our mouths and our noses, as if
its holiness that's necessary
like oxygen for the soul's good health
and survival like vitamins which
we eat in oranges, tart and sweet.

XV

The Lord cries, "Return! Come home, my Bride,
to our great canopy where we two
join Spirits becoming one Spirit
and yet two Spirits distinct in that
they never lose track of their Being
God and the Other outside of God.

XVI

Our affection like espoused lovers
does resemble the Rose of Sharon
"My beloved is mine," she says,
and I am his—my beloved's, too."
As one Soul together we shall be
if Israel will return home to
be in love with your Groom whom is God!"

Dialectic of God

I

How long will you waver,
O rebellious daughter?
Jeremiah 31:22:1-2

II

"My child; come back home," says Lord YHWH.
"Come back to the earth promised to you.
When I found you, you were an orphan,
one abandoned since Abraham in
the poverty of slaves in Egypt,
for Joseph's nobility was lost.

III

"In dessert sands you tormented Me,
you undeserving towards we two—
that's towards Moses Lord YHWH—
and yet you were my beloved if
you'd realize adolescence ended
years ago; and adulthood had long
since begun, and it was time for you
accept Lord YHWH commands yourselves.

IV

"My daughter, end this rebelliousness—
for although I'm long suffering I
have limits just like earthly parents
do because after they're gone your chance
to apologize ends with their death.
They might want to say that they forgive
and yet they're unable to until
you join them within the grave itself.

V

Best not to wait in life with regrets.
For the sins plaguing us in the end
For the sins plaguing us in the end
are unbearable as death itself.
Yet best not to wait for God either.

VI

Come to your Divine Father as if
he were a beloved friend in love
who will embrace like earthly Fathers.
"Our Father, protect us," we reply.

VII

"We long for promises to us to
be fulfilled and yet when embraced we
our Divine Father lonely for Him
we find that we are persecuted
for keeping His Law given to us.

VIII

From Spanish Inquisition's fury
to the great Holocaust of Europe
we have died sanctifying Your Name.
When will You redeem us, Your chosen?
When will 'A chosen people become
a nation like the nations' as You
had promised ages ago to us?"

VIII

The dialectic of God and scroll
with individual praying to Him
in order to have faith one more time.
For faith has been though difficult to
the individual, necessary
to Maiden Israel en mass, too.
Don't wait to ensure YHWH's grace with
it's bounty of love and of worship.

Courting Men

I

(For the LORD has created something new on earth:
A woman courts a man.)
Jeremiah 31:22:3-4

II

There was a nefarious book called
The Rules which, written a few years back
which tried to elicit the customs
of courtship women ignored only
at peril to their marriage ventures.

III

The secret, it said was to say "No,"
but more, to never ask a man out
on a date and play "hard-to-get" with
the gentleman who hunted like
the arctic foxes for white coats.
The book says that by becoming like
the fox a woman attracts her mate.

IV

Now Woman proposes but God says,
"Let arctic foxes chase hounds for once;
the change will do both foxes and hounds
good because foxes will choose hounds that
are gentler and the hounds will see fox
as friend and the hunt will be over."

V

The fox is the Jews as a people.
It is not good that hunted people
should hunt wild creatures in the forest.
According to the Oral Torah
the act of hunting is a sin for
the Priestly Nation to teach others
that it is sinful to Lord YHWH
in the way murder and theft are, too.
For killing for sport remains sinful
if one would follow YHWH's mitzvot.

VII

Yet just as women can court husbands
so Jewish women can court their God.
In dresses worn for Shabbat they pray
for Him to come to them by themselves.
They prepare for him in minds and hearts;
they prepare candles and the children.

VI

This hardly is a diffident act;
they should now perform it with great pride.
When as teens considering a crush
they should at least think, "Should I ask him
to go out on a date with me now?"
God wishes women to be brave, bold
and spirited, not cunning at best.

VII

Yes, God will praise those women striding
to ask their men folk to a movie.

The Wheel of God

I

...with the corpses of men whom I struck down in My anger and rage, hiding My face from this city because of all their wickedness: I am going to bring her relief and healing...; And I will purge them of all the sins which they have committed against Me, and I will pardon all the sins which they committed against Me, by Me. And she shall gain through Me renown, joy, fame and glory above all the nations on earth, when they hear of all the good fortune I provide for them. They will thrill and quiver because of all the good fortune and all the prosperity I provide for her.
Jeremiah 33:5a-33:6; 33:8-33:9

II

O Lord, You gave our History its
own unique dialectic, one which
is defined by our relation to
You, as a simple melody in
a minor key with strong woodwinds
which take the floor to dance slow but sure.
Yet that same melody's flow has cracks
as though the instruments will revolt.

III

We revolted, Lord, to find Your wrath
poured upon us like lava burning;
yet we knew it would cycle because
we believe when we are good, good comes
to us in terms of developing
the ability to harbor friendship

and gain a reputation that's good.
An honest man gains trust from people.
A man who works hard has food to eat.

IV

Like Hindus we have karma
of a sort, but an uneven sort,
where evil and good together rise
and fall as unsorted till judgment.

V

The wheel of time is alien less
than we in the West think that it is.
First God gives, and then Israel sins,
God punishes and Israel cries
in her pain that she repents her sin.
Then God gives to the Israelites like
a mother cow to her young suckling.
And Israel sins once more so that
She evades reward otherwise due
to Israel with good works and grace.

VI

God chastises his chosen once more.
Then once more Israel does repent.
The cycled universe is where we
are until finally we succeed.
Does the test grow more difficult with
each time as, perhaps, the bar is raised?
When Romans destroyed the Temple
it's said that Israel was punished
for despite their works their hearts were hard.

VII

The Talmud promulgated this tale.
So will the messiah come to us
or a great Messianic Age with
God reconciled with human beings
in an act of great compassion from
Lord YHWH whose embraced at last by
the humanity made by YHWH
in YHWH's likeness, reflecting back
at last the love which YHWH gave first?

VIII

Or will our human end be Auschwitz?
Lord, we have bled for you; hear us…
Lord we call to You; Israel is
the bleating calf that cries out for You.

God's Romancing of Israel

I

Thus said the LORD: Again there shall be heard in this place,
which you say is ruined, without man or beast...the sound of
mirth and gladness, the voice of bride and bridegroom.
Jeremiah 33:10-33:11

II

The Lord shouts that there will be joy,
just as God prepares ecstasies for
the devout in a bridal tent where
the Maiden Israel shall be
the wife of the Lord in his glory.

III

For Israel is espoused of God,
God and the Israelites feel passion
each for the other like a pair of
the lovers entangled in romance.
For just as mystics speak of God's love,
so the bride with her bridegroom partake
of marital bliss between God and
the Israelites beloved by
their Divine Incorporeal Spouse.
For God's love though not physical is
an almost erotic love of us.

IV

For blasphemy and insightfulness
are not as separated as we
are prone to imagine with our minds
as God woos Israel as if she
were indeed a fresh maiden with Him,
a gentleman and virgin as well.

V

For Eternal Spouse celibate yet
wed like one betrothed soul mate to us
in eternally yearning to share
with us life's sadnesses and joys
as though he bore them on His back for
His beloved bride Israel who
sits waiting for His coming to her.

VI

Like Rose of Sharon in the Song of
Songs, the bride Israel knows her Spouse
will come to fulfill her chaste desire.

Jewish Artemis

I

In those days Judah shall be delivered and Israel shall dwell secure.
And this is what she shall be called: "The Lord is our Vindicator."
Jeremiah 33:16

II

The virgin body Judah displays
for her Lord and her Savior reveals
the beauty of a Venus surpassed
and sanctified like a young bride cloaked
in niave pristine chastity made
more lovely than the goddesses of
the ancient pagans, Greeks and Romans
and their great admirer much later
in Renaissance Art funded by Popes.

III

In particular, Israel is
like Artemis in appearance with
this goddess of the hunt praised over
that of her shining twin the sun god;
more natural in grace than he was
fleet Artemis was like a young faun
and untainted by love of mere men.

IV

It's perhaps ungracious to suggest
that Israel is like the best of
the goddesses of Ancient Greece yet
this goddess possessed innocence like
the soul of the deer in the forest.

V

As for the People Judah of God:
her skin is 'swarthy' like the Rose who
had ensnared the King's heart in the Book
the Song of Songs called 'Holy' the sage
called Akiba who prized love of God
like a grave coquette gently wooed who
will inevitably yield to Him
who is her Husband as well as Lord.

VI

While dark and comely, this young bride is
clean with clipped, ground-down fingernails and
curls carefully brushed out of her face.
Each woman cries, "I am the Rose" and
each husband adds "She belongs to me;
the virgin Israel whom God loves."

VII

Both are ones beloved of their Lord
who will bring forth new children through them.
As God breathes a soul into each one
the Jewish children are as a whole
the firstborn of the human race and
yet others have their separate tales
where they search for God in parched deserts
of the soul for the waters of God.

VIII

The Jewish child is bathed in them,
the waters of God ensoul all born
and yet he or she's consecrated
so growing to be part of Judah.
It is as though the child at birth
is purified as though a convert
in a great mikveh preparing them
for life both inside and out of shul.

IX

While Jewish parents supply bodies
the Jewish God grants souls to children;
the Jewish people are kept youthful
through unsatisfied longing for God.

Free at Last

I

The word which came to Jeremiah from the LORD after King
Zedekiah of Judah in Jerusalem to proclaim a release among them—
that everyone should set free his Hebrew slaves, both male and
female, and that no one should keep his fellow Judean enslaved.
Jeremiah 34:8-34:9

II

Slaves male and female rejoice for God
Lord YHWH declared freedom for them!

III

This day will belong to the Lord as
a consecrated day in justice,
in an end for the drudgery of
the menials forced to sell labor
to richer Jews than they, the slave will
now return home from bondage nearby
not enslaved in a foreign land yet
bound by her brethren as a mere slave.

IV

The slave embraced liberty when freed—
a butterfly would open wings to
not simply flutter but fly—like birds—
with delicate claps towards the sky.

V

Yet remembering freedom we should
still remember its defect: it was
the Jewish people granted freedom
not all of those who, entitled by right,
lived in the land of the Lord's chosen.

VI

Why this strange omission, one might ask?
The Canaanites would surely have flocked
to the cause of God had it promised
their freedom with their neighbors, the Jews.

VII

Yet perhaps even this flawed freedom
in Jews made civil activists first
in America in disproportion
to their own number because they hear
the cause of God like destiny to
make freedom the fate standard for all.

VIII

As Martin Luther King stood in for
the prophet Moses crying his cry,
"Free at last, free at last," they join Jews
in proclaiming the freedom God grants.
Then and now we are bound by Laws that
will guarantee our freedom with God.

Cry from Israel's Slaves

I

But now you have turned back and profaned my name; each of
you has brought back the men and women whom you had given
their freedom, and forced them to be your slaves again.
Jeremiah 34:16

II

The cry of the slave calls to the Lord,
"Grant us our promised freedom, YHWH,
for bondage should not follow us to
our promised Israel like a hearse
of Egypt picking up the poor who
along the way are overburdened.

III

"The sick and the lame will fall down if
they are not cherished by the healthy—
for the Lord cherishes God's children
who make up the weak link in the chain.
In fact, it is the injured best loved
by the Lord, for the Jews were weakest
of peoples whom they live among as
slaves, foreigners and separated
for those that Pharaoh chastised with whips
to take their fellows to abuse them.

IV

"God intended that both be free and
to serve their Maker in their prayers.
God's beloved is the slave Egypt
had produced in the promised land of
their ancestors and in worshiping as
they waited during slavery, too.

V

"O Lord, we ask for mercy from you
as human chattel to our masters.
Do not let Jewish masters become
like Egyptian ones who were in the past."

VI

So spoke the Israelites slaves against
the usurpers of freedom given
by divine grace to all of the Jews.

Alien Traditions

I

[The Lord says,] *Go to the house of the Rechabites and*
speak to them, an bring them to the House of the LORD,
to one of the chambers and give them wine to drink.
They replied, "We will not drink wine, for our ancestor,
Jonadab son of Rechab, commanded us:
'You will never drink wine, either you or your children. Nor shall
you build houses or sow fields or plant vineyards, nor shall you
do such things; but you shall in tents all your days, so that you
live long upon the land where you sojourn... we never drink
wine, neither we nor our wives nor our sons and daughters.
Jeremiah 35:2; 35:6-35:8

II

The descendents of Jonadab said,
"We possess private traditions of
our own, on top of those of Judah.
We abstain from wine, living in hills
like Jonadab for whom we are named.
Our womenfolk keep traditions of
our denial of the flesh with us.

III

"In fact, our women's cooking is free
of intoxicants within the things
used as the ingredients to make
the foods so that there won't be mistakes.

IV

"As kashrut is for Jewish people
so abstention of alcohol is
an abstention of certain foodstuffs
for Jonadab's clan inherited
from descending sons of their fathers.

V

"We are thus different from others
a nomadic group without roots which
can be pulled out when conquerors come
and we leave for a safer venue.
We reverence our ancestor as
a guiding star in the black of night.

VI

"For honoring our parents extends
to grandparents to forefathers who
are distant as the stars yet live through
their descendents in tribal living.

VII

"For in our day and age it is true
that a man's children are his future
not just in taking care of him in
the frailty of his decayed old age
but in his continuing line down
through centuries of pain and joy.
So Jonadab lives through his children—
in other words, he lives on through us."

VIII

And to the family of the Rechabites Jeremiah said: "Thus said the Lord of Hosts, the God of Israel: Because you have obeyed the charge of your ancestor Jonadab and kept all his commandments, and done all he enjoined upon you, assuredly, thus said the LORD of Hosts, the God of Israel: There shall never cease to be a man of the line of Jonadab son of Rechan standing before Me."
Jeremiah 35:18-19

IX

So it is that God bids us respect
the variants of religion that
will and have existed in others,
the traditions of outsiders who
may also receive the word of God.

Zedekiah's Peace

I

King Zedekiah said to Jeremiah, "I am worried about the
Judeans who have defected to the Chaldeans; and they [the
Chaldeans] might hand me over to them to abuse me."
"They will not hand you over," Jeremiah replied… "For this is what
the LORD has shown me if you refuse to surrender: All the women
who are left in the palace of the king of Judah shall be brought
out to the officers of the king of Babylon; and they shall say:

II

The men who were your friends
Have seduced you and vanquished you.
Now that your feet are sunk in the mire,
They have turned their backs [on you]."
Jeremiah 38:19-38:22

III

The wives of Zedekiah added,
"Men can be seduced easily as
the womenfolk they 'protect' from harm.
An only female army might prove
as impregnable towards the sins
that accompany seducers as
the wayward male whom prostitutes court.

IV

"The Babylonian hordes courted
the men of Israel as allies.
The womenfolk know better because
a female pursued who is seduced
is then held accountable for it
while males get a slap across the wrist
and complain bitterly of wives deemed
as 'shrewish' regarding the same thing.

V

"So women closely watch their own steps;
men expect forgiveness by contrast."
So Zedekiah's wives warned further,
"Heed your wives and faithfully serve
Lord YHWH lest God strike out towards both
the king and citizens of the land
and remember Lord YHWH will choose
the women to hurt first and foremost;
for the king will be injured through them
as though it's women who are soldiers
for God in the king's defense instead
of male foot soldiers fighting for them."

VI

The wives and children pleaded their cause;
yet the king listened reluctantly.

VII

They will bring out your wives and children to the Chaldeans,
and you yourself will not escape from them. You will be captured
by the king of Babylon and this city shall be burned down.
Jeremiah 38:23

VIII

So Zedekiah heeded these words
and sued for unpopular peace with
the lonely support of Lord YHWH
and also his own multitude of
the royal wives and concubines in
his harem persuading the king to
hear Jeremiah, saving his life
and preserving the city he loved.
For even more than his life he loved
the city Jerusalem herself.

The Peace of Gadaliah

I

*The officers of the troops in the open country, and their men
with them, heard that the king of Babylon had put Gedaliah son
of Ahikam in charge of the region, and that he had put in his
charge the men, women and children—of the poorest of the
land—those who had not been exiled to Babylon... Gedaliah
son of Ahikam son of Shaphan reassured them and their men,
saying, "Do not be afraid to serve the Chaldeans. Stay in the land
and serve the king of Babylon and it will be well with you."*
Jeremiah 40:7; 40:9

II

The Babylonians picked a man
named Gedaliah representing
their cause to those who, subjugated
to Babylonian rule, were Jews.
He was to represent their cause to
the poorest members of the country.

III

So he spoke to the Judeans thus,
"When oak trees are felled by the great wind,
the grass bends to it, living as though
the roughness of the wind were a spur.
Now listen and fight another day;
the cause is just but the time is wrong.
Do not fight against the Lord's decree.
For the Lord's punishment is justice
and the best people will have setbacks."

IV

Yet the Jews hearing replied to him,
"Yet surely God hears righteousness when
it calls to his thrown from here below.
Lord, we Your people demand You come!
Come to us, O Lord! Come to us, now!"
"Ah!" Gedaliah cried out to them.

VII

"The Lord will announce it when He comes!
Mere prudence impels us bide our time
and wait for the Lord's coming to us
for although He may tarry the Lord
will come while we, in Babylon, stay
for however long we will outlast
the Babylonian foe with whom
we are in conflict against right now."

VIII

The citizens of Judah agreed—
but reluctantly, bitter with grief.
They felt in their hearts if their leaders
had been a differing kind they could
force the Lord to act on their behalf.
The cry of peace had thus been spoken.

The Beating of the Prophet

I

Instead, Johanan son of Kareah and all the army officers took the entire remnant Judah—those who had returned from all the countries to which they had sojourned in the land Judah, men women, and children; and the daughters of the king and all the people whom Nebuzaradan the chief of the guard had left with son of Ahikam of Shaphan as well as the prophet Jeremiah and Baruch son of Neriah—and they went to Egypt. They did not obey the Lord.
Jeremiah 43:4-43:7

II

"Though the Lord sends His rebuke to us,"
so spoke the Israelites headed
for Egypt from the land of Judah.

III

"We sin yet hope for forgiveness while
we commit disobedience we
hope the Lord will see desperation
is our sole alibi and forgive
our indiscretion towards the Lord
as forgivable because we are
like a bird wounded by an arrow.

IV

"For the truth is we're driven towards
the despair Dante's Inferno shows
in the first circle of those damned for
not grasping either good nor evil
but swaying according to the winds.

V

"We flee our Judea in panic
for mighty Babylonia is
now upon us as we lack defense.
Think of us chosen by You, O Lord.
Do not turn Your back on us, our God.
For if You don't we will kill him, Lord.
We will kill Jeremiah, the Lord's prophet.

VI

"As it's said, 'if God lived on earth there are
those who would break His windows,' and Lord
we are they if you won't grant us more
than errant pests like Jeremiah
have even promised us in good times.

VII

"We want our homes back, but we will take
the homes of Egyptians if that is
all that we can get from Lord YHWH.

VIII

Oh God we've carried Jeremiah
Your prophet with us so if evil
comes to us in the hands of Egypt
we can force Your hand on our behalf
so that if Your heart towards Judah
will remain hard, You will think of him."

IX

Then Jeremiah cried to the Jews,
He will come and attack the land of Egypt, delivering,
Those destined to the plague, to the plague,
Those destined to captivity, to captivity,
And those destined for the sword, to the sword.
Jeremiah 43:11

X

Thus the Jews beat the prophet once more.

The Queen of Heaven

I

Have you forgotten the wicked acts of your forefathers, of the
kings of Judah and their wives, and your own wives, and your
own wicked acts and those of your wives, which were committed
in the land of Judah and in the streets of Jerusalem?
Jeremiah 44:9

II

"Cry all you want old man," they replied.
"We will go our own way with you as
a bartering tool against your will.
For meanwhile we'll return to Her,
the Mother Goddess in whose breast we
find enveloping warmth and the strength
of a great she-wolf suckling her pups."

III

Yet they'd said more to Jeremiah.
There upon they answered all the men who knew that their wives
made offerings to offerings to other gods; all the women present, a
large gathering; and all the people who lived in Pathros in the land of
Egypt: "Who will not listen to you in the matter about which you spoke
to us in the name of the LORD. On the contrary, we will do everything
that we have vowed—to make offerings to the Queen of Heaven and
pour libations to Her, as we used to do, we and our fathers, our kings
and our officials, in the town of Judah and the streets of Jerusalem. For
then we had plenty to eat, were well off, and suffered no misfortune."
Jeremiah 44:15-44:17

IV

While Jeremiah chided the Jews
for faithlessness to their Lord YHWH
the Jewish people celebrated
the Queen of Heaven, ravishing Her
as Lady after the Jews own heart,
a Canaanite with golden wings and
a body made of ivory from
the luckless elephant's tusks for goods
sold by the upper classes of
the relocated Judeans.

V

She was the goddess of earth from whom
the wheat stalks sprang to harvest their bread.
They declared Her the consort of earth,
with its great bounty caused by falling
as it was cast down from Her heavens.
She was a terrifying goddess;
like the Lord she would inspire great fear.

VI

But God will tolerate no rival;
He demands steadfast devotion from
His chosen people, whom He loves with
a tender harshness created by
a husband's jealous care for His wife.
The Lord will demand fidelity
while providing His beloved with
the gentleness she lives by with Him.

VII

For husbands should be gentle with wives;
it is the Lord's own decree that if
a man is cruel to his wife he is
a boor who deserves no more mercy
than idolaters receive from Him.

VIII

The poorer Jewish citizens were
now Pharaoh's exiles themselves forming
an army to fight Babylon's might
brought forth this Native Goddess with
sheer impudence in sculpting her in
the clay of Egypt's pyramids made
in similar bricks as those made by
their ancestors, the Israelites who
the Lord led out of this same kingdom
to which they'd shamefully now returned.

IX

This Queen of Heaven's statue must have
now revealed in their betrayal of
poor Abraham's God who had waited
their repentance in Egypt before
yet even as they returned to sin
felt remorseful for the sake of those
who, following the fate of Joseph,
were Egyptian slaves waiting for God.

X

Now this 'Queen' was held the Jew's true God—
and admittedly she had allure.
She looked as insouciant as sin,
and yet she was made for the hearth, too:
her physicality begged to be
embraced by the heart and the senses
while YHWH was of Spirit only
as if his love while consummated refused
the fleshly desires of his small flock
like the great unconsuming bush which
the prophet Moses discovered when
they waited faithfully years before.

XI

O burning bush that's once more betrayed!
How could this happen? Descendents cry,
how could our ancestors have done this?
Must we live down sins committed by
that generation those years ago.
Yet perhaps their sin was not so great:
they wanted the God they had to be
one they could understand with their hands,
a God as touchable as the earth—
and hence they molded her from the earth.

XII

She was a goddess lascivious
and vapid, feeding human hunger
but not the mind which beheld the Queen.
She bewitched Israel's souls far from
Lord YHWH, Judah's husband once loved
as children revere father's when small.
The Lord was supposed to be both of
the Judeans own parents to them—
they're Mother as well as their Father
with divine attributes which are like
a Mother's feminine traits by which
small children thrive or acquire illness.

XIII

The God Jews broke faith with had loved them
with tenderness and devotion which
a mother bird will tend its young with.
When the Lord withdrew the Jews took up
with a god of their devising which
like what the pagans have as goddess.
This angered the Lord and He left these—
those Jews who'd abandoned the Lord's ways—
to die ones unmourned in the land of
the Egyptians where they had trespassed.

XIV

Jeremiah replied to all the people, men and women—all the people argued with him. He said, "Indeed, the offerings you presented in who argued with him. He said, "Indeed the offerings you presented in the towns of Judah and the streets of Jerusalem— you, your fathers, your officials and the people of the land—were remembered by the LORD and brought to mind!... When the Lord could no longer bear your evil practices and abominations you committed, your land became a desolate ruin and a curse..."
Jeremiah 44:20-44:22

XV

The Queen of Heaven, however, had possessed
the worshippers of the Lord's people.
The women particularly loved
their Divine Mother who filled them with
the spirit Pentecostals believe
is poured down upon them like fire on
the parched wood of the burning bush of
the prophet Moses traveling in
the wilderness in search of his sheep.

XVI

This frenzy whipped up by their desire
called up a demand singular and
yet audacious in what it suggests,
"The Lord must marry our Queen so that
the femininity of the Queen
can heal what a Lord alone cannot."
Then Jeremiah turned to the wives
who worshipped the Lord's female rival.

XVII

Jeremiah further said to the people and to all the women: "Hear the word of the LORD, all Judeans in the land of Egypt! Thus said the LORD of Hosts, the God of Israel: You are your wives have confirmed by deed what you spoke in words: 'We will fulfill the vows which we made, to burn incense to the Queen of Heaven and pour libations to her.' So fulfill your vows!"
(Jeremiah 44:24-44:25)

XVIII

Then without listening more the Jews
cried with one voice, "Harrah! Harrah!
The Queen of Heaven and the Lord shall
be joined as one at the side joint!"
Yet they did not miss Jeremiah
in his next words of condemnation.

XIX

"Yet hear the word of the LORD, all Judeans who dwell in the Land of Egypt shall ever again invoke My name, saying, 'Lo, I swear by My great name—said the Lord—that none of the men of Judah in all the land of Egypt shall ever again invoke My name, saying, 'As the Lord God lives!' I will be watchful over them to their hurt, not to their benefit; all the men of Judah in the land of Egypt shall be consumed by the sword and by famine, until they cease to be.'
Jeremiah 44:26-44:27

XX

And yet God promised both men and wives,
in private without Jeremiah,
"I will grant you my Holy Spirit
my Shekinah, my feminine side,
if you will return home to find me.
My Holy Spirit cries our for you
on your own behalf, go back home to
the land of Israel which is yours."

XXI

And, indeed, hearing thus, there some who
then returned home to Israel and
yet Jeremiah was left behind.
He stayed while begging repentance from
the remaining Jews on God's behalf.
The feminine side of God wooed them
more gently, begging them to come home.

The Apology of the Egyptians

I

Go up to Gilead and get balm
Fair Maiden Egypt.
In vain do you seek many remedies,
There is no healing for you.
Jeremiah 46:11

II

God hears the Egyptians prayers
as God hears Jewish prayers as well;
and Egypt cries out to Lord YHWH,
"Don't begrudge us sins against the Jews
For we have recognized them praying
to You Lord regarding the promise
You make to forgive repentant souls
for asking they repair their life,
the piece of tikkun olam which is
each person's possession, and do good
once more so that God's people proclaim,
'God bless the Egyptians' on Pesach
'for we they gave twice what was taken.'

III

The Jewish people, incredulous
at first say, "Is this truly Egypt?
The enslaver when forgetting that
the patriarch's son Joseph healed her
by interpreting Pharaoh's dreams and
so helping make the plans to save her?

Does she now forget hate and so to
embrace love gained when forgiveness is
made complete as the sons of Isaac?
Embracing Jacob nobly Esau
caused the two's rebirth together as
if neither supplanted the other."

IV

Then Egypt welcomed Jacob's children
with open arms so that they'd survive
the incoming hordes from the north from
the Assyrians conquering Jews
and Egyptians, crashing waves that
land on North Africa's sand isthmus.

V

For despite the fact it is as hard
to forgive the one who is victimized
to the one who had injured her as
it is for the one injured to give
up on her injury done towards her.

VI

And as has often happened throughout
the world's history, a threat from
the outside caused a forgiveness to
be necessary to former rivals.

Saving Egypt

Equip yourself for exile,
Fair Egypt, you who dwell secure!
For Noph shall become a waste,
Desolate, without inhabitants…
The mercenaries, too, in her midst
Are like stall-fed calves…
Jeremiah 46:19; 46:21

II

O Egypt! Israel cries, you who once
had wronged us yet who will be punished
with us for committing sins towards God
the beloved Lord YHWH injured
by errant children disobeying
a Lord they love while playing the fool—
for Israel has always loved God—
but selfishly like human children.

III

Yet there is one worse off than we are,
one further from God's love than us
and that is Egypt, slavery's land,
and yet the country containing wealth—
not just the material wealth of goods
but the sheer creativity that
went into making a part of
the African's great northern culture.

IV

We needed Egypt to be our foe.
as strong in fighting as we became
or perhaps secretly we admired
the pyramids we never spoke of
or would have had we ourselves not been
the ones who sculpted the bricks to build
the triangular buildings made from
mud mixed with straw by hapless slaves who
were nascent Israel in Goshen.

V

Those castles for the Pharaoh's corpses
climbed the skies celebrating humans
by accomplishing architecture
that's matchless even in our own time.

VI

"Ah Lord!" cries Israel, "Spare Egypt!
For Egypt was a genius during
an age when Israel was only
a backwater to 'civilized' men
long before the Greeks judged it as 'old.'

VII

It would take longer for the children
of Zion to win sympathy and
the appreciation they deserved—
as even now it is not always
a granted that they receive respect
for surviving their history which
had dished out its worse to God's chosen—
as they would continue to believe
they were as heritage from their God.

VIII

Our subjugators become those whom
we pray for as a once proud culture.
Lord, do not destroy the Egypt
we recognize as grand in the past!
For despite its crimes, we can't wish for
its death in history's mill spanning
the millennial backwards in time.

Down with Pharaoh!

I

[Egypt] shall rustle away like a snake
As they come marching in force;
They shall come against her with axes
Like hewers of wood.
They shall cut down her forest.
Jeremiah 46:22

II

For indeed as the hapless Adam
would smack down the snake's risen head to
bite his heal, so it was that Egypt
the symbol of our servitude from
past ages despite its great comfort
for the task makers Israel had.

III

O Egypt, rattler by the Nile,
stick of the Pharaoh writing in pain
as Moses's staff swallows it up.
Like skilled magician the Pharaoh
will give an incantation which
he pronounces the Lord's name backwards.

IV

"Oh HWHY!" Pharaoh cries his stick,
his idols turned to slithering snakes
to be a creatures devoured by one
Great Snake of Moses, an image of
the prophet Moses slaying rivals
to Israel's God beheading them
on the ground where they'd them
on the ground where they'd been cast to prove
the man-god Pharaoh supreme over
the Lord and Moses, YHWH's prophet.

V

Why would God command idolatry?
Would YHWH create the means to sin?
Would YHWH desecrate God's own Name?
Or would the Prophet Moses take it
on himself unintentionally
to form a powerful image of
the sins of humankind with his hands
while believing it honors YHWH.
Is this snake the cause of why Moses
come enter Israel with YHWH.

VI

Or perhaps, having used this idolatrous
the prophet Moses should have destroyed
it because despite YHWH's sanction
it outlived its true purpose and so
like Moses himself needed to leave.

VII

For perhaps Israel when Moses
stayed in the dessert was in danger
of worshiping him with Lord YHWH.
The sin of Moses in not give
the credit YHWH dressed when he
hit the rock producing pure water
for Israel in Canaanite land
was creating a situation
where Israel might worship Moses.

VIII

Yet despite this prophet died with
Lord YHWH's blessing in the dessert.
For wasn't Moses forging his staff
so doing creating an idol?

IX

The carved snake reminiscent of he who
first seduced that pair in the garden
from whom we humans descended from
was dangerous to behold itself.

X

Did Moses's staff incite the Jews
to worship gods from Egypt, Canaan,
and all of the lands between the two.

XI

For certainly it bewitched as though
it were the serpent with legs who would
not eat dust like the one cast out of
the Eden where he'd debased the pair
both Adam and Eve for, so neither
could enter Eden again until
the future Judgment Day of their heirs.

XII

Ah! Serpent beguiling the children
of Israel, could you be Egypt,
the land abroad of wealth and glamor
who cowed the prophet Moses into
the using of his magic serpent?

XIII

Like slavery our sins shall be purged
in wilderness free of Egypt,
land lush and indolent with the ease
of vanquished subjects by their Pharaoh,
a watermelon broken with their juice
that attracts mosquitoes to the sight.

XIV

The Pharaoh's might will surrender to
the Israelites who once served Egypt.

On the Madness of Men

I

Moab glory is no more
In Heshbon they have planned evil against her:
"Come, let us make an end of her as a nation!"
You, too, O Madmen, shall be silenced;
The sword is following you."
Jeremiah 48:2

II

O Israel is faced with madness
of Moabite sons, descendents of
Lot by his eldest daughter after
his family had elected to
flee Sodom from the mountains close to.

III

These children unnaturally born
of lust a father bore his daughters
came harassing the Israelites
They come to harass Israel with
their weaponry of bows and arrows
this scourge of Israel's ground held as
one being sacred soil to the Jews.

IV

The madness they bring descendents down
on the Jews' holy living space is
a plague of the soul from which Jews
beg God's aid against enemies whom
like illnesses have pursued the life
of the Jews have in time immemorial.

V

It is the madness persecuting
a chosen nation that means no harm—
for Jews have preferred peace to all things—
in fact it persecutes by falsehood
in saying Jews are uniquely bad
like grass spurs animals catch on hairs
when they rub accidentally on
but unlike women soldiers only
give birth to the death of their brothers
the fellow human beings who are like them.

VI

O battles pounding plough shears into
the swords made for the battlefields so
young men can die in needless warfare!
Yet humankind keeps fighting despite
the fact God wishes warfare to end.

The Battle Against Moab

I

For thus said the Lord:
See, he soars like an eagle
And spreads out his wings against Moab!...
In that day, the heart of Moab's warriors
Shall be like the heart of a woman in travail.
Jeremiah 48:40; 48:41:3-4

II

Like women, soldiers give birth in pain
but unlike women soldiers only
give birth to the death of their brothers
the fellow human beings made like YHWH;
in YHWH's transcendent image of
both male and female in God's likeness.
Yet just war is still tragedy as
the soldiers pour blood onto the earth.

III

O battles pounding plough shears into swords as
if human lives were themselves as cheap
as the sands lying on the floor of
sands lying on the dusty floor of
the nation Israel's great desert.
In the heat of war, individuals
give up their life as Kiddush Hashem[2],
but afterwards, the widows cry with
their orphans in their helpless arms as
they try to mend what became broken
in acts of Tikun Olam[3] because
their menfolk aren't there to cure the world
with the ones who will recall their love.

---

[2] "Kidush Hashem" translates as "sanctification of the names" and refers
to martyrdom, lawful and unlawful, in Judaism. It is specifically given in
the Talmud to those who died because they refused to break the rules of
Shabbat—the Sabbath. However, it is a general word which covers other
dying for Judaism as well.

[3] Tikkun Olam means repairing the world. According to Kabbalah there
was a point in which there were holy vessels broken in this universe.
Their 'shards' splintered and the job of the pious person is to 'repair' the
universe by putting the pieces back together again. The putting of these
pieces together is done by keeping the mitzvot.

The Moabites Cry to God

I

Woe to you, O Moab!
The people of Chemosh are undone,
For you sons are carried off into captivity,
Your daughters into exile.
Jeremiah 48:46

III

"O Lord," the Moabites cry to God,
"Are we not equally your children?
Do You love only Israel as
You hate Your sons and daughters who were
bound at birth to Lot's Uncle Abram.

III

Howl, O Heshborn, for Ai is ravaged!
Cry out, O daughters of Rabbah!
Gird on sackcloth, lament,
And run to and fro in the sheepfolds.
For Milcolm shall go into exile,
Together with his priests and attendants.
Jeremiah 49:3

IV

The Heshbonites cry out to YHWH,
"Show mercy on us, Israel's Lord;
grant mercy towards us in
our repentance and we will restrain
lusts wreaking havoc on those You
who are made holy as Your chosen people.

V

"God forgive both the Jew and non-Jew
for it is Your own proclamation,
that 'Though your sins be red as scarlet
I will make them white as snow' fallen
like delicate white lilies upon
the fallen earth which then lies covered.

The Petition of the Pagan Cities

I

Howl, O Heshbon, for Ai is ravaged!
Cry out, O daughters of Rabbah!
Gird on sackcloth, lament,
And run to and fro in the sheepfolds.
For Milcolm shall go into exile,
Together with his priests and attendants.
Jeremiah 49:3

II

The pagan citizens of Heshbon,
of Ai and of Rabbah cry out,
"Show mercy towards us, O YHWH
of enemies the Israelites and
then we shall abandon our own gods,
in particular the god Milcolm.

III

O restrain Your arm against us and
we'll join with Your people ourselves.
Allow us our own equality
with the Jews under Your Law and we
will be as faithful as the Jews themselves;
we will shun eating pork and shellfish.

IV

We shall love our Lord YHWH on high
with 'all our heart and with all our soul
and with all our might,' yielding to You.
Grant mercy toward us and make us
a holy people like the Jews, too.
Lord YHWH forgive Jew and non-Jew
for it is your own proclamation.

V

'Though your sins be as crimson,' You say,
'They can turn snow-white; be they red as
[a] dyed wool, they can become like fleece.
If then, you agree and take heed, [then]
You will eat the good things of the earth.'

VI

Lord grant Your favor with Your chosen
and we shall forget Milcolm for good.
We shall keep Your Law within our hearts
and it will purify our deeds with
the blessings of Your justice itself.

VII

You have said that the nations observe
in faithfulness 'gods who are no gods' and
now we shall destroy our own idols
and join with Jews in faithfulness which
You believe in which Your own wavered.
Our wickedness has outstripped the Jew's;
now our love will not be less than theirs.
O Lord grant our hearts to be joined
with Your own beloved as Your own.

VIII

O Lord for eternity we wish
to be ones remembered as ones who
have repented like Nineveh with
the prophet Jonah bring them to
see the great evil of their ways, too.
Our desired memory is of peace
and of our forgiveness by You."
So these three cities acquired God
and became chosen like God's people.

Children of the Edomites

I

But it is I who have bared Esau,
Have exposed his place of concealment;
He cannot hide.
His offspring is ravaged,
His kin and his neighbors—
And there is none to say,
I will rear them;
Let your widows rely on me!
Jeremiah 49:10-49:11

II

The Edomites cried out to YHWH,
"O Israel's God remember us
as Abraham and Isaac's children.
Why favor Jacob's children over
the children Esau's wives bore Esau?
For Jacob was a trickster to him
yet Esau forgave Jacob who'd wronged
his elder brother two times over.
We do not resent Jacob's being
the father of a chosen people.

III

"We only ask that we be chosen—
as Isaac's son and Jacob's brother.
We are as family to the blessed.
O YHWH, each soul wrestles with God
in the sense of their trying to get
back to the home in which we belong.

IV

Please look at Esau with a kind heart,
and do not bar it from the promise
of the land inhabited by Jews.
Although the Edomites have a name
which to the Jews is wicked they have themselves
still we aren't unlike them in our ways.
We share our patrilineage with
Jews, Ammonites and Ishmaelites, too.

V

Our father Abraham is father
to many nations and not just one;
the Middle East are progeny to
this one great father blessed by his God.
God promised Abraham his offspring
would be as numberless as the stars.
Grant Abram's other offspring their due;
don't expunge them from the earth itself.

The Demands made of Israel

I

I have received tidings from the LORD,
And an envoy is sent out among the nations:
Assemble, and move against her,
And rise up for war!
For I will make you least among nations,
Most despised among men.
Jeremiah 49:14-49:15

II

The maiden Israel cries to God,
"Lord do not send the nations after
our lands and our lives in this home of
sweet milk and honey in the raw comb.

III

"It is a good land You have given
to Israel Your servant who loves
Lord YHWH despite inconstancy;
in fact it was this love for which she
was chosen as God's coquettish spouse;
a creature lovely to the Lord's eye.

IV

"For despite such love rebellion is
not unnatural on the Jew's part;
for Israel fears nations who make
her look as small by comparison
when thinking of her physical size
as if she were an tiny ant faced
with a great anteater, as hungry
to devour the ants as if they were
the sweetest confections they'd eaten.

V

"God demands unrelenting faith that
can withhold tragedy and dark days
when God's care holds no transparency;
for although human rulers answer
as fallible guides to their peoples,
God demands absolute trust from us.
Yet Israel needs consolation
to survive our test's severity.

VII

"Poor Israel needs God to remove
the veil of gloom which covers our face.
In tragedy and triumph You are
our God; do not bear down hard on us.
We wait for redemption in Your time."
And so the God of Israel was
thought to have repented the designs
of evil He had planned for the Jews.

The Defense of Edom

I

See, like an eagle he [Edom] flies up,
He soars and spreads his wings against Borzah;
And the heart of Edom's warriors in that day
Shall be like the heart of a woman in travail.
Jeremiah 49: 22

II

"O YHWH," cry the Edomites to
the Lord of Israel[4] their brother,
"Why do You condemn us for a deed
You Yourself willed us towards the Jews;
if free we might have avoided
the crimes we committed as those who
have benefited at the Jews' expense.

III

If human beings are born free than
could God "cause" the sins committed by
the Edomites when Jacob stumbled,
with their guilt springing against the Jews?

---

4   Israel, the reader may recall, is Jacob and therefore Esau's (the ancestor
     of Edom's) brother.

IV

"Yet if the Edomites chose to sin
could God have made us, Esau's children
act in a way we were not going
to act in responsibility
for the sins committed with the Jews
as victims of their brother Edom?"

V

All of Time is One to me.
I see all human history for
I am both in and outside of it
for having created it Outside
the Universe in unfolding space.

VI

Existing in part outside of it,
God says, there is a Time existing
in areas existing outside
of the Time human experience.
Whole Universes have existed
when YHWH gave birth to this One and
Lord YHWH will exist when it dies.

VII

Lord YHWH grants us opportunity
to join our Lord above this time frame
but YHWH's greater than Death Itself--
Lord YHWH is Life's Source Itself.

VIII

Lord YHWH can how reveal one time
to a time elsewhere, experienced
at once as physicists watch Time
more backwards within other spots in
our Universe with telescopes on
Lord YHWH can how reveal one time
to a time elsewhere, experienced
at one as physicists watch Time
move backwards within other spots in
our Universe with telescopes on
the earth as we search to find meaning.

IX

So YHWH sees All at once because
it all exists at the same time in
the Eyes of God our Creator who
both transcends and dwells in Time.

X

Now Esau became despondent and
said to Lord YHWH, Creating Lord,
"How is it anyone is able
to stand up before Judaism's God?
How could our relative in Abram
come argue for the citizens of
the wicked cities Gomorrah and
it's sister city Sodom itself?

XI

Lord YHWH chuckled, "Scripture begins
with the words, 'When God created' of
our universe and making this place
I created time within it I have changed—
God repented man's creation when
I sent the flood to Noah's earth and
I may change again within the time frame of
the universe which itself changes.

XII

"I and the universe have and will
both commingle, a piece of it will
last into eternity itself
and a piece of Me forget Myself—
as I have promised that I'd forget
the sins of Israel in My time.
O Edomites, the reason I know
Your deeds is because I am there now—
just as the past will not cease to be."

XIII

"O Lord," cried Esau's children, "Spare us
as You have spared the Jewish people,
for people will say You were not fair,
if you have forgiven them while
not forgiving us while not us
and also forgive for our fathers
for Abraham and Isaac; they are
our father's as much as they're Jacob's."
"No, you're more," spoke God, "You are
the sons and daughters both of Adam
and Eve, the humans made first on earth,"
Lord YHWH spared poor Esau's children
so that his descendents were sprinkled
like pepper sprinkled on the nations.

The Earth's Syrian Children

I

The children of God's pagan lands have
as their staunch supporter the Earth who
God made to love all peoples throughout
their homes they wait for redemption of
the entire human race by their God
so that while Buddhists wait for heaven
or nirvana they will have themselves
an advocate who nurtures their souls.

II

Damascus has grown weak,
She has turned around to flee;
Trembling has seized her,
Pain and anguish have taken hold of her,
Like a woman in childbirth.
Jeremiah 49:24

III

Will Damascus give birth to stillborns
a future stymied by Lord YHWH
in exhaustion that's unfulfilled as
no good's come of her labor or pain?

IV

For women who give birth to nothing
amongst the creation's most sad as
they go through so much so that they
see only a dead child born within
their tired arms, a pitiful thing
both beloved and already missed.

V

Can a whole nation suffer stillbirths
so that their efforts all go to naught?
Will this great city's glorious past
be swept from the earth along with gods
who represented its own culture
which would not be lost in the sands of
the ages fossilized by times past?

VI

O YHWH you are immortal and
through You the Jewish people, are, too.
We have no tie to Judaism
yet we beg that our culture live on.
We are in fact the enemies of
Your people and yet we beg of You
that Damascus's children live on.

VII

Just as a mother mourns the death of
her children as much as her life's end
so we mourn the death threatened by You.
Assuredly, her young men shall lie fallen in her squares.
And all her warriors shall be stilled in that day
—declares the Lord of Hosts.

VIII

In Damascus, the mothers begin
to mourn the deaths of their sons whose loss
is final, a grave gaping open
for soldiers on fields of woe thirsting
for young men's blood as it pours onto
the moist and maternal earth which gave
the first pangs of birth ages before
Lord, why do You will these young men's death?

IX

In vicious battle young men cleave here
on gentle Mother Earth, our Savior.
O Earth! O Fecund Mother given
to human beings as a cradle!
How we have mistreated You since birth!
Yet resting on your sanctuary,
the soldier breaths his last breath because
a forgotten man to the king whom
he fought when the cause was just.

X

The soldiers comforted and chastised
by the Earth YHWH gave us are blessed
by Her embrace as they sleep until
the Judgment of all human beings—
the slain in the fields dead for causes
both noble and extremely wicked.

XI

O Earth! O fecund mother given
to human beings from the cradle!
How we have mistreated you since birth!
Yet resting on your sanctuary,
the soldier breaths his last breath although
a forgotten man to the king whom
he fought for whether the cause was just.
The soldiers comforted and chastised
by the earth God gave human beings.

XII

For the rain causes the mud soldiers
tramp through as they have traveled through lands
on dry bread and dry wine which ages
to the place of their destination
as they will ration it out to drink.
Yet the earth also supplies game to
eat after hunting it down to kill.

XIII

The Syrians are the earth's children;
all human beings receive blessings
from her and so these soldiers die at
her breast which once gave them life itself.
For the earth loves both Jews and non-Jews;
and bereft of the Lord these soldiers
will make their graves in the Earth's bedding.

XIV

And bereft of God, they will die there
in the arms of the impartial earth—
and there the soldiers caress the earth
in blessing it with final breaths while
in wretched squalor they die at war
look up to see the colors of dusk.

XV

For even enemies of the Lord
are ones let to view handiwork made
for them as equally as the Jews.

The Search for Forgiveness

I

Some archers against Babylon,
All who draw the bow!
Encamp against her roundabout,
Let none of her people escape.
Pay her back for her actions,
Do to her just what she has done;
For she has acted insolently against the Lord,
The Holy One of Israel.
Jeremiah 50:29

II

The Babylonians cry to God,
"Can guilty nations expunge their guilt?
Is remorse itself enough to cleanse the self?
Or is guilt inextricably tied
like Karmic relations to Hindus
who believe the soul bound by its works
save when it enters in Divine Release
in moksha[5] "liberation" to those
who studied goodness from the Ganges[6]
the trees and India's great jungles.

---

[5]   "Moksha" is the Hindu term for "Release" or "Liberation" from the constraints of the cares of this world in favor of oneness with God.

[6]   The Ganges River is considered holy by the Hindus.

III

Can people break free of their past sins
or are they bound like slaughtered sheep to
the altar of God to have their throats
slit Kosher-style for what they have done?"

IV

In Judaism came the reply,
made always possible for prayers
and good works to wash one's sins from one,
yet Babylonia had waited
till it was too late, when it faced death
and whimpered prayers to gods unknown
as it had failed to connect to God
in believing the Jewish people
were of no consequence to her fate.

V

For Babylonia had believed
the Jews among the multitudes of
the conquered nations powerless save
for their strange resolution to remain
one people despite the odds which were
so against the Jews remaining Jews.

VI

The Babylonians felt contempt
for Jewish people in their land in
a form of servitude far from home—
the citizens of Babylon felt
their strength in relation to the Jews,
this despite the fact that when conquered
they could not survive this fate themselves.

VII

For indeed, Babylon is no more.
The vital purpose Israel serves
Would outlast Babylon's cruel regime,
built as if it was on power only.
The Jews, by contrast possessed all things
save Babylonia's great power
and lasted ages despite this lack.

VIII

So Babylonia has deserved
no mercy corporately from God
and yet there are good individuals
in Babylon who will be counted
with other righteous people living
in nations outside of Jews ourselves.

O Lord, Return Us Home

I

Declare among the nations,
Hide nothing! Say:
Babylon is captured,
Bel if shamed,
Morodach is dismayed.
Her idols are shamed,
Her fetishes dismayed.
Jeremiah 50:2

II

"O Lord," cries Israel to YHWH,
"When will you free us from the yoke of
the idolaters of the country
of Babylonia so that we
may begin our lives at home anew.
We wait and yet as we plead and cry
an anger swells deep within our breasts
that we are not allowed to go home.

III

For centuries we've been kept from home.
We long for nothing more than taking
and shattering the idols which have
in foreign captivity enslaved
the sons and daughters of Lord YHWH
who sent the Jews out from their own land—
and yet made promises of return.

IV

For the land of the Jew is ensouled
by Jewish people its own spirit
the body in which they live the Law
that the Lord gave us at Mt. Horeb
in the great wilderness where Jews were
once born a chosen people of God.

V

The Sea of Reeds was a birth canal
from Egypt into Israel where
the children of God formed an infant
while the Lord proved as diligent as
a mother and a father combined.

VI

The Lord cries, "How can I give you up,
O Ephraim" with devotion to
God's chosen people who are children
in the heart of their Divine Father
their corporate soul is made holy
as Israel's was made for the land.

VII

As other peoples have lands they own
the Israelites mark out for the Jews
for all time perfectly fit as though
the Israelites were Cinderella
whom their Lord provides a glass slipper
for as a dainty wedding gift to
as the Prince Charming whom she loves back.

VIII

As God speaks to the exiled Jews they
have recalled the milk and the honey
of their land itself waiting for them.
The Jews swear "If I forget thee," to
both God and Jerusalem itself
all manner of harsh curses shall come
to pursue Jews like the Greek furies
or a cloud of flies overtaking
the Jews like horses on a hot day.

IX

Just so the enemy of the Jews
in Babylon shall be as hunted
in worshiping their own god Marduk
shall be as hunted by the flies of
their own great Babylonian horse
the Persians until the Jews return
to their home Israel once again.

X

Just so, Lord YHWH is One
who has sworn never may he forget
the Jewish people—they're his children.
The city Jerusalem is left
a city incomplete while they're gone.
The Jew's true resting place lies therein.

We Pray for Justice

I

For see, I am rousing and leading
An assemblage of great nations against Babylon
From the lands of the north.
They shall draw up their lines against her,
There she shall be captured.
Their arrows are like those of a skilled warrior
Who does not turn back without hitting the mark
Chaldea shall be despoiled,
All her spoilers shall be sated
—declares the Lord.
Jeremiah 50:9-10

II

O Babylon, we do not pray for
your death for the sake of our revenge;
we pray for the sake of our freedom;
for we love freedom more than our lives.

III

O Babylon who's conquered because
our YHWH removed protection from
us, the Lord's people, we Jews who love
our Lord and yet are faithless towards
our God at the same time as though we
were the spoiled children without limits
set by the Lord who is both Father
and mother to us punishing and
yet nurturing us with love as well.

IV

You, Babylon, are punished for us
so that we're able to go return
to our home, Israel while Persia
the conquerors of Babylon was
a nation considered blessed as they
sent Jews home from their captivity
in, Babylonia far from home.

V

O Lord we sing Your praises for You
have sent the Jewish people back home;
for while we left our land bodily
we left our hearts in Jerusalem.
O Babylon, you're chastised so for
the sake of slaves you've oppressed too long.

VI

For God loves the least of his people
and you dragged them to Babylon, chained.
We don't speak harshly to gain revenge.
We speak this way to assert our rights.
For Jews are history's most oppressed;
the slaves of Egypt and gassed victims
of the great concentration camps which
the Nazis slaughtered Jews in with the names
of Treblinka and Buchenwald and
of Auschwitz where the millions vanished
with none asking questions at all.

VII

Yes Nazism would disappear and
the Jewish people remain on earth
and scarred though we are we will live on—
Yes, Hitler dies an unmourned tyrant.
The name of Anne Frank becomes one blessed
and Hitler's memory shames those who
had conspired murder with this monster.

VIII

So Babylonia will become
a symbol of the oppression of
the Jewish people after she's gone.
For ancient Iraq is not a place
with any resemblance to the place
which is now Muslim with the gods of
the Babylonians gone along
with the dust of the skeletons which
the average man decayed into.

IX

Though it was not the Nazi's homeland
it was a place of infamy like
the Temple prostitution itself
but also efforts of Jews living
in the land to assimilate them
yet resistance would make the Jew strong.
The Nazis killed more Jewish people
than Babylonia could swallow
in its assimilation-ism which
they tried to make Jews into non-Jews.

X

Yet we the Jewish people remain!
This is the proof that freedom's power
will overcome the servitude we
have born since our time spent in your land.
This evidence is stronger than death.

The Death of Babylon

I

For you rejoiced, you exulted,
You who plundered My possession;
You stamped like a heifer treading grain,
You neighed like steeds.
So your mother will be utterly shamed,
She who bore you will be disgraced.
Behold the end of the nations—
Wilderness, desert and stepped!
Because of the Lord's wrath she shall not be inhabited;
She shall be utterly desolate;
Whoever passes by Babylon will be appalled
And will his at all her wounds.
Jeremiah 50:11-50:13

II

O Babylonia the edge of
the abyss which all men fear the most
that chasm swallowing up nations
and rendering our efforts futile.
This is death; for the Babylon of
won't survive mortality itself;
as Jews will survive until Judgment.

III

Just as the kings of Babylon fought
and afterward were forgotten by
the many peoples ruled once by them
so Babylonia is recalled
by enemies like those they conquered
the Jewish people's recollection
the Babylonia was bad
and Herodotus second of this
with the land of Greece, siding, for once,
with Jewish people in their viewpoint.

IV

While Babylon lies forgotten its
own smallest victim will be judged as
the Righteous Servant[7], homely in face
but beautiful in devotion to
Lord YHWH gave the Jews one Soul which
Lord YHWH's reflection looks back at
the creator of one great mirror.
So God will smile on his own great world.
This contrasts with the selfish conquests
by ancient empires like you who
once conquered YHWH's priestly people.

---

[7] The "Righteous Servant" of Isaiah is alternately interpreted to be the messiah or the Jewish people themselves.

The Last of Nebuchadnezzar

I

Range yourselves roundabout Babylon,
All you who draw the bow;
Shoot at her don't spare arrows,
For she has sinned against the LORD.
Jeremiah 50:14

II

"Who is it we've sinned against? Who? Who?"
cries Babylonia on the news.
"We know of no 'Lord' outside Marduk?
There are, true, plenty more gods besides
the great god in his holy palace
but this 'Lord' speaks with arrogance to
our great King Nebuchadnezzar who
is Babylon's Kings of Kings himself.

III

"From whence do armies surround us with
their legions of great flaming arrows,
these arrows torched with glowing fires tall.
The castle goes down in bursting flowers
of orange and red colored petals,
like sunset's ambiance of dark hues
still lighting up the starless night sky
I who had worshiped all gods the same
which divinity did I neglect?"

IV

Raise a shout against her all about!
She has surrendered;
Her bastions have fallen,
Her walls are thrown down—
This is the LORD's vengeance
Take vengeance on her,
Do to her as she has done!
Jeremiah 50:15

IV

Who has sent these large armies to us?
King Cyrus the King of the Persians
said to King Nebuchadnezzar that
"I am of Zoarastrian birth
but 'I AM' sent me in the conquest
of Babylonian in speaking
to me as a friend to the Jews when
my people are first secure at home.
Now I heard from Lord 'I AM' written
the Tetragrammaton's[8] name pronounced
as Ayer Esher Ayer a pun
on the Lord's holy name called YHWH."

---

[8] The Tetragrammaton is written in four letters Yod Hay Vov Hay, traditionally too holy to be pronounced. (Before it was destroyed the only place it was said was in the Holy of Holies of the Jerusalem Temple itself. Scholars argue how it is pronounced but according to Etz Hayim it means "I am whatever I choose to Be," "I am pure being," "I am more than you can comprehend." It is discussed in the footnotes to Exodus 3:14.

V

"The Jews?" King Nebuchadnezzar cried,
"Why those poor wretches—who cares for them?
They are least powerful among men
they are made isolated at heart
for the sake of their God—one only!—
one lone God all by Himself without
the others obeying him at times
and disobeying Him at others—
how can this be a true God when all
the other gods are not included?
They are mere atheists, these Jews, who
eat their food all alone for His sake!
Their sole good seems to be to survive.
Bah! So much for them! Why have concerned
your kingship regarding a people
so dedicated to one lone God?"

VI

Make an end in Babylon of sewers,
And of wielders of the sickle at harvest time.
Because of the deadly sword,
Each man shall turn back to his people,
They shall flee everyone to his land.
Jeremiah 50:16

VII

King Nebuchadnezzar was taken
and beheaded and the Jews were told
they could now return to their homes in
the land of Israel, it's people
once again a ghost to the body
which had housed its soul while it lived.

321

Marathaim's Plea for Mercy

I

Advance against her—the land of Marathaim
And against the inhabitants of Pekod;
Ruin and destroy after them to the last
—says the Lord—
Do just as I have commanded you.
Jeremiah 50:21

II

O YHWH have You considered that
the citizens of Merathaim
are human beings as much as we?

III

O Lord we ask on behalf of them
that You will reconsider their fate
that they won't prematurely come to
a death they fail to warrant because
they have been no worse than their neighbors
for even we have strayed from Your Laws.

IV

O God Your people have erred often
but remain rendered holy through You;
please listen on our behalf to us
that we have been no better than she
who is our enemy who pillaged
our towns when we were helpless victims.

Untitled

I

Come against her [Babylon] from every quarter
Pile her up like heaps of grain,
And destroy her, let her have no remnant!
Destroy all her bulls,
Let them go to slaughter.
Alas for them, their day is come,
The hour of their doom!
Jeremiah 50:26-50:27

II

Lord, even Babylon has deserved
some mercy from the Lord God of all.
Of this we're certain within our hearts
for even while we review the crimes
she committed we cannot say that
it's justice to trade one eye of ours
for one eye of theirs, instead it is
mere revenge, beneath the Lord YHWH
as we argue in the tradition of
our father Abraham who it was
who argued on the wicked's behalf
in cities Gomorrah and Sodom.

III

To say our captivity earned us
the Babylonians' dead corpses
in big piles stinking under the sun
at noontime in a punishment which
is unmitigated by the fact
that most Jews survived despite the wrongs
dealt us by Babylon as a whole.
We survived Babylon and flourished.

IV

The Babylonians when measured
by these are ordinary in that
their crimes were unspectacular as
they were a simple conquering group
who meted injustice out to all.

V

O Lord, if Babylonia will
give its last breath let it be a death
that's placid as the grave itself
and let her descendents go in peace
with her crimes forgotten by the Jews.

A Plea to God

Assuredly, her young men shall fall in her squares,
And all her warriors shall perish in that day
—declares the Lord.
Jeremiah 50:30

II

"Ah!" Babylon sings despairingly,
"For my young men I cry out to God!
Don't trample our sons under Your feet
as they aren't responsible for crimes
the Lord says we have committed as
if leopards towards Jewish born sheep.

III

"For, indeed, the Jews were seen as sheep
when Babylonia had conquered
the Southern kingdom Judah so that
the Jews could then be deported from
the province within the great empire
built by the Babylonians there.

IV

Yet although complacent in regards
to the Jews ourselves, surely our guilt
should not be inherited by children;
of this, O Israel's Lord we pray
to You as ones who've awakened from
a deep sleep's lethargy which recedes.

V

O Lord, don't slaughter our sons in war
with bloody battles fought in the fields.
For You shall recall Jewish infants
and realize that in between children
the differences between nations
are small with our sons exactly like
Jews in their ability to feel;
For it is from this that their rights come.

VI

Our sons are out of infancy yet
their possibilities in peace are
as endless as imagination
is itself with its murkiness in
its substratum yet with fire central
its processes that exist within
the hearts of human beings themselves.

VII

Their creativity adds up dreams
That can form future realities."
"It is true," said God, "that these young men
did no wrong themselves towards the Lord
but the truth is that causally there's
a connection in deeds done causing
the consequences of these actions.

VIII

"The accountability of acts
is needed so that there can be virtue
and individuals acquire justice
at Judgment Day while groups will receive
the justice deserved collectively
that occurs the day before that day before."
So Babylonia was silenced
by YHWH"s awful decree on high.

To the Lady Insolence

I

Insolence shall stumble and fall,
With none to raise her up.
I will set her cities on fire,
And it shall consume everything around her.
Jeremiah 50:32

II

O Lady Insolence who's fallen
on the Jews like wolves upon a deer
and basks in her own punishment as
if she's a living spirit herself
and not an abstraction, pure and cold.

III

She's insouciance personified
an experience abhorred by those
who, despite circumstances, are still
as devout as Jews should be to God
who bring peace like the dove that Noah
sent out just after the flood God sent
which plucked a spring from the green tree leaves
which abundantly covered the earth.

IV

O Insolence which is the same as
pride, explicating to its Maker,
"This is how You should have made us, Lord,
not according to Your will but ours,"
do you so presume understanding
as to know your own interests as
well as God know them and cares for them?

V

O Insolence that does not regard
its Maker, our Lord YHWH who made
existence in the universes
both past and present in swaths of time
vast in their conceptualization.

VI

O grasshoppers who populate earth
how dare you challenge that which made you
Lord YHWH made all humanity
out of Grace and Love for God's servants.

VI

We each were granted the choice
to choose our destiny on our own
so long as it was blameless towards all.
Lord YHWH bequeaths to use the will
to say what we most desire to be
and although not all succeed in terms
of their dreams, tireless dreams receive
their in Heaven itself at last.

VII

An artist painting creates a work
of free will beside's beauty itself
and housewives baking bread take part in
the Divine gift of freedom itself.

VIII

The person walking a dog is free;
so is one resting after having
spent Shabbat morning in prayers each week
this whether 'rest' means reading novels
on sleeping outright because they're tired.

IX

Yet we are free to choose as we please;
this is God's gift of freedom to us.
We're granted choices by the dozen
large and small people decide themselves
what matters working and on days off.

X

O Insolence you ignore God's gifts
and do not see that those things which are
not forbidden are allowed choosing
the forbidden and not the given.
This is the essence of your bad deeds.

The Women's Protest

I

A sword against its [Babylon's] horses and chariots,
And against all the motely crowd in its midst,
That they become like women!
A sword against its treasuries that be pillaged!
Jeremiah 50:37

II

"O Lord," cries Israel's own daughters
"Why do you compare weakness to us?
Have we not proven strong as Sarah
of whom her husband repeatedly,
lied, saying, "She's my sister,"
so leaving her to YHWH's mercy.

III

Its surely Abraham who warrants
the title "weakness" if her husband
could no more protect her than she could.

IV

O Lord, did Isaac protect his wife
when following the example of
his father Abraham in Egypt?

V

But what of Moses? You say to us.
For surely Moses shown forth courage.
True, Moses was a brave man, we say,
but Moses' sister Miriam was
just as brave as her brother Moses
as one who'd rescued him in childhood
from Pharaoh's cruel grasp in the rushes
of the Nile, hiding her dear brother.

VI

So courage is a woman's valor
as well as a man's; why is Woman
called cowardly next to mere Mankind.
It's said that Man will fight as soldiers,
but Woman gives birth in pain so that
in danger herself Woman make sure
the continues existing.

King Cyrus the Great

I

Lo, a people comes from northland;
A great nation and many kings are roused
From the remotest parts of the earth.
The king of Babylon has heard the report of them,
And his hands are weakened;
Anguish seizes him,
Pangs like a woman in childbirth.
Jeremiah 50:41; 50:43

II

The Persian Zoastrian came from the north,
King Cyrus remembered in the words,
"Thus the Lord spoke to the King Cyrus,
His anointed one—treading down on
the nations before him,…" in order
to free the Jewish people despite the fact
he was of a faith differing from
that of the chosen people, the Jews.

III

The Persian Zoastrianism
was dualistic worshipping as
a head god 'Beneficent Lord' while
they recognized the Destructive or
the Evil Spirit which strove against
the Good Lord who then created both
his servants, human beings with bulls.

IV

They were the Iranians known for wars
fought against the Greek Athenians.
Then later Alexander conquered
the Persian Empire for them
to become their own liberators.
While Rome ruled the West, Persia controlled
the Mediterranean Sea's East
right next to India as it was
when Pakistan was part of the land.

V

But when the Muslims came to Persia
it turned out differently; Persia's army
was not the great force it had once been
and eventually Iran became
two percent Zoroastrianism
their history was not quite ended.

VI

As Islam came, some of them escaped
to India, where tens of thousands
live today, sheltered by the Hindus.
In India now Parsees live as
the remnant of this religion which
once helped the Jewish people rebuild
their Second Jerusalem Temple.

VII

So Cyrus the Great Persia's great king
served as the benefactor to Jews
and through them Muslims themselves today.
For Muslims would not exist without
the Jews those centuries in the past.

VIII

As for the Jewish people today
we recall friends as well as foes;
just as the righteous gentiles within
the Holocaust are remembered we
will also remember King Cyrus.
We should now recall Persia fondly
for Persia's Cyrus sent us back home.

The Last Cry of Babylon

I

I will send strangers against Babylon, and they shall winnow her.
And they shall strip her land bare;
They shall beset her at all sides
On the day of disaster.
Let the archer draw his bow,
And let him stand ready in his coat of mail!
Show no pity to her young men,
Wipe out all her host!
Let them fall slain in the Land of Chaldea,
Pierced through in the streets.
Jeremiah 51:2-51:4

II

When Babylonia heard news of
her punishment from Lord YHWH Himself
she cried, "Lord will you ravish our lands?
Will the God of the Jewish people
so despoil Babylon's fair maidens?"

III

"O God your mighty hand comes down in
the person the king Cyrus the Great
of a great people, esteeming the goodness
above all else the individuals
who've done good to the Jewish people
as something reminiscent of God.

IV

They are not Jews and yet they are friends
to the Jews, indeed beloved to
those who have recalled history well
in regards to God's holy people.
They will send the Jews back to their home
in Israel where the Jews were born
a chosen people beloved of
among the many nations of earth."

V

Those doomsday words to Babylon were
once spoken centuries long ago.
The Persians, who were powerful once,
have largely disappeared as the Jews
have survived to tell the tale of them;
it is up to the Jews to recall
their benefactors sent by YHWH.

VI

Yes, Persia was a civilization
as dazzling as its competitors.
And Persia's tolerance for the Jews
was even greater than theirs would be.
It has been said that of the ancients,
it's only the Jews who have survived
yet Jewish people's memories are
what have kept the Jews planted in life
this world and not just Heaven Itself.

VII

At the time, the Lord spoke to those who
had conquered the Jews, "You shall suffer
far less than you had meted out to
my people the Jews, but you'll convert
as conquered Babylonians to
the Zoroastrianism faith with
no fight for your own culture, you will
not be forced, peacefully you'll convert
the religion that sponsors the Jews—
and you will be the better for it."

Arguments Between Babylonians and Jews

I

Flee from the midst of Babylon
And save your lives, each of you!
Do not perish for her iniquity;
For this is the time of the vengeance for the LORD
He will deal retribution to her.
Jeremiah 51:6

II

As the French guillotine chopped off heads
so Babylonian heads roll:
the just fall with the wicked in life;
the blameless with those who are guilty
and Babylon though largely unjust
has guaranteed that innocents will
fall suffering for the sins a few
had refused to be participants
while the great multitudes did enjoy
the benefits of persecuting
the Babylonian Jews living
among the many cultures within
the civilization which had conquered.

III

Our Father Abraham once asked You
to You that for ten Sodom should be
a city preserved despite its sins.
He asked for pardon for the wicked.
Yet he spoke to Lord YHWH in awe
as one whom he would sacrifice all
including his son Isaac for when
he personally was asked by God.

IV

"Does Babylonia have likewise
ten righteous men or women for whom
to spare her punishment due to sins
which wicked Babylonians had
once visited on the Jews so that
they are now remembered as the ones
who were the greatest enemy of
the Jews in ancient Biblical times?

Have mercy on our innocents, Lord."

V

Yet Jewish people replied to them,
"It is not revenge for which you die;
it is not even justice itself, either.
It is for our sake, beloved of
the Lord whose Israel's God for you
would tear us apart if God ignored
our pleas and your guilt, letting us go
and punishing you for our own sake.

VI

"God cannot risk their being no Jews;
short of death to the villain Jews are
too prized to be left to Foes.
Jews because of his design on earth.
We suffer for God and God saves us.
So therefore Babylonians die
both good and bad with promises that
those good will someday be ones reborn
and receive rewards in God's own time
while the bad ones will remain within
their graves, as forgotten by us as
if they had never lived lives at all.

VII

"If justice does not come, Jews suffer;
good people suffer for the sake of
the chosen people whom we've laughed at."

VIII

Then the Jews returning to their home
went further, saying their last words to
the Babylonians who they left,
"Yet like Lot we turn our back on you;
you are our past and we search at night
for a great beginning of new light;
we pray for the light of a new dawn,
one reminiscent of leaving Egypt
one reminiscent of our own Eden."

The Great Dialogue

I

Babylon was a golden cup in the Lord's hand,
It made the whole earth drunk;
The nations drank her wine—
That is why the nations are mad.
Jeremiah 51:7

II

O Babylonia is not just
a nation but an idea which
has pervaded our consciousness since
the captivity of the Jews by
the Babylonia which Christians
will later label 'the Whore' who is
a drunken, licentious slut who drinks
the wine of oppression and hatred.

III

It became prejudice aimed at Jews;
if in the times when Christians ruled lands
where Jews lived, Jews were persecuted
as heirs to Babylonia by
the descendents of Babylon and
the multitudes of former pagans
who became Christians and then Muslims
though the phrase 'whore of Babylon' is
whom Christians recall in their scriptures.

IV

Or at least, the Jews hated those named
as Babylonian when they lived
if they are indifferent to those
who live now as their descendants where
the many conquests left a group which
no longer knows Fair Babylon's gods.
Yet there are those among the Christians
who conflate Babylon and the Jews.

V

For Jews the identification
with the old enemy is one that
is irrational, sadistic and
with a streak of the masochism
that speaks to the dark side of a faith
based on the innuendo prejudice sews.

VI

The metaphysical Babylon is
one which has corrupted for reasons
the sages of the Talmud say that
the Jews lost Israel; they say that
there were a plenitude of good works
and yet there was a gnawing hatred
in the Jews' collective heart which said
that it was alright to hate others.

VII

I dispute this claim that Jews hated;
but admit that it's hatred that warps
all good in purposes like one's faith.
But their heirs remember the old grudge.
For Christians inherit the Bible.

VIII

So hating Babylonia is
as wicked as they themselves, causing
its bile to spill on other people,
a nastiness that's recurrent in
the harm it does to others as well
as itself and Jews' persecution
has been fueled by lust and hatred
the very thing Jews supposedly
feel towards outsiders who've hurt them.

IX

"O Superhuman Babylon," comes
the cry of traditionalists who
are Christian anti-Semites themselves.
These pray as much to anti-Christ's as
to Jesus Christ the man in himself,
and never let go of the apocalypse
that is soon, so they say, in coming.

X

"We never understand you as you
are relentlessly stiff-necked towards
our truth and hunt us as wolves as lambs."
"O you are the true inheritors
of Babylonia," cries a voice.
"You persecute the chosen people."

XI

Yet those who persecute don't listen.
It occurs to this humbled person.
Suddenly Babylon has fallen and is shattered;
Howl over her!
Get balm for her wounds
Perhaps she can be healed.
Jeremiah 51:8

XII

O Babylonia, a shout comes,
can ancient hatred be cured at last?
Are you an irredeemable land
and can your connections to Jews be
now finally shown fallacious to
the masses of minds corrupted to
the stultifying hate which poisons
the soul as well as both mind and heart?

XIII

We tried to cure Babylon
But she was incurable.
Let us have her and go,
Each to her own land;
For her punishment reaches to heaven,
It is as high as the sky.
Jeremiah 51:9

XIV

Long after Babylonia fell
its impress remained misapplied to
the Jewish people themselves by those
who hated them for millennia
and carried Europe's numberless Jews
from Germany and France to Poland
and Czechoslovakia to be
the ones who have been murdered inside
a massive aute de fe-style death.
Not even Babylon did this to
the Jews in distant millenia.

XV

A black smoke still hangs over Europe.
The LORD has proclaimed our vindication;
Come, let us recount in Zion
The deeds of the LORD our God.
Jeremiah 51:10
With the Jews Babylonians are
ones vindicated in time and place
as Abraham came from a city
called Ur as part of Babylon, too.

Untitled

I

She is all we have left in our pain.
She is the land of milk and honey.
We return to the land of our birth.
The Jewish birthplace calls us back home."
Oblivion
Polish the arrows,
Fill the quivers!
The Lord has roused the spirit of the kings of Media,
For his plan against Babylon is to destroy her.
This is the vengeance of the Lord,
Vengeance for His Temple.
Jeremiah 51:11

II

Lord YHWH's punishment is meted
out to the Babylonians who
have conquered Jerusalem itself
and carried Jewish people from home
thus intending to destroy the Jews
as the one people chosen by God.

III

Now God seeks that same destruction for
the Babylonia which conquered
the Jewish people's bodies despite
still leaving intact the Jew's essence,
that gentle but proud commitment to
the salvation God promises us
which extends beyond the Jews themselves
to humanity beloved of
the Lord of the Jews who plead for God.

IV

The Babylonians have tried
to stem that gentle pride in the bud
and so face oblivion themselves—
not that they will meet bloody tortures
but that they themselves will so forget
their culture that it will be through books
like Judaism's Bible that they
shall be a group that's remembered by
their descendents and others living
in the lands that were Babylon once—
the villains in the Jewish story
is how they shall be recalled by them.

V

For to the wicked oblivion
Is their fate, the great chasm of death
while those who are those counted rightous
and shall be resurrected to God.
So Babylonia meets its death;
yet it was mighty in its own time.

God's Battered Wife

I

With you [Israel] I clubbed man and woman,
With you I clubbed graybeard and boy,
With you I clubbed youth and maiden...
Jeremiah 51:22

II

O YHWH You have battered Your own
so that if she could say so under
the Orthodox Law, the poor woman
would say, "I divorce You," with her heart
still beating for her beloved spouse.
Why have you, YHWH, so abused us?
We cry to You as our advocate and
not just our Judge in Heaven itself.
Yet you've abused Your devoted wife.

III

Just as the wife abused cries for him
who had abused her inventing for
him justifications a lawyer
could formulate and listens to him
for he says, after intimacy,
he was once beaten by his father
and needs her sympathy to protect
him from the world with its harsh judgment
to him as her own tormentor as
well as the tender lover in pain.

IV

But I will requite Babylon and all the inhabitants of Chaldea
For all the wicked they did to Zion before your eyes
—declares the Lord.
Jeremiah 51:24

V

O Lord, if those who mock us suffer
a worse fate than we do at your hands,
still will it lighten our great burden
of loving You while feeling pained on
Your behalf as Your beloved spouse
who will not give up despite our pain.

VI

Lord, they way we know we aren't that wife
is through our hearts; the love we feel is
You, the warmth of Your presence is You
and not the imagination as
it recreates images made of
a false god who'd abuse the Jews, too.

VII

This wife abused sees what is not there;
the love she has for him has become
his love for her in her mind's great eye
with neediness still hovering like
a single flower's honey bee which is
as unnaturally treated as if
it was a murdered blossom by him.

VIII

Yet God's love is felt directly and
the Lord's image is unclouded by
the fear and hatred angry men have.
For indeed even God's wrath will be
a judgment tempered, being tender,
the parental rule of love itself.

IX

O YHWH, forgive us that we doubt
that we have imagined that we are
the beaten wife by her God Himself
for we wish ardently that those words
You spoke as promises be fulfilled.

X

It is this yearning that causes
our faith to waver in the face of
the concentration camps, yet without
our yearning waiting would lose sweetness
and we might in our sadness become
like the old accusation of tombs
which are ones white-washed on the outside;
not because we'd be hypocrites but
we would die of our strangling grief which
would kill us in our lack of our faith.

The Fall of Babylon

I

Raise a standard on earth,
Sound a horn among the nations,
Appoint nations against her,
Assemble kingdoms against her—
Ararat, Minni, and Ashkenaz—
Designate a marshal against her,
Bring up horses like swarming locusts!
Jeremiah 51:27

II

"O Babylon shall fall at long last!"
cries many conquered minorities,
those subjected to being taken
and assimilated by force of
the sword in slicing through these peoples.
They exult in great Babylon's fall;
for Babylon had subjugated
these luckless subjects to their king's law.

III

"O Nebuchadnezzar has brought down
the Lord's wrath upon his own people
just as the Germans will be brought low
for that worse monster, Adolf Hitler.
For rebuilding the Germans shall be
done for the sake of others outside
of Germany for the sake of peace.

IV

And Nebuchadnezzar's foul attempt
at a great painless Auschwitz results
in Nebuchadnezzar's own culture
to undergo an erasing which
is painless towards deities which will
be forgotten for millennia
for the sake of God's chosen people.

God's Lambs

I

A point nations for war against her—
The kings of Media,
Her governors and all her prefects,
And all the lands they rule!
Jeremiah 51:28

II

The Persians took up the cause of Jews
and others mistreated by the king
of Babylon and those who serve him.
Yet it was God who granted success
to Israel through Persia's army.

III

For despite Babylonia's blood pouring
down onto the earth in God's own time;
it will die painlessly and without
the help of the Jews whom they'd despised.

IV

For the Jews are to be God's lambs
the gentle sheep whom God will shepherd
to holy Israel in order
to be ones tended by Lord YHWH.

V

For God loves his sheep or else he would
not possess anger towards those who
have persecuted the sheep he loves
as he put the great Shepherd Moses
in charge of caring for God's great flock.

VI

For just as Israel's well-being
Is for the sake of humanity,
so humanity is bound to God
to preserve them with their God's message
to the world and not merely the Jews.

VII

The Jewish message transforms those who
embrace it and its bearers with love
so transcending birth making converts
in Isaiah's words to them "better
than sons and daughters" native born Jews.

Women fight the War

I

The warriors of Babylon sit fighting,
They sit in the strongholds,
Their strength is dried up,
They become women.
Her dwellings are set afire,
Her bars are broken.
Jeremiah 51:30

II

O Babylonia's fair maidens,
those women who are at the age of
their being able to give birth to
the Babylonian's own children
but who have not so chosen themselves
to marry husbands yet or ever,
have become mightier than soldiers
made of the iron dangerous in
the hands of ancient smiths who smelt it.

III

O unwieldy yet hardened maidens
if men can't defend Babylon than
we'll depend on the women to fight.
Yet they will follow leadership that
is decidedly male as a group
and which is resentful of women
when empowered above the levels
the menfolk they mind in times of peace.

IV

For these proud fighting women will prove
that women can be strong just like men.
with skill and acumen they're able
to overcome mere brute strength in war.
"Ah Alack!" cry the Persian armies, seeing
the sweeping army coming towards
them from the Babylonian walls.

V

"What shall we do? These female soldiers
are ferocious as tigers coming
for us from the walls beyond the hills."
"I know," cried Persia's general who
was brightest of the lot, "We shall bring
our maidens to do battle against
these indefatigable females
so that we may still win the battle—"
and so the Persians regrouped and sent
back to their homes so they could find those
who they knew ensured victory to
their cause, which are the Persian maidens.

VI

Thus Persian soldiers desisted in
the fighting against Babylon's maids
till finally from across mountains
came Persian women as the soldiers
than Babylonia was subdued.
So it was the men who would become
like women and the women became
the soldiers, fighting the war for them.

Wrenched from the Land

I

For thus said the Lord of Hosts, the God of Israel:
Fair Babylon is like a threshing floor
Ready to be trodden;
In a little while her harvest time will come.
Jeremiah 51:33

II

O Lord, You teach us that what we sew
so we shall reap; and Babylon sewed
a harvest of great wickedness which
now clamors at their doorway, begging
to enter Babylonia's gates.

III

This judgment is harsh and is greeted
with evil replying from inside,
"Now we shall eat, drink and be merry
for tomorrow we shall die as one,"
with no thoughts towards repentance and
their hearts as directed to their sins
as though they relished punishment more.

IV

So Babylon drinks the wine of sin,
and waits to be one overcome with
the bleak night of that despair which will
yet overcome the wicked eating
in comfort at the expense of Jews
and other conquered peoples.

V

So Babylonia will be wrenched
out of the earth by shallow roots which
won't survive elsewhere as a culture.

VI

The Jews' roots are in Israel's land
yet miraculously they've survived
as migrants throughout ages as if
they were but tumbleweeds which can live
life nearly anywhere at all where
there's water in the topsoil itself.

VII

But when the Jewish people return
once again to their homeland they will
be able still to reconnect to
their roots as sons and daughters of God,
and of the land in Jerusalem.

The Drying Well of Hate

I

Assuredly, thus said the Lord:
I am going to uphold your cause
And take vengeance for you;
I will dry up her [Babylon's] sea
And makes her fountain run dry.
Jeremiah 51:36

II

O Babylonia's sea is death's
the abyss between the two rivers
the Tigris and the Euphrates from
which Abraham the Hebrew began
his journey to the promised land of
the Israelites, his descendents who
would be the slaves of Egypt's bondage
to rise up against masters who have
so badly oppressed masses of slaves
as servants of death in the form of
the pyramids built for the Pharaohs
in denying their mortality.

III

These pyramids prove that the Pharaohs
were aggrandizers of the self who
flocked shamelessly to the faith that they
would never die at last as they were
in both here and the hereafter kings—
and owed their divine rights in death.

IV

The Babylonians took no airs
that such was the case with their own gods;
they believed their gods to be as mean
as they were and so only viewed it
as necessity that death ended
all human hopes and desires at last.

V

The well of Babylon would say that
all good or bad in people ended
with their death, causing them to say that
no virtue mattered in the end of
the day and that their rulers had rights
to whatever they could take now as
the gods were indifferent to rights
of human or beast down here on earth.

VI

From this well Babylon was held to
be salacious and corrupt to Jews
and even the Greeks, conquering those
who existed in ancient countries
that existed just nearby them as
the cities lazy and flush with cash.

VII

This well, said the Lord, will run dry as
the corruption of nations always
has in the end, in history's wheels.
But as the Torah tells us, "But the word
of YHWH is yet always fulfilled,"
an indication that our souls will
not wither from us like the flowers
that Pharaoh's dream is made real for Jews.

VIII

For both our souls in the next world and
our strivings in this world shall be those
which will be remembered in all times.
Our God is immortal and yet loves
the Jewish people humanly in
our own times and in future ones, too.

IX

The wickedness of those like Hitler
will be mowed down eventually
by the God of his enemy whom
he made his enemy—Lord YHWH.

When God Created...

I

Assuredly, days are coming,
When I will deal with Babylon's images;
Her whole land shall be shamed,
And all her slain shall be in her midst.
Jeremiah 51:47

II

Ah! Land of corpses, that was mighty
in which great roses of blood rise up
from the earth surrounded by barbed wire,
the thorns that sting the bleeding earth from
which they spring piercing out of the ground
by moving upwards underneath it—
and so were reminiscent of World Wars.

III

O Babylonia's men lay dead
in heaps on arid desert ground in
the parched land of our modern Iraq,
their corpses will be buried deep in
the pagan earth where they will die on.

IV

For despite real barbed wire not having
been invented by humanity,
the weapons Babylonia knows
have crushed the skulls of innocents from
the land of Israel where they died.

V

The Babylonian's made themselves
images they called their goddesses, gods
and other spirits under YHWH—
which, however, they worshiped as 'Him.'
Their gods were ivory and stone cast.
Yet their gods were gods of war itself.

VI

But Babylonians gods were more
than wickedness as portrayed in script
of their own conquered peoples later.
They fight with issues regarding death
and immortality and evil.
They question their god's goodness
while never doubting gods existing.

VII

And harsh as Nature appears at times
how, without prophets, could we know God?
For if a person knowingly prays
to wickedness—while Jews know YHWH—
how can that person be good to God?
If other nations aren't strong in faith
the Jews as priests should prepare them for
the holiness of YHWH's Spirit
when it finally comes to Earth.
"The Righteous of the Nations are saved"
but Jews must prepare for the era
when there is no King save for YHWH.
That a God who is not good is not
yet truly a God to His people?

VIII

Or are there Babylonians who
will secretly break bread with the Jews
who fix them vegetarian meals
so they can swap their stories so Jews
can write those tales down afterwards and
be recorders of ancient tall tales.

IX

This tale was taken from *From Distant Days: Myths,
Tales and Poetry from Ancient Mesopotamia* edited by
Benjamin Forster (Bethseda: CDL Press, 1995)

In the Wake of the Great God Marduk[9]

i

The world was once an ocean vast
in immensity as the verse
from which it arose being in
scope and size a broad universe
in and of itself compared to
the limited skies on planet Mars.

ii

In the skies gods like eagles flew,
their talons raping the earth for
the fishes that it gave birth to.
They swallowed, 'O my little fish!'
as they choked 'delicacies' down
they digested the fishes' faith.

iii

An august tower burst forth from
the deeps of Babylon which lay
far beneath the waves of the sea,
a tower of the Babel that
would come when man was born on earth.

9

iv

The voice of Babel's tower then
burst forth through tides drawn by the moon,
"I am the great god Marduk of
the Babylonians and I
will demand of you allegiance—
as slaves to I and other gods.
You will live at our pleasure and
not because we love you like sons."

v

The fishes hummed and sang that they
would obey the gods ruthlessly
and be ruled ruthlessly in turn.
So below the gods were feared by
the fish of Babylonia.

vi

Then finally a story came
to be told by the fishes that
one of the gods, an Erra was
in revolt against Marduk's rule.

vii

The fishes rejoiced that the new god
had arisen from the deeps
for though the wisdom of the god was
so unquestioned and manifest
that none of the fish abandoned
due to the timidity of
the waters themselves which were in
the ponderous' god's shadow on
the oceans watching below him.

"O Marduk!" wailed the fish, "Die and
leave us to die as unmourned as
a fishy despot would leave us"
as Erra claimed gifts given from
the eagle—the first of its kind—
called Anzu, almost himself god."

As the gods had once hunted fish
so Anzu made it possible
to hunt down the gods with the fish.
"O food of the gods which is like them!"
Yes, the fish and the birds were each
as vulnerable to one whom
they offered themselves as though they
shared lineage and faith as one.

These gifts were given by the bird,
the offspring of the eagle who
had flown with the gods themselves as
if the fish they gorged themselves on:
the first was to spread terror with
a pain of panic biting teeth
in the guts of all mortal lives;

the second was fire, sizzling flames
that licked the salty, screaming fish;

xii

the third was a beast with a face like
a lion, that inspires dread in all;

xiii

the fourth a mountain collapsing
on soldiers of an army picked
as victims by the owner's whims;

xiv

the fifth a wind which overtakes
the circumference of the earth;

xv

the sixth a deluge sparing none
in its the path of its storm's rage;

xvi

the seventh and last a venom that
which slays all the things in its way.

xvii

So Erra filtered the seas through
his diabolical tool,
a sifter numbering the fish
more numerous as victims than
had been the case when Marduk ruled—
an evil malformation in
the fish world dominated by
the ocean gods that the fish spawned.

xviii

The great god Marduk looked down on
the state of affairs granted and
he said in ponderous, stiff words,
"If only I had known what had
been intended by Erra when
cruel Erra asked to wreak sad havoc
on the fish, for I assumed he
did not mean to do quite as much
to end the fishes live's in all—
not altogether, completely.

xix

I only meant for a few fish
to die and not all of sea's life.
Then Erra said, "I meant less harm
but my own bloodlust overtook
me as I swept through waters on
the reckless ocean beneath me.

xx

To stop my plague now requires fish
to die in such large numbers that
to do such would be inhumane.
We will just have to make the best
of a bad situation that
does entail, perhaps, allowance
of more fish to die needlessly."

xxi

So Erra chortled to have fooled
the great god Marduk in this duel,
sure Marduk would be silenced by
the fact he had known beforehand
and granted afterwards that fish,
in numbers beyond numbers, died
in gruesome deaths while Marduk watched
as impassively as a statue.

xxii

Then Marduk turned from a great god
to a huge statue of the god
of iron, clay, bronze, silver, gold,
with the head made of fine white gold,
its arms were silver, belly and thighs
were bronze with iron and clay mixed
in its feet standing on a stone that
was roughly hewn like the stones of
the Temple come to life so it
could be cast to the ocean's depths.

xxiii

So Marduk was the statue and
a giant hand threw the statue to
the waves, and mocking Erra was
then silenced forever with gods
shamed by the loss of Marduk in
his sacrifice for many fish—
his body became continents
as two fish stepped out upon them
and unzipped their skins, undressing
to reveal humans, the first pair.

xxiv

Then the Lord God breathed them to life.
This is all which shall remain of them;
but Babylonia would also
give birth to Judaism itself:
for Abraham was born in Ur while
the scrolls were written down there, preserved
for future generations to read.

X

The flood tales originated there;
as a great Babylonian myth.
If there had been no Babylon then
it's perhaps the case the Jews would not
have discovered God within wreckage
of a great empire's ashen remains.

Two Sides of One Coin

I

Assuredly, days are coming
—declares the Lord—
When I will deal with her [Babylon's] images,
And throughout her land the dying shall groan.
Though Babylon should climb to the skies,
Though she fortify her strongholds up to heaven,
The ravages would come against her from Me
—declares the Lord.
Jeremiah 51:52-51:53

II

O Lord, you are harsh in your decrees
both towards the Jews and their rivals—
and You say Babylonia is
as irredeemable as the snake
who pulled Eve astray in the Garden—
and irredeemable as Balaam
when he tricked Israel by using
loose women in their seduction of
the men of Israel out at camp.

III

You say her idolatries add up
to a great mountain of sins heaped high
like garbage heaps with the trash piled high—
a tribute to the worst of refuse
to be left excreted on the earth.
Yet is this all there is left to say
of this great civilization which
had lasted millennia on end
with epic poems celebrating
its grandeur as a city which was
as large as any in its own day?

V

Was Gilgamesh's Epic written
in vain in regarding its own thoughts?
Can Babylon's fall not be tragic
as it proves human endeavors will
end as the Gilgamesh tale says it,
as ending in great futility
and after greater efforts than that
of ants which bury food in the earth?

VI

Our Lord has denied futility
as the end of our endeavors and
has instead insisted that each day
our small acts matter greatly to God.
No, what is positive is our Lord
in telling the Lord's Jewish children,
"Does any grain of sand fall without
our universe as a whole being touched and

so that no speck leaves unaffected
the great whole of life's being at large.

VII

No single life goes without impact for good
or for ill on the family of
the human race as one great whole with
God's presence permeating our space
and outer space which reaches outwards?"

VIII

These are two sides of the same coin which
on one side portray God as having
once acted as the creator of
the universe and then the flip side
that God acts within the soul itself.
We believe in the ultimate that
we experience within ourselves.

Forgiveness of Babylonia

I

For the Lord is ravaging Babylon;
He will put an end to her great din,
Whose roar is like waves of mighty waters,
Whose tumultuous noise resounds...
Her warriors shall be captured.
Jeremiah 51:56-51:57

II

O Wickedness! Is this not your root!
To enjoy what's sinful without
once giving rest for food and water!
O Babylon why can you not give
your fleshly pleasures up for good now?

III

Up in the heaven the din on earth
can be heard wafting from the sin-filled streets
which have reached upwards, resplendent with
the grime of the heart covering up
what's good in Babylon with its sins
amongst the nations are quite the worst.

IV

Although quite civilized they were thought
as amorally brazen as they
were rich in luxurious living—
at least for Babylonians who
were wealthy kings and priestesses with
the majority were poor eating
their bread with onions drinking their beer.

V

The majority was poor enough;
the wealthy had wealth for that time but
were not as fortunate by standards
which are set by our times save that they
held power absolutely over
their subjects, Babylonians and
the conquered peoples they brought back home.

VI

Yet perhaps that was what they wanted.
They provided their pagan subjects
with license, temple prostitutes and
and beer made of cheap barley to drink.

VII

While they eat lightly because they're poor,
these subjects are still pandered to in
the form of pleasures they do not need.

VIII

For if she would still receive her need
she'd receive forgiveness with virtue,
the requirement to admit doing
a wrong to somebody else is what
is forgiveness's greatest burden.
Would forgiveness not be enough
to make the mending of ways worthwhile?
Start anew, Babylon, you have time.

The Fool

I

I will make her officials and wise men drunk,
Her governors and prefects and warriors;
And they shall sleep an endless sleep,
Never to awaken
--declares the King whose name is the Lord of Hosts.
Jeremiah 51:57

II

The drunkenness of the fool is that
he lacks the sober person's wisdom;
for sobriety is a knife that is
a tool that's wielded cautiously and
with skill as though the sober person
was carving their own legacy in
block of pure marble, a great poet
of sense like Michelangelo in
his medium of creating art.

III

The fool cuts himself, bleeding, and dies.
Fools, lunatics and children are said
to need the special care of YHWH
it's possible to be a holy fool whose
roots of their muddle headedness springs
for YHWH Itself transcending that
which is deemed sanity by mankind.

IV

There is another kind of fool who
is mad with power, money or lust.
This is not YHWH's foolishness but
the foolishness of vicious living.
This was the foolishness of Babel
which granted Babylon its name which
was taken from great Babel's Tower
from whence the languages of humans
were confounded by YHWH because
they'd scale it to drive YHWH from it.

V

Now Babylonia plays the fool
as one drunk on the wine of power
for power can so corrupt a fool
that interacting in life he will
say out loud, "I am God," assuming
that he is safe from others and God;
that he's above mere human questions
what he wills and what YHWH wills are
the same and he needs listen only
to the one single person he trusts—himself.

VI

King are ones who are especially
ones susceptible to this plague,
this malady of the mind and heart
but entire nations block out others
as if alone abroad they matter.
This is both unjust and yet unsafe;
for egocentric behavior costs
its actors because it blinds them to
the reality which surrounds them as
they may be betrayed, but by themselves;
if they saw clearly they would see that
lines exist between what they want and
what others want who surround themselves.

VII

The fool is his own victim who sees
the world as if it were his only.
He needs to know that others exist;
or he will do his injuries to
the self-same person doing the harm.
Such drunkenness kills Babylon now.

Babylon's Last Breath

I

Thus said the Lord of Hosts:
Babylon's broad wall shall be knocked down,
And her high gates set afire.
People shall labor for naught,
And nations have wearied themselves.
Jeremiah 52:58

II

O Babylonia! It's decreed
that soldiers pound against the gates.
This labor will be fruitful at last
with mighty Babylonia torn
to the ground while its uprooted with
the battering ram pounding inwards
to despoil Babylon if it were
now possible to violate such
a wicked city in the sight of
God and the peoples who knew her best;
her captive peoples like the Jews and
those travelers who go through the land.

III

Still to be brutalized in the way
that the Lord proclaimed Babylon will
seems a cruel fate for any nation.
If deserved it's an awful fate still.
Yet nations weary themselves so that
they may live for yet one day longer.
The Babylonians have cried out,
"The gates! Hold up fair Babylon's gates!"

EZEKIEL

The God of Ezekiel's Wife

I

When Ezekiel lived he saw that
the nation behaved sinfully and
so he then withdrew from the nation
in the Lord's Temple to spend his time
in giving prayers up to YHWH.
"If I can't live a just life outside
of the walls of the Lord God's Temple
than I'll live inside those walls only
and never walk out of them even
to eat, and have my wife bring my food."

II

But in the Temple YHWH pursued
this anti-social prophet, saying,
"I expect you to foretell my word
but first eat this scroll which I provide."
And Ezekiel ate a scroll which
had written down on both sides dirges
and psalms that came from the Lord YHWH.

III

His beloved wife watched as he wrote
God's dirges and psalms on a piece of
thick parchment, which he then ate himself
he told her after wards when she asked
him "Tell me of the scroll you've eaten."
The prophet Ezekiel replied,
"The scroll God gave me tastes of honey;
It is fresh honeycomb to my lips."

IV

Now Ezekiel's wife could not see
the YHWH delivered God's message
to Ezekiel, yet she believed
that his truth was her truth, that God came
and spoke with Ezekiel as he
had described to her and to those who
would gather in the Temple to hear.

V

But privately, the prophet revealed
to his wife, "My Lord torments me so.
It is as though God will not grant me
the peace I sought in God's Temple where
I thought that nobody would disturb
the prophet of the Lord as one who
is dedicated to the mitzvoth."

VI

"I keep the mitzvoth yet I am bid
to publicize my devotions to
the Lord as a great king's true servant."
"But you had wanted privacy first,"
said Ezekiel's beloved wife.

VII

"I know," he cried in torment. "I wish
I could at least be lonely in peace,"
but secretly the prophet's wife would
search his face enviously as if
he were the keeper of a seal that
was given to him by a great king.

VIII

It was not just his following that
she envied, it was his great belief
in YHWH; she wished she had it, too.
She was not the sole person who thought
her husband a saint to Lord YHWH.
The people Israel thought so, too.

IX

They revered Ezekiel and she
would listen reverently to them
as they would recall miracles which
they attributed to the great saint.
He cried in regards to the sins of
the people Israel who would not
put up their idolatries which kept
them from Lord YHWH whom he loved, too.

X

For Ezekiel observed scruples
of the Law that were hard to keep to
those living outside of God's Temple.
He ate no meat save what was butchered
by the Lord's Temple priests whom he would
give instructions to direct himself.

XI

He was known for his docility,
a kind and patient man of the faith.
When he had married his wife she was
a virgin while she afterwards would
deal with her impurities that both

their oral tradition and their laws
both circumscribed and proscribed cures for.

XII

She practiced them in accordance with
those laws which were the smallest to men.
And on the Sabbath they would observe
all prohibitions against that work
which Jews are not to do on Shabbat.
And Ezekiel told all that they
must have faith in Lord YHWH Himself.
"For to fear God is wisdom itself."

XIII

And yet the prophet seemed sad himself,
as though God was a burden to him.
And Ezekiel's wife would envy
her prophet the great knowledge he had.
So finally, the prophets wife asked,
"O Ezekiel, I am your wife,
show me the Lord whom you so revere
that you will refuse human contact."

XIV

And Ezekiel said to his wife—
for he loved her as greatly as if
she were the greatest beauty living,
"I will see what I can do for you."
So Ezekiel bent down and prayed.
And Ezekiel's wife heard the voice,
"Dear Ezekiel, what is your wish?"

XV

"Lord my wife is flesh of my flesh and
bone of my bone; she completes my life.
Yet she has not been chosen to see
You intimately the way I have.
Please come to both of us now so that
we'll participate together in
the worship You granted me, a mortal.
This is all I wish from You, O Lord,

and if You never again came I

would still fill fulfilled for my wife's sake."

XVI

Her eyes were closed; she waited hoping
that patiently he would tell her
that God was near to her as to him.
Of course, it is said also that she
heard wasp-like buzzing of the armies
which he would describe within his work.

XVII

But tradition says that she heard God
in her heart beating, 'Do not listen
to visions only; listen to your own heart.'
Did Ezekiel's wife see the Lord?
It is not recorded. It can be hoped
that she was not left disappointed.
For truly Ezekiel believed
in the God he saw; and what she saw
was enough for her in her belief.

Chariot of the Lord

I

Thus said the Lord God: I set this Jerusalem in the midst of nations,
with countries round about her. But she rebelled against My rules
and My laws, acting more wickedly than the nations and countries
round about her; she rejected my rules and disobeyed My laws.
Ezekiel 5:5-5:6

II

"Rise, Israel's great prophet," God spoke.
"You shall be the one revealing to
the Israelites the will of the Lord."

III

From stormy winds which swept from the north—
a huge and radiant cloud flashing,
like a great storm on the sun itself
a tumultuous mix of colors,
the oranges, reds and gold of dusk—
fierce as though it was lightening struck
like the great blinding light and thunder
of the sky's breaking in the night sky.

IV

In the fire's center is the gleam
of a yellowish brown newspaper save
for its light piercing those down below
like looking directly at the sun.

V

But in the center are four figures—
who despite the light are quite distinct—
there are four creatures appearing thus:
the legs of each one are fused into
one rigid leg with one hard calf's hoof.

VI

Their sparkle is the luster of bronze
when burnished into a hue lamp-like—
and they are darker to the sun when
they're compared to the surrounding storm
like a more grainy sunset than most
with a deep reddish cast in the light;
like they were intermixed with green sand
if they had been a sculpture next to
the great light surrounding the figures.

VII

Each figure has four human faces
which are both genderless and beardless
with almond colored eyes that look out—
and within as well as God's presence knows all—
of coffee and cream colored flesh tones.

There are four faces looking outwards at us
as they see all of existence now
and in the past and in the future
for the Lord's presence *is* in all times
and places pervading them making
all of them together one great thing.
These faces are remote contrasted with
the warmth that emanates from the light.

IX

Yet because of their omniscience they
are keenly aware of the prophet
who hides his face by looking downwards—
but possesses their impress within
his mind as of the likeness of God—
for Ezekiel believed himself
to have come as close as a mortal
could come to seeing YHWH and live.

X

It never occurred to the prophet that he
might be one experiencing what
in modern people would call madness;
he would not acknowledge that he could
be experiencing delusion or
that anything save his God, YHWH.

XI

Each human face looks forward at him
a lion's face on the right and
a red brown ox's face on the left.
The lion carved out of gold with eyes
like sapphires and a ruby tongue.
The ox was made of bronze like a shield.

XII

On the back of the human faces
were four bald eagles with brown wings outstretched.
These creatures are all identical
in their great faces and their bodies.

XIII

Next to these gargantuan figures
were coals that burned next to wheels turning,
that gleamed bright turquoise blue-green like
the polished stones in jewelry that
is made and worn as a craft item.

XIV

Above these four is a great expanse
of crystal clear like diamonds and yet
bright as the noonday summer's hot sun.
This expanse made the prophet's head spin
and below the figures were two pairs of
wings colored like clouds in mists and fogs,
one covering the figure's bodies
one reaching to sounds of an army
above the crystal expanse laid out
is the Lord's semblance, the form made out
of a just barely observed human.

XV

This figure was the one which Moses
saw the back of while in the desert.
So Ezekiel indistinctly saw
the Lord of the Jews from that dessert.
Lord YHWH's great waist, was an amber
but below he was made of great flames
which flicker and lick the Lord's great throne
made of green sapphires and gold metal.

XVI

The prophet Ezekiel flung down
his body in front of Lord YHWH.
And Ezekiel nearly fainted
yet managed to keep the Lord's command.

XV

"O mortal," spoke the Lord, "Your people
has sinned as greatly towards me now;
their love has run cold towards YHWH.
You shall warn them of my wrath coming
and then you will go console them in
the Land of Babylonia where
they shall be sent as punishment for
crimes against me they've committed which
have outnumbered those pagans have done.

XVI

Warn them and join them in their fall down
from the great heights they've enjoyed from me."
Then God sent Ezekiel with this,
this message serving to warn the Jews,
Here is the day! See, the cycle has come round; it has appeared. The
rod has blossomed; arrogance has budded, lawlessness has grown into
a rod of wickedness. Nothing comes of them, nor of their abundance,
nor of their wealth: nor is there preeminence among them. The time
has come, the day has arrived. Let not the buyer rejoice nor the seller –
for the seller shall not return to what he sold so long as they remain
among the living. For the vision concerns all her multitude, it shall not
be revoked. And because of his guilt, no man shall hold fast to his life.
They have sounded their horn, and all is prepared; but no one goes
to battle for My wrath is directed against all her multitude.
Ezekiel 7:10-7:14

XVII

So the Lord declared the Lord's warning.
"Rise, Israel's true prophet," said God.
"You shall be the one revealing to
the Israelites the will of the Lord."

Tammuz

I

Again He spoke to me, "O mortal, you have seen what the elders
of the House of Israel are doing in the darkness, everyone in
his image covered chamber? For they say, 'The Lord does not
see us; the Lord has abandoned the country.'" And He said to
me, "You shall see the abominations which they practice."
Next He brought me to the entrance of the north gate of the
House of the Lord; and there sat a woman bewailing Tammuz.
Ezekiel 8:12-8:15

II

On closer inspection the woman
was elderly, quite old yet singing
of earthy lust in regards a god
who died young only to be redeemed
by his own divine lover, Ishtar.

III

She sang the words in regards to them,[10]

"i
The Goddess Ishtar decided
to visit uninvited in
the Netherworld, home of the dread
and ruled by Ereshkigal who
was Ishtar's jealous sister as

---

[10] This tale was taken from *From Distant Days: Myths, Tales and Poetry from*
Ancient Mesopotamia edited by Benjamin Forster (Bethseda: CDL Press,
1995)

she would have liked to Ishtar's role
as Goddess of Sex, Love and War—
and dispenser of desired things.

ii

Now Ishtar had breasts resembling
crab apples hanging on her like
a tiny apple tree whose limbs
were tough and lean like tree's stiff limbs.

iii

Yet despite being ugly she
could inspire insatiable lusts—
which provoked Ereshkigal to
a molten jealousy at heart.

iv

Imagine Erishkigal then
when Ishtar came to the gates of
the Netherworld with these words to
the gatekeeper on the way in,
"You open up your gates for me!
If you won't open these gates then
I will break the door and its gate
I will smash both door and gate, too
The dead will devour living souls."

v

The gatekeeper than consulted
Queen Ereshkigal of the dead
and came back explaining to she
who pounded to be let in gates
no mortal ever returns from,
'O Ishtar, welcome inside here!
Let me take you through these gates as

I introduce you to rules
which govern Ereshkigal's home,
the underworld where the dead
will reside until time ends for
the human race beyond it.'

vi

So Ishtar started to walk through
the first gate when the gatekeeper
stopped Ishtar, lifting her crown from
her head, the tiara she wore.
'Why do you move my tiara?'
asked Ishtar, puzzled in her heart.
'Such are the underworld's rules, Queen,'
were the words of the gatekeeper.

vii

He spoke with subservience now
as one who recognized that he
was in a goddess' presence for
the first time in his existence.
Then Ishtar followed the man to
the next gate, where her earrings were
the second things he took from her.

viii

'Why do you take my earrings, too?'
'Such are the underworld's rules, Queen'
were the words of the gatekeeper.
The gatekeeper brought Ishtar to
the third gate, removing her beads.
'Why do you take my necklace, now?'
'Such are the underworld's rules, Queen,'
were the words of the gatekeeper.

ix

The gatekeeper brought Ishtar to
the fourth gate, removing from her
her breastplate and pin from her chest
and letting her clothes fall down to
the ground on which her feet stood firm.
'Why do you take my breastplate and
the pin which upholds my clothes, to?'
'Such are the underworld's rules, Queen'
were the words of the gatekeeper.

x

The gatekeeper brought Ishtar to
the fifth gate, removing from her
the girdle of birth stones she wore.
'Why do you take my girdle now?'
'Such are the underworld's rules, Queen,'
were the words of the gatekeeper.

xi

The gatekeeper brought Ishtar to
the sixth gate, removing from her
the anklets and the bracelets which
she wore on her arms and her feet.
The gatekeeper brought Ishtar to
the seventh gate and removed from
her the while loincloth that she wore.
'Why do you take my loincloth now?'
'Such are the underworld's rules, Queen.'

xii

If Ishtar had been watching she
might have then noticed that this man
now sounded obsequious to her,
but Ishtar assumed he meant it.

By now she was as naked as
a newborn baby freshly born.
Her breasts were pert and tiny hips
like those of adolescent girls'.
Yet she was pretty in her way.

xiii

Now Ereshkigal saw her and
was trembling, furious with her.
And Ishtar, without thinking, sat
in the place designated as
as that of honor at the head
of Ereshkigal's table laid
out for the occasion with food.

xiv

'A curse of all the diseases
that I have power on to you.
All sixty diseases on you!
Eye disease and side disease and
heart disease and head disease, ALL!'

xv

And defenseless in her nakedness,
the victim Ishtar fell down sick
and died of Ereshkigal's curse.

xvi

Now, after Ishtar left the earth,
the bull would not mount the cow and
the humans refused sex as well.
So the gods were left in a state
of consternation; they lived off
of humanity's servitude.

xvii

So Ea, god of wisdom, sent
down a male prostitute he made,
named Asushunamir for she
who ruled the underworld as Queen.
So Asushunamir went down to
see Ereshkigal, flirting with
this Queen by stroking her long thighs
and singing songs of pleasures to
Queen Ereshkigal of the dead.

xviii

It was intoxicating for
the queen of the dead below us:
for nobody spoke such words to
death's mistress Ereshkigal who
lived below the earth's sandy crust.
'Now, what would you like for your wares?'
asked Ereshkigal, Queen of Death.

xix

'Swear you will give me what I ask?'
'I swear,' said Ereshkigal with
as little thought as if he were
a merchant asking pennies for
a supply of sweats eaten cheap.

xx

'I want Queen Ishtar's body dead
or living so the case may be
so as to leave the Netherworld
with it as my prize for the gods.
This is above all what I want.'

'Swine!' Ereshkigal cried, 'Tricked! Tricked!
May you die impoverished with
no food to eat on filthy streets!
May public sewers provide you
as water to drink in that time!'
So Ishtar returned beyond ground—
this even as Asushunamir
lived out his curse for doing right.

Now Ishtar hurried back to find
her consort Tammuz enjoying
his time with prostitutes in song.
Both did not suspect that he
had been tricked by the death god who
gave him a flute to play that brought
the gorgeous whores to him to play.

'Shame!' Ishtar cried. 'You revel on
my apparent death, and with whores!'
'Ack! Forgive me,' cried Tammuz then,
'Else I will myself go to die.'

'Do!' Ishtar cried. 'Prove your love to
me as your beloved and Queen.'
So Tammuz took a spear right through
his heart with her hand on the spear."

IV

Then the old lady sang one last dirge
in regards Tammuz himself who died.

V

"i

O beautiful young shepherd, loved by
the goddess Ishtar, grant me this wish:
that your great fragrance wafts up to me!
For in that fragrance is youth's sweet smell!

ii

Give to me the life of a goddess
through the throbs of your gentle purring,
like a lynx in heat please be towards
your earthly servant worshiping you!

iii

O almost god whose flesh is young
who lives on in fresh youthfulness
who even in death tenderly
will regard female servants like
me myself in my arms a faun."

VI

Now this old crone seemed lascivious
in regards to her Tammuz as though
he were one serving her as well as
the jealous Ishtar, goddess of love.
The prophet Ezekiel crossed past
the woman invoking her prayers
he said not one thing regarding her.

Israel Falls to the Cherubim

I

*Now the presence of the God of Israel had moved from the cherub
which it had rested to the platform of the House. He called the man
clothed in linen with writing case at his waist; and the Lord said to
him, "Pass through the city, through Jerusalem, and put a mark on
the foreheads of the men who moan and groan because of all the
abominations that are committed in it." To the others He said in
my hearing, "Follow him through the city and strike; show no pity or
compassion. Kill off graybeard, youth and maiden, women and children;
but do not touch any person who bears the mark. Begin here in my
Sanctuary." So they began with the elders who were in front of the
house. And He said to them, "Defile the House and fill the courts with
the slain. Then go forth." So they went forth and began to kill in the city.*
Ezekiel 9:3-9:7

II

The prophet Ezekiel was pulled
by YHWH's hand which outstretched grasped his
in order to find that instead of God
he grasped the ghostly spirit's hand of
the holy presence manifested
of the Lord Incorporeal which was
the Holy Spirit reaching for him
yet not the Godhead itself which was
barred from the view of Moses himself.

III

For Moses saw God's back but not front;
for nobody sees the Lord and lives.

IV

They weren't like cherubs depicted on
that Christians give on Valentine's Day.
These mawkish greetings have more to do
with cupid in Greek tradition than
the mighty Jewish Cherubim whom
the ancient Israelites had faith in.

V

No Cherubim wear linen garments
worn surrounding waists like a diaper
draped over newborn infant bottoms
in olden times when mothers used cloth.
Real Cherubim were with the prophet.

VI

The Cherubim were terrifying
yet inspired awe on YHWH's strange terms:
of beasts with four heads, buzzing like wasps.
The Cherubim would have been mistook
for gods by any other culture
as fearsome as an Aztec god to
whom live flesh was a sacrifice made.

VII

For though abhorring such gifts from us
Lord YHWH has their ferocity
to a small degree combined with this:
God demands respect for God's Justice.
This would make YHWH austere
were it not for the gentleness of
Lord YHWH as God's shepherd to sheep
whom are the Beloved of YHWH.

VIII

This ferocity made mild creates
the great image of Mother Tiger
who however feared in the jungle
is beloved by Her cubs at night.

IX

"Ah Lord!" cried Ezekiel, "My faith
rests on the fact I've even seen You
up nearer to You than You've been
to any man saved Moses himself
and seventy tribe elders with him.
For Moses asked Me to see Me close
and so I passed by letting Moses
see Me back with the elders watching.

X

"And others have felt their Lord without
their being able to see Me there,
with My own presence suffuses hearts.
You will find believers in the Jews.
It may take time but they will believe."
Then YHWH gave God's message to them,
"Through you I will warn Israel now."

X

God's message through the Cherubim was
"I demand fidelity of You.
While other peoples I may forgive
You will have your Lord YHWH only.
I'm sending these two Cherubim to
cut down the souls of the bad but leave
the good ones standing firm like the oaks.

XI

"But you have betrayed Me in your gods
who are the alien revelation
that's recognized as foreign to you.
You've absorbed Canaanite gods;
now I will send my avengers to
my people to cut down their gods."

XII

So the first of the Cherubim went
through Israel in search those who'd been
good and left his mark on their foreheads.
This mark was like a tiny red rose
and yet the eyes of human beings
could not see this stain marking the good.

XIII

Another Cherubim came to us
and slew the people who did not bear
the sign of the rose written upon
their foreheads marking salvation from
the Lord's wrath poured down from God on high.
The people writhe in pain who were bad
and fall to the ground, dead as their gods.

XIV

Yet the Jews ask the Lord in prayers
"Among the gods there is none like You
O LORD," who breathed life into humans
and graced the animals with the grace
of a rich imagination unmatched
by humanity's greatest poets.

XV

The Jewish people are left special
for Jews are rich in love for their Lord.
The love of the Jews is God chose them.
The love of the Jews is why they will
be forgiven all their sins against
their Lord in the Jew's transgressions when
in adolescent rebelliousness.

The Suffering of the Good

I

The word of the LORD came to me: O mortal, if a land were to sin against Me and commit a trespass, and I stretched out My hand against it and broke its staff of bread, and sent famine against it and cut off man and beast from it, even if these three men—Noah, Daniel and Job—declares the Lord God.
Ezekiel 14:12

As I live—declares the Lord God—those three men it would not save neither sons nor daughters; they alone would be saved, but the land would become a desolation.
Ezekiel 14:16

Should Noah, Daniel, and Job be in it—declares the Lord God—they would save neither son nor daughter...
Ezekiel 14:20

II

Lord YHWH spoke to Ezekiel,
to warn the Israelites in regards
to the sins practiced in the land of
the Jews in Judah saying through him,
"I will not forgive that the people
have competed with Sodom's sinning.
I will say instead that I demand
that virtue overflow in the land
and not lie buried in a desert."

III

Yet Ezekiel begged God to know,
"But suppose that at Sodom there had
been ten such men while the rest were dross?
Is it not the case that You promised Abram
that if there were ten such souls buried
as a great freshwater well under
the sandy soil beneath a parched desert
that lacks the moisture that is goodness,
You would spare the people's parched land
on behalf of the underground well
that oozes goodness on their behalf?"

IV

But God said, "I have higher standards
for the Jews: they must love My Torah
in spirit and in letter given to them—
for spirit is the same as letter
in Judaism's essence as though
it fills the injunction of one to
do what the other demanded with
both Kashrut being kindness practiced
on animals in painless slaughter
in order to be abrogated
when meat is eaten no more by Jews.
I will not forgive that the people
have competed with Sodom's sinning.
I will say instead that I demand
that virtue overflow in the land
and not lie buried in a desert."

V

And Ezekiel regarded this
with wailing at its harshness towards
the Jews to be told, "Desist prophet,
for the Jews have sinned greatly and they
will accordingly reap what they'd sown.
For those who've acted justly will reap
their reward; so will wicked people."

VI

"But I've seen people who were good die,"
said Ezekiel. "Misfortune stalks
the just with wicked people dying with them."

VII

"Their sufferings will end," said YHWH.
"And I will claim them once more as mine."

The Conversations of Ezekiel

I

The word of the Lord came to me: O mortal, proclaim
Jerusalem's abomination to her, and say: Thus said the Lord
God to Jerusalem: By origin and birth you are from the land of
the Canaanites—your father was an Amorite and your mother
a Hittite. As for your birth, when you were born your navel cord
was not cut, and you were not bathed in water to smooth you;
you were not rubbed with salt, nor were you swaddled.
Ezekiel 16:1-16:4

II

"Lord! Ah I remember You so well!"
the prophet Ezekiel cried out
while in the temple as his wife walked
by the great Temple's Inner Sanctum.
For in his heart he knew he was part
of Israel who had sinned towards God
his Father as well as the one who
he held as Beloved to himself.
he had on earth here below who had
died angry with his son the high priest.

III

"I longed for You to be my Father
and yet You seemed so remote to me;
it was as during maidenhood I
reached out for You as my dear Father
but frostily You kept far from me
and reproached me as if the sun to
a blade of grass in fall or winter.
You said I was Your bride-to-be but
the world at large would be my Father.
Yet I loved You while waiting for You.

IV

No one pitied you enough to do any one of these things out of
compassion for you; on the day you were born, you were left lying,
rejected, in the open field. When I passed I passed you by and saw you
wallowing in your blood, I said to you: "Live in spite of your blood."
Ezekiel 6:5-6:6

V

On reflecting on Israel's plight,
the prophet spoke up regarding her.
For Ezekiel saw her plight as
if it were his own, as if he were
the Bride called Israel as
more than one individual, loving
the apostate child, she who loved God.

VI

"Was she not a Jew, O Lord? Did You
not love her as a beloved child?
I did not see the futility
of loving You, I reached out to

my Lord and Divine Husband whom I

had myself devoted to while young.
Why wasn't Israel a Jew, Lord?
I believed in Your goodness, O Lord.
I longed to fulfill mitzvoth to please
my Divine Husband who rules my soul.
Yet am I merely a poor gentile?"

VII

"Is Israel not beloved, Lord?
Do You not love Your Daughter as child?
For we have never wanted to be Consort
to God; we've only wanted Your love
as children; penetration destroys;
the mind of Israel is too weak
to hold the injury of union
with the Lord's Divine Spirit on High!
You have called grasshoppers! We can't give
to You what You seem to want from us."

VIII

*I let you grow like the plants of the field; and you continued
to grow up until you attained to womanhood, until your
breast became firm and your hair sprouted.*
Ezekiel 16:7

IX

The beauty of the girl he knew outshone
the city Jerusalem's glory?
"God, we were only youngsters grown up
in the fields when my father found us.
She and I meant no harm; he hurt us.

X

We did not deserve what he did to
the two of us in the field to us on;
I admit it for it made me see
the depravity of the world which
had cursed such a sweet girl by making
her a mere foreigner to my house;
I was a Kohen; it was sinful.

XI

Yet I can't forget the girl despite
the fact I have tried very hard too.
For even my own beloved wife
can't completely take her place in me.
I live with that sin every day."

XII

The prophet's vision dimmed in seeing
a devout woman uncovered right
in front of him, her limbs white and pure—
like the bare ivory in idols
yet put to holy purposes as
the bride of God, Jerusalem
made pristine for the Divine Husband.

XIII

You were still naked and bare when I passed by you [again] and saw that your time for love had arrived. So I spread My robe over you and covered your nakedness, and I entered into a covenant with you by oath—declares the Lord God. Thus you became Mine. I bathed you in water and washed the blood off you, and anointed you with oil. I clothed you with embroidered garments, and gave you sandals of dolphin leather to wear, and would fine linen about your head and dressed you in silks. I around your neck. I put a ring in your nose, and earrings in your ears, and splendid crown on your head.
Ezekiel 16:7-16:12

XIV

"Yes Lord," said Ezekiel, "But why
did You take so long to come to me?
I prayed all of my childhood that You
would take me with you from my father.
I prayed all my life to Lord YHWH."

XV

Then Ezekiel's wife called him from
the hall where she had his food prepared,
"My Husband, I am waiting for you."
So Ezekiel out of the room
where he prayed near the altar of God.
"Yes, wife?" said Ezekiel, her spouse.
"What has the Lord said today, dearest?"
"Bad tidings, dearest companion and
the light of existence next to God
who formed me before I was born and
I do not know when they will get well."

XVI

Then Ezekiel lingered within
the Inner Sanctum, the Lord's great house.
And he went into a trance, mouthing,
a beauteous description of the dress
of Israel in splendor at last—
that is just before growing corrupt.

XVII

You adorned yourself with gold and silver with gold and silver,
and your apparel was of fine linen, silk and embroidery. Your
food was choice flour, honey, and oil. You grew more and
more beautiful, and became fit for royalty. Your beauty won
you fame among the nations, for it was perfected through the
splendor which I set upon you—declares the Lord GOD.
Ezekiel 16:13-16:14

XVIII

"Now God is telling me of how God
has seen the iniquities that are
those being practiced within the land,"
said Ezekiel to his dear wife.
"The scribes will write it down, dear," she said.
"Do you know," Ezekiel asked her,
"That sometimes while I speak to my God
I will imagine Father is there?"
"Is that true?" she asked. "Why is he there
when you had never liked him in life?"

Further Conversations of Ezekiel

I

... Confident in your beauty and fame, you played the harlot:
you lavished your favors on every passerby; they were his.
Ezekiel 16:15

II

"Ah, Lord," cried Ezekiel "She is
a graceful woman degraded to
the point of becoming a serpent
and eating the dust of the parched earth!
O Israel is debauched, covered
in refuse like the garbage dumps which
the seagulls overhead steal food from."

III

"Yet, Lord, you neglected her during
her childhood, observing she'd survive
in blood till she was marriageable
and in that period she grew till
her spirit become mercurial;
both temperamental and shrewish.
She grew up playing beside trash heaps
alone on the undrinkable Dead Sea.
Yet with Your care she became more than
an ordinary beauty, her sad eyes in
which the world reflected Your likeness."

IV

"'My Lord,' she would say, 'You're my savior.'
Yet she would wonder, 'How is it You
did not come for me sooner instead
of leaving me to poverty as
the chattel whom You neglected there?'
And so young Israel went to play
the harlot towards her Lord whom
she secretly loved despite betraying."

V

*You even took some of your clothes and made yourself
tapestried platforms and fornicated on them—
not in the future; not in the time to come.*
Ezekiel 16:16

VI

"You hardened her heart like the Pharaoh's;
and lovers came in droves to her bed
as though she were a sacred priestess
in Babylonia, that symbol
of lust to Jewish people living
in that same polluted state the Jews
were forced to live their exile within.
While Jews ate no meat in the land of
their desolation they were
the greatest sinners in their homeland
the land where they ate milk and honey
as sweet as sugar cane bleached out white."

VII

You took your beautiful things, made of the gold and silver that I had given you, and you made your phallic images and fornicated with them.
Ezekiel 16:17

VIII

" 'Lord,' Israel cried to Lord YHWH,
'I wanted my dear Husband
to be a physical one so that
I could love Him the better as Spouse—
for though the Lord was good as Father
God's undesirable as Husband
as though his orphans love him better
than widows he has husbanded, too.'"

IX

Then Ezekiel paused in shock at this;
although he loved Lord YHWH greatly,
the shock of the two's meeting when he
was young still staggered Ezekiel.
For Ezekiel's God was searing
in love and pain in one fixed moment.
Could Israel have failed the YHWH?

X

Yet Ezekiel in rare moments
when he walked Jerusalem's streets saw
the sinfulness of fellows praying
to gods who were as foreign to Jews
with practices ranging from sex
to giving children to gods who they
would believe demanded this cruelty—
the suffering of Jewish infants.

XI

You even took the sons and daughter you bore to Me and sacrificed
to those [images] as food—as if your harlotries were not enough, you
slaughtered My children and presented them as offerings to them.
Ezekiel 16:20-21

XII

"O Israel is mad! She is mad!"
cried Ezekiel, "For do any
save madmen sacrifice their children?
Would any person who is sane do
such despicable thing to a child?
It is a dreadful act to the Lord:
for the Lord defends children against
the wicked who would injure the young.
This madness is one not to be born:
that children suffer at the hands of
their parents, as if they were cattle
and slaughtered on the altar of God."

XIII

In all your abominations and harlotries, you did not
remember the days of your youth, when you lay naked
and bare and lay wallowing in Your blood.

XIV

"'Ah Lord,' cried Ezekiel, 'When she
was little Israel was treated
with neglect by you, withering in
the land of Egypt; then as she aged
she rebelled despite her new freedom
and in her largess she turned wicked.
Her infancy's wounds had not healed yet
and that is why she behaved badly.'"

XV

"'Please forgive Israel for her crimes;
send consolation acknowledging
that You have maltreated the people
and they will give up their sins towards
You, believing once more in God's love.
For it is the love that is missing in them;
God needs to tell them they are valued.

XVI

They need to know Lord YHWH has not
and will never abandoned them to
a grim fate undeserved as those who
who died in Treblinka or Auschwitz.
Send them a sign, our redeeming Lord."
And Ezekiel told his wife to
go home and fix him a stew to eat.

Found in Blood

I

In all your abominations and harlotries, you did not
remember the days of your youth, when you lay naked
and bare and lay wallowing in your blood.
Ezekiel 16:22

II

The prophet Ezekiel spoke to
the Jewish people, relaying this,
"It was in this blood that I found God.
My father—my God—the two are linked—
my father came up upon we two
and punished us as brutally as
if we were mere brutes in the wheat fields
who would maul human beings themselves.

III

"For the Lord discovered me in fields
of wheat where I lay in tears because
my beloved and I were taken
and separated—divided like two cells
of unicellular sea cucumbers that
float on the waters of the ocean."

IV

"My beloved screamed—Israel cried—
for I can't distinguish between the two.
I only know that wickedness reaps
its reward—yet I have such trouble
in believing what was done was wrong.
For it was as though Israel was
a neglected, abused young girl while
I and the girl I loved meant no harm."

V

"My father bloodied us for our sins
like YHWH he would punish children
who were as disobedient as
the stiff-necked Jezebel and her spouse.
The bleeding we did resembled that
of intimacies between we two—
I like a divine being in love
she like the daughter of men found fair
in the eyes of the divine beings—
for it is said that this sin led to
the flood of Noah which he escaped."

VI

"My bleeding fed the parched earth itself.
It is in Israel's blood she found
the God of Moses crying to her.
It was in this blood that I found God."

The Virgin in the Fire

I

*You built your mound at every crossroad; and you sullied your beauty and
spread your legs to every passerby, and you multiplied your harlotries.*
Ezekiel 16:25

II

"On hearing of adulteries in
words made as severe in their phrasing
I was shocked by the vigor
of YHWH's anger regarding them
as though Lord YHWH was a Father
as Husband cuckolded by his wife.
And in another's arms God found her—
the other being Lord Baal of Tyre—
a hot stud with taut, muscular arms
and long beard falling into his chest
in curling brown locks matching his eyes."
So Ezekiel saw this treason
as it was committed to YHWH.

III

Yet that 'he' resembled the prophet
an eerie reflection of his youth
with Israel a foreign woman—
and yet a pretty young girl with eyes
as innocent as a faun nursing
at a doe's tit just after its birth.
For despite the act's shamefulness she
seemed pristine as snow newly fallen.

IV

They were both younger than the prophet;
they reminded him of she who was
his first love to his father's chagrin.
His beloved wife barely replaced
the sprightly girl his father injured
and sent way before, enraged
with his son Ezekiel, he took up
a riding whip while shouting, "You are
a Kohen, descendent of Aaron;
you will leave gentile women be and
not look at them or into their eyes."

V

Next Ezekiel went unconscious and
dreamed of Lord YHWH and the angels,
to wake up in his mother's arms while
still lying in the fields the girl worked.
She was left to the vultures by
his father who was the priest before
the prophet Ezekiel himself.

VI

There Ezekiel saw how wicked
the world was, never believing in
its goodness because he knew he was
not to ask question of Lord YHWH;
he felt a longing deep and strong which
would surpass his love of the girl he
had loved in his youth, and yet he cried.

VII

Yet he saw Israel as that night
the daughter of some pagans working
those nearby fields as slave owners
who were Jews, wealthy slaveholders and
so often creditors to the poor—
both to the Jewish and non-Jewish.
For Jews are supposed to help the poor;
this family had merely fleeced them.

VIIII

But Ezekiel remembered them
not for their sins but because he loved
their slave, a very pretty girl who
worked near the Temple from where he saw
the girl he loved far beyond rubies—
the beloved his father made watch
be sold far after discussing it
with the girl's owners with bribes to send
her far from his son Ezekiel.

IX

Now witnessing her likeness pictured
in Israel, a lovely woman
who debauched herself for the reason
that Ezekiel had his virgin
when he was young in the wheat fields when
both of them swore vows eternally—
and on the Divine Name which itself—
when Ezekiel confessed this to
his mother she told him that it was
both blasphemous for him to have sex
and swear to marry a young gentile.

X

But now she was as purified as
Lord YHWH condemned for sins towards God.
She became Israel now herself;
for Israel was born a pagan.

The Lost Israel

I

You played the whore with your neighbors, the lustful
Egyptians—you multiplied your harlotries to anger Me.
Ezekiel 16:26

II

"Lord, Israel did not do these things
to anger You or kindle Your wrath.
She was young, vivacious and foolish
with a nose delicately upturned
in futile passion lacking spite
which You then assumed that she shared with
the girl who shared the wheat fields with me.

III

I would have married that girl I loved
if You and Father had so let me
have my will at that age years before.
Those afternoons like watermelons
are sweet to remember in spite of
the abrupt end with which they would meet.
The sex we had seemed holy despite
It being forbidden as lobster."

IV

Although he never missed the lobster
the prophet Ezekiel still loved
that girl he'd known in wheat fields in which
they shared their love's sweet conversations.

V

The Egyptians who bought her for gold
were swarthy and smooth—handsome in fact.
This did not stop her tears from falling
or reassure him regarding what
would come of Ezekiel's first love.

VI

When Ezekiel was by himself,
he poured out his grief to Lord YHWH
and discovered in repentance God—
yet he still missed his beloved girl.
In the girl he saw beauty itself—
and Israel the cause he treasured.
He could not separate those two things.

VII

The Egyptians who bought the girl might
have molested her body with hands
as unwanted and dirty snakebites
but they still could not tarnish her soul.

The Girl

I

Now, I will stretch out My arm against you and withhold your
maintenance; and I will surrender you to the will of your enemies,
the Philistine women, who were shocked at your lewd behavior.
Ezekiel 16:27

II

The prophet Ezekiel crooned to
his God in the Great Temple himself
to all save the God that he adored.
"My father said that she was worse than
a Canaanite, the girl I recall
in childhood as my beloved friend.
He said she possessed Philistine blood.
The Philistines were wicked people.
Yet this one Philistine touched my heart;
I adored her for she was purer
than the air beyond mountain tops at
high altitudes in Greece's mountains."

III

"She was a flower blossoming for
me in the hills near Jerusalem.
I believed in my beloved's gaze;
I touched her hair and wondered if she
was shocked at my 'lewd behavior' when
I reached for her nose, kissing the bridge,
and pressing her hand close to my own.
She was a gentle lamb in my heart."

IV

And indeed, he thought he saw her form,
the slight and delicate girl he'd loved
in front of him with a shy smile and
a doe's eyes peeling into his soul.
The prophet's sad heart pounded for her;
for memories were all he had of
his beloved chaste and hard working—
for she did all of her work before
the sunrise so they could meet by day.
He believed in his heart that she would
have believed in Lord YHWH with him
and surrounded by faith she'd believe.

V

"God if you love me send her back to
Your prophet in a reunion so
that on my deathbed I may bid her
the farewell on the doorway leading
out of this life to the next because
I would be joined in the grave with her:
God if I must go to hell to be
with the girl I loved, send me to her;
but do not force me separation
from my own beloved for all time.
For eternity without her is
worth nothing to me whatsoever."

The Assyrian Jew

I

In your insatiable lust you also played the whore with the Assyrians;
you played the whore with them, but were still unsated.
Ezekiel 16:28

II

The prophet Ezekiel spoke to
his long lost beloved with these words,
"Ah Woman! Carried far from Judah
like northern Israel's lost ten tribes.
Yet are those Assyrians brought to
the province Samaria not us?
They grew up in the land of Canaan
and practice some of Israel's rites.

III

They claim our Pentateuch which Moses
Wrote down for Israel at Sinai.
Are these not the Lord's children like us?
For they have recognized Lord YHWH;
they're bone of our bone, flesh of our flesh.
They're siblings to us, forgotten and
for millennia continue to
live beside neighbors, Arabs and Jews."

"Yet I see more in them; they remind
me of my beloved, the one that
was taken from me by my father.
For they are come from foreigners yet
are Jewish people within their hearts.
They are said to have converted here;
but should mere ancestry keep them from
the God of the Jews, children of God?
For Isaiah says converts who keep
the Law of the Lord are those granted
a given name 'better than sons and
than daughters' beloved of the Lord."

V

"My beloved had already kept
the Law of Moses because she was
the slave of wealthy Jewish people.
She believed in the Lord for my sake;
I swore by YHWH's name I could not
love her as though she were my own wife.
I always wonder if in marriage
I betrayed the girl I loved while young;
for I love my wife much as I loved
the girl whom I called Israel as
the feminine bride of Lord YHWH."

VI

The bride of God spoke to the prophet,
"Your beloved will see you before
you die, O prophet Ezekiel."

No Mere Whore

I

How sick was your heart—declares the Lord God—when you did all
those things, the acts of a self-willed whore building your eminence
at every crossroad and setting your mound in every square!
Ezekiel 16:30-16:31

II

"Ah, Father called the girl whom I loved
a self-willed whore like Israel whom
I protect as a flower within
my heart as the girl whom I tried
to protect from the outside world who
did not care regarding the love felt.
Now I call Israel one such whore—
and yet I regret these words I say
the Israel I love as if they
were Father's words, not my own phrases.
For she is not self-willed or a whore."

III

"My Lord, the girl I visited in
hills covered with wheat where we would walk
each holding the hand of the other—
how could our love be profane? I asked.
Her hair was colored the burnt umber
that painters use in painting pictures,
yet possessed softness like a rabbit
in softness like a lop ear's brushed fur.
So were her eyes, with a doe's love and

the innocence of her faun nursing
at her tit, nourishing him or her
as if they were joined for all their life.
Yet she was also thin and graceful
with a deer's delicate face and legs."

IV

"My father said our affection for
each other must be nipped in the bud;
for it was illicit for a son
of priestly family to love one
born outside Judaism's bloodlines.
O immoral act, so-called.
O uncleanliness of the body!"

V

"Yet, still I refuse to call the girl
whom I loved condemned in my sad heart
this even though I married a wife
in another who is kind and good
but not the girl I adored while young.
Now I am responsible for her,
the other Israel, the nation,
a chosen people who need service
from their priests serving the Lord's Temple."

VI

"Lord YHWH she was no whore to me."
So Ezekiel cried in prayer.

Rubies

I

Yet you were not like a prostitute, for you spurned fees; [you were like]
the adulterous wife who welcomes strangers instead of her husband.
Gifts are made to all prostitutes, but you made gifts to all your lovers,
and bribed to them to come to you from every quarter for your
harlotries. You were the opposite of other women: you solicited; you
paid fees instead of being paid fees. Thus you were just the opposite!
Ezekiel 16:31-16:34

II

The prophet Ezekiel proclaimed,
"O YHWH! She took no fees because
she was a virgin, young and pristine;
my Lord has misjudged Israel for
she's stayed as devoted and constant
as though she were like Naomi's Ruth:
the Moabite who epitomized
the friendship that two people can have.

III

The girl and I had such a friendship;
our friendship's tenderness was the mark
that she was in love for the first time
as was I: we were lovers for life.
Although she was one taken from me
my father she still remains one who
is unforgettably lovely to me.

IV

She gave her favors freely, O Lord,
but she gave promising that the one
she gave to was the only lover
she would have, sewing together robes
with wool he bought for her to use for
the Temple garb I still have to wear
for prayers in the Holy Center
of the Great Jerusalem Temple
which I keep with a wooden box of
the flowers she gave me from the fields.

V

And I gave pebbles to her because
she would not admit rubies from me;
for she felt it would be mercenary
and compromise our relationship.
But she valued those gifts she saw
as more acceptable than rubies.

VI

Ah! Rubies! The girl's value compared
with those cheap objects greatly outshone
them as though they were grains of hard sand.
She was no common strumpet who walked
the streets of Jerusalem itself
in plying it for lusting sinners.

Child Sacrifice

I

Now, O harlot, hear the word of the Lord. Thus said the
Lord GOD: Because of your brazen effrontery, offering your
nakedness to your lovers for harlotry—just like the blood of your
children, which you gave to your abominable fetishes:—
Ezekiel 16:35-16:36

II

She admitted to Ezekiel
that her own parents sacrificed one
of the girl's sisters to the gods of
the Canaanites on behalf of both
her parents and their Hebrew owners.
On recalling this Ezekiel
was enraged; sacrifices scared her
for the girl wondered if she was next
in line for slaughter to the cruel gods.

III

The girl begged Ezekiel with words,
"O Ezekiel, never slaughter
a child to any god if you love
the friend who adores you as sweetheart
from childhood to the end of all time.
For it still chills me to hear the cries
of little sister on the altar of gods
who fed on human children as though
these children were the entrails of sheep
in my imagination at night."

IV

In the dark Ezekiel saw her watching
her infant sister wailing out to
her sister lonely without the child.
Although the prophet's beloved girl
was young when sacrificed the child
was herself merely a small baby.
And Ezekiel stopped this practice.

Saving the Children

I

I will inflict upon you the punishment of women who commit adultery
and murder, and I will direct bloody and impassioned fury against you.
Ezekiel 16:38

II

In Ezekiel's mind the baby
that was his beloved's own sister
was not the only sacrificed child
to Canaanite gods worshipped by Jews.
The children who were murdered cried out
to the God Ezekiel worshipped.
So Ezekiel spoke out against
the crimes of Israel as high priest—
on behalf of the infants of God.

III

For children were those consecrated
to the Lord through their circumcision—
that's physically for the young boys
and spiritually for the girls who
are capable as boys of goodness—
both possess circumcised hearts, says God.

IV

For God loves children as his builders—
they create the new Israel as
they grow to their adulthood through rites
taught to them by both of their parents
with elderly Jews given children
as a crown to hold in their old age.

V

Yet the Lord's especially fond of
the children Israel bears because
they are made vulnerable by youth
as delicate young saplings which God
loves as though he were their own Mother.
For God loves Israel as daughter;
they possess tender warmth which is that
not associated with men.

VI

God mothers like a female bobcat;
in early morning she sends forth food.
She tucks us in at night with prayers,
and prays her qualities are such that
her gentle traits will overcome traits
that are harsh or strict towards children.

The Loss of Ezekiel's Beloved

I

I will deliver you into their hands, and they shall tear hands,
and they shall tear down your eminence and level your
mounds; and they shall strip you of your clothing and take
away your dazzling jewels, leaving you naked and bare.
Ezekiel 16:39

II

When Ezekiel's beloved was
sold, deeper into slavery he
watched as she bled on the ground crying,
"Let me keep my stones," to her owners.
Not knowing the 'stones' significance,
her owners laughed, "Of what stones do you speak?"
and she took them to the box she kept,
"These are my things," and ascertaining
the things in it had no value they took
the girl to auction and sold her off.

III

They reported this to the high priest,
the prophet Ezekiel's father,
and he grew red with rage, "Why have you
not given me the box so those things
so that they may be destroyed by me?"
but it was too late; the girl took with
her the gifts that the prophet gave her.

IV

Their sentimental value was what
she took with her; there was no other.
The girl left bloody and bruised yet she
still possessed Ezekiel's sad heart.
Her body was left naked and bare.

A Dream of the Prophet

I

They [your lovers] shall put your houses to the flames and execute you in
the sight of many flames and execute you in the sight of many women;
thus I will put a stop to your harlotry, and you shall pay no more fees.
Ezekiel 16:41

II

The other women surrounded her
with stony faces darkening as
a hurricane in surrounding seas.
Adulteresses are stoned because
of her crimes against their own husbands.
So, in his nightmares, is the girl whom
the prophet Ezekiel once loved.

III

She was short with coarse hair and large eyes—
both colored the burnt umber used by
oil painters creating their landscapes—
as tree bark surrounded by the fall
of orange, yellow and red leaves which
lie scattered on the surrounding ground
the tall tree's branches up from their fall.
Her skin was golden like some leaves were
but with red bleeding out of her veins
and onto the skin's surface which hold
the body together with skin cells.

447

IV

For indeed the girl who had blossomed
in Ezekiel's arms years before
in his dreams was a rose torn up on
the ground with 'lovers' standing ready
with stones in their hands, ready to kill.
The prophet Ezekiel cried, "No!
She is as innocent as a lamb
of the crime committed! It is mine!
The punishment is also my own."

V

Then he saw two great cherubim come,
"Great prophet Ezekiel, God wills
that you shall be a lesser Moses!
Your beloved, will however be
one denied you for long time to come!"

VI

Then Ezekiel fell at its feet,
"Lord forgive me my all of my sins!
And spare my friend the punishments that
we may both deserve as we both loved
You and each other as man and wife—
but I will give up her love if only
you promise no ill will come to her."

VII

The cherubim laughed, "before life's end
you shall see her once again if You
will until then love your Lord as once
you loved your mistress and she loved you.
For Moses was blessed because he loved
his sheep and would love Israel, too,
and God sees your love for this girl and
so concludes you will love God's people."

VIII

"Lord, Lord," spoke Ezekiel, "I will
love Israel with the Lord because
of Your great kindness towards me, too.
For You have answered prayers which I
had thought were unanswerable now."
The cherubim gave him a scroll to
read, digesting by eating it, too.

IX

"And since I am now already wed
to a young woman who loves me, too,
I beg for her sake, faithfulness till
her death when my own beloved comes.
The sad truth is I love both women.
This causes me grief at my love life;
for I feel I wrong both the women.
But I have finally loved You as much
as I love those two in my own life."

X

When Ezekiel awakened from
his slumber his wife asked him,
"You mentioned a scroll, dearest prophet."
"Yes," Ezekiel said, "God sent one."
"Is it good news?" his wife asked him now.
"It is mere confirmation of what God
has told me regarding past events."

XI

Then Ezekiel paused, "But God says
'You have the right wife for the works which
you have been given to by your Lord.'"
"Well," she said, secretly pleased, "That's good."
"I could not have asked for a spouse who
was any better," said the prophet.
"But now I must go to the Temple.
My work waits for me as I stand by."

XII

"Of course, my beloved," his wife said.
And then the prophet traveled to God.

The Trains of Death

I

Since the girl's disappearance the prophet
has heard the voice of God as it speaks
to him while awake or while sleeping.
Have you not committed depravity on top of all your abominations?
Ezekiel 16:43

II

The abominations that I see
are committed to crimes of passion:
that's idolatry, prostitution,
abuse, adultery and, worst, murder.
These are epitomized by one crime:
child sacrifice, a ferocious lust,
which decimates the population
and yet is worse than that will imply—
a savage act on infants born pure.

III

*Why, everyone who uses proverbs applies you the proverb, "Like mother,
like daughter." You are the daughter of the mother, who rejected
her husband and children. And you are the sister of your sisters, who
rejected her husband and children. And you are the sister of your sisters,
who rejected their husbands and children; for you are daughters of
Hittites mother and an Amorite father. Your elder sister was Samaria,
who lived with her daughters to north of you; your younger sister was
Sodom and her daughters did not do what you and daughters did.*
Ezekiel 16:44-16:46

IV

O mothers, daughters, sisters, alas!
I see in you a web of sins which
catch Israel in their net grasping
like spider web does ancient railings.
O metal and tile which trains run down
you are the future which I see out
in a great distance stretching outwards.
These trains lead to the camps of death for
the millions of Jews who were remnants.

V

At the end of tiles envisioned I

see the blood of Jews drenching the earth.
Has Judaism overpaid for its sins?
the murderers will themselves ask when
it's over with the tracks reaching out to
the concentration camps of Auschwitz
and Treblinka and Buchenwald where
the tentacles of Europe cry out
for justice which is rarely granted—
in this life, at least, for each of us.

VI

Did you not walk in the ways of their abominations? Why,
you were almost more corrupt in all your ways?
Ezekiel 16:47

VII

Lord, You have taken too much for sins
that were mere youthful indiscretions.
And compared to these large crimes I'm struck
by the small consequence of prophets,
so Ezekiel thought to himself,
not writing down this prophesy for
he feared the knowledge of it would be
too much for Jewish people to bare.
For knowledge of their impending doom
would cause them to flee from Lord YHWH
to apostasy and worse escapes.

VIII

Yet Judaism's message would be
one vital to the human race and
the Jewish people will be paid with
a reward dwarfing suffering which
they experienced in Auschwitz itself.

IX

Then Ezekiel troubled by this
was heard to mutter, "the trains of death!"
and reflect that his sufferings were
those of a madman; he'd seen far worse.
Why would Just YHWH give us such things
the bitter fruit which we don't deserve?

Bafflement of the Israelites

I

*As I live—declared the LORD God—your sister Sodom
and her daughters did not do what you and your daughters
did. Only this was the sin of your sister Sodom: arrogance!
She and her daughters had plenty of bread and untroubled
tranquility; yet she did not support the poor and the needy.*
Ezekiel 16:48-16:49

II

The prophet Ezekiel spoke to
the God from whom he derived this from,
"Lord, in this respect Jews are humble:
we love one another as though we
were one great family—which we are."
The prophet Ezekiel reflects
on this truth while his wife makes breakfast.
His fellow Jews have been kind to him
when baffled by his message;
although they believed him they wondered
what his words possibly could mean to
them when he spoke of cherubim and
the distant likeness of God's presence—
the man in the throne speaking to him.

III

They were both intrigued and yet disturbed
as idolatry's brilliant likeness
was made so vivid as to shame what
the physical world contained in it.
The Jewish people believed in him
when his abusive father didn't
and besides that he doubted whether
God's goodness because he had suffered.

IV

These were images vivid compared
to the calf of gold formed of the sins
of Israel in having escaped
the Egyptians who kept them as slaves.
The Jewish people heard his visions
and puzzled what the words meant to them.
They were the family who shared with
the Jewish people their faith itself.

V

For indeed it was his strange visions
that convinced him of the Lord's goodness
and his own special mission given
to him on behalf of the Jews who
were believers of his words themselves.

The Lord was there in the Darkness

I

*Truly you must bear the disgrace of serving as your sister's [Sodom
and Samaria] advocate: Since you have sinned more abominably than
they, they appear righteous in comparison. So be ashamed and bear
your disgrace, because you have made your sisters look righteous.*
Ezekiel 16:52

II

"O sinless virgin Canaanite girl!"
cried Ezekiel, the Lord's prophet.
"I gladly pray on behalf of you!
For tender heartedly you loved me!"
In his mind he made her an idol.
She was all those things beautiful to
the prophet when he was still young
and reminisced of when he was old.

III

The prophet cried with his whole heart words,
"O YHWH, I pray willingly for
the Sodomites and Samarians
with no shame because I know myself
to be born needing redemption for
the crimes of Israel for we know
although we need God's forgiveness we
feel that to forgive is a gift which
goes beyond our not sinning itself."

IV

"For to love and be love is the same.
In particular, it is goodness
if no sin results from a first crime.
Sin often results from pain and yet
if there's no suffering there's also
no beginning of compassion as
the development of the soul is
based on one's giving from one's heart till
there seems no more to give yet finding
a bottomless pit from which love comes."

V

"The saints of Auschwitz will be redeemed.
The sanctification of God's Name—
the holy breath which pronounces this:
"O Beloved Lord YHWH Itself"—
is holiness in itself when faith
would seem to be weak in the face of
the wicked, proud of being evil.

VI

"And salvation will come to all Jews
with righteous non-Jews saving those few
whom they were able to hide from those
who are called iniquities doers.
The evil doers from that time will
meet oblivion for their sins as
the pits of gehenna aren't enough
to cleanse the hearts of Nazism.
Yet if not forgiven they will be
ones forgotten to victims of hate.
Those saved shall be ones collected to
grant holy offerings to their God."

VII

Then Ezekiel cried tears for those
would sanctify God's Holy Name as
if that pain overwhelmed his senses.
"O Lord, spare Sodom who was not bad
in comparison with these thugs who
have committed the ultimate sin.
O Lord, spare Canaan itself because
it is less guilty than these monsters.
O Lord, if we meet this fate ourselves
still be our consolation when we
are awakened from our soul's bleak night
when Jews are face with killers who are
as merciless as spiders are not."

VIII

"This pain-filled night is filled with death,
with howling of the innocents who
bleed for the sake of YHWH only.
God let their souls rest until judgment;
than carry them like swaddled infants
to the home they longed for while living."
Yet the Lord was there in the darkness.

The 'Punishment' our Crimes Afford

I

I will restore their fortunes—the fortunes of Samaria and
her daughters—and your fortune along with theirs.
Ezekiel 16:53

II

When Ezekiel heard these words he
was ecstatic and said to the Lord,
"O YHWH, slow to anger at us
and quick to forgive Jewish children—
we will love our crimes' punishment which
You have placed on us not to burden
but to save the Jews as a whole.
This burden is light despite the pain
it temporarily will afford
the Jewish people carrying it."

III

"The Jewish Father loves all people—
and in his judgment is kind to all.
We'll delight in our punishment as
such because it proves the Lord is just.
Your mercy to the nations as well
as Your love for us as You forgive
the guilty of crimes committed in
those ages when the world was still young."

IV

"For indeed, our Lord, we want to prove
that our Lord remains merciful to
most of the human race, not just Jews.
The Lord will redeem sinful people
as well as the just when he decides
on final judgment day the fate
the individual souls on that day
in accordance to their deeds they've done."

The Second Chance

I

Thus you shall bear your disgrace and feel your disgrace in such a way that they could take comfort. Then your sister Sodom and her daughters shall return to their former state, Samaria and her daughters shall return to their former state, and you and your daughters to your former state.
Ezekiel 16:54-16:55

II

The prophet said this should bring gladness
for it proves the Lord gives the same chance
to even wicked people that he
gave to the Jews to repent their sins
and that one life is not the sole chance
the wicked person has to repent.
We just have no way to know who is
one reborn and who lives their first life.

III

You Israel, shall now be tested,
right along with the sinners Sodom
and Samaria not to compete
but repent wicked deeds done by you.
For since the Lord gave you a chance
once after you first it was judged just
to grant them the self-same chance given
to Jewish people born twice over.

IV

O second chance! It is the Lord's gift!
Lord YHWH may grant to some
among the wicked who live earth.
For gehenna is like a prison
in which the wicked spend the term which
is judged appropriate for the crimes
a person committed alive and
there are those given second chances
for YHWH does not rejoice in that
the wicked receive punishment from
Lord YHWH through his children on earth.

VI

Your test and Sodom's are judged the same;
and yet should Sodom do well it is
to their own credit but not your blame.

VII

For the Lord independently will
alike judge the just and the unjust.
So perhaps Israel's sins are like
the sin of Joseph's being sold by
his brothers into slavery and
so ultimately for the good as
the saintly Joseph assured them when
he revealed that he was their brother.

VIII

"You meant ill, but God did well," he said.
And Israel's sins are turned into
the blessing to both she and Sodom
and Samaria, who since dead will
both receive second future chances.

Becoming Goodness

I

Was not your sister Sodom a by word in your mouth in the days of
your pride, before your own wickedness was exposed? So must you
now bear the mockery of the daughters of Edom and all her neighbors,
the daughters of Philistia who jeer at every side. You yourself must
bear your depravity and your abominations—declares the Lord.
Ezekiel 16:56-16:58

II

O YHWH, we're are made desolate for
the cause of pride in regards others:
we said, "we commit none of the sins
of Samaria, Philistia,
or Sodom; we are sinless people."

III

For too long, Ezekiel spoke up,
"The Jews have spoken the words themselves,
'We are good because we have bloodlines
on our side rather than mere mitzvoth.'
Lord YHWH wants the mizvoth kept by
the pious Jew to visit the sick;
for dying humanity is judged
to be a 'Holy Thing' to YHWH
near death on immortality's cusp.

I V

The duties YHWH demands of us
are to be keepers to our sisxters
if we see an act committed which
is criminal we should do all to
stop this act—even if there are
a thousand other witnesses there.

V

Most of us are not called to become
a rescuer of victims within
the Holocaust—thank YHWH for that—
but we are called on to do our duty—
the good Jew's dharma's[11] and the Hindu's
at some point to a fork in the road
where destiny is made this way:
a person decides to work their best
in holy battle for Lord YHWH.
The path is unexpected and comes
to all who would climb back home to God.

---

[11] "Dharma" is the word for duty in both Hinduism and Buddhism. Although they differ on what precisely a person's "duty" is, the both agree that it should be done unselfishly.

VI

True, Mother Teresa's and Gandhi's
but even ordinary people
can walk the walk of YHWH
or decide to choose ease and comfort
for themselves treading downhill at night.
The Saints like Sisyphus[12] climbs their hill.
But, so do ordinary people.

VII

One day on a bus you see a man
he is a beggar and it is cold.
You notice he has no coat to wear.
You ask him if you can help him then;
you join him to the local shelter.
You take him there and once a week come
the first one with a gift: a new coat.
You have thus saved a world for YHWH.
As the great sages have said to us:
"You can't save the world; you may be one
who is the world to somebody else."

---

[12] Sisyphus is the figure in Greek mythology who in punishment for his sins must push a rock up a hill—only for that hill to roll down over him so it both damages him and he has to push the rock up the hill again. He is considered one of the two biggest sinners in the Underworld. However, one might keep in mind that if one purges one's sins with good deeds in this life it is all the better in the world-to-come.

VIII

These are the acts of goodness God wants.
Now despite YHWH calling to us
there are still beggars filling the streets.
This insouciance God calls wicked.
To believe arrogance is what will
be the Jew's justification when
times are hard is a blindness of heart.

IX

It ignores impoverished people.
It ignores values such as caring
for friends and relatives, as well.
God demands humility and love.
God makes an counterexample
of this pride humanly and towards
the divine essence expressed in us.
This humility attracts others
to the cause of the Jewish people.
It's humility which brings us near
to our God who is Father to us.

X

For Jewish people should strive towards
the goodness of a Moses himself,
but without arrogance to those
who belong to faiths outside of ours.
"There never was a man as meek as
the prophet Moses" the scrolls tell us.

XI

We should be "lowly like the dust" which
lies on the ground in humility.
The Lord told us that humility
is why Mt. Sinai was picked out for
the spot of where the mitzvoth God gave
were given to us somewhere where we
would not find afterwards or again.

XII

So the Lord's leveling of the Jews
with other people who'd been wicked
is not just punishment, it teaches.
The Jews are to be people to all,
not simply other Jewish people.
For Sodom was known as a city
which practiced inhospitality.

XIII

To be kind to those ignored by them
is thus the goal of fidelity
to our Lord YHWH is their being
kind to both Jew and non-Jews they meet—
as we're told by the Talmud as well.

XIV

More, it's said that, 'the righteous man is
kind to his beast' and our own footfall
on the rocks should be gentle so that
we can so avoid harm to the ants.

XV

Be better than the Sodomites were
and forgiveness will flow like those words
"let justice flow down like a river,"
with mercy replacing hard justice.
By becoming the mitzvoth called "do justly,
love mercy and walk humbly with God,"
we'll become goodness ourselves flowing
out towards the world changing it so
that it will itself become goodness
and reaching the God creating it.
We create God's world; the Lord commands
such to be the case shining through us.

The Israelite's Siblings

I

*You shall remember your ways and feel ashamed, when you receive your
older sisters and your younger sisters, and I give them as daughters,
though they are not of your covenant. I will establish My covenant with
you, and you shall know that I am the LORD. Thus you shall remember
and feel shame, and you shall be too abashed to open your mouth again,
when have forgiven you for all that you did—declares the Lord GOD.*
Ezekiel 16:61-16:63

II

O Lord, we do not begrudge siblings,
the Edomites and Sodomites or
as (perhaps) Christians and as Muslims
for being related to our claim
if they will be as righteous gentiles
to us in their faiths for we believe
that if a person acts with goodness

III

Lord YHWH is a god good enough
that He will forgive those who love God
in their hearts whether understanding
of YHWH is there within their minds.
The Jews aren't YHWH's only children.

IV

The connection is relational
of Mediterranean cousins
born across borders joined at the roots.
For fratricidal though the cousins
have been at times, when Constantine made
his conversion, the Christians went to
the Jew's own synagogues to pray at
and Mahomet learned half his faith from
Jews in the Meccan proximity.

V

Why they left the faith's family is
the only regret; they should have stayed.
For if the Catholic Church had said
they recognized Jews as their partners
and Mahomet said they would see Jews
as equals without converting them
things would have been much better than now.

V

Yet perhaps there were times when Jews were
as unkind to them as vice versa.
For it is easy to see how come
crimes towards Jews seem the worse when Jews
for centuries been positioned low
in Catholic and Muslim places.
We do not resent their good luck when
they have it; but we have a path carved
in accordance with our own genius
which the Lord gave us in the womb of
the wife of Abraham called Sarah.

L'Chaim!

I

Thus, if a man is righteous and does what is just and right: If
he has not eaten on the mountains or raised his eyes to the
fetishes of the House of Israel; if he has not defiled another
man's wife or approached a monstrous woman... if he has
followed My laws and kept My rules and acted honestly—he is
righteous. Such a man shall live—declares the Lord God.
Ezekiel 18:5-18:6; 18:9

II

Life! The man who is righteous is one
alive more fully than the wicked
for moral people experience
a wealth of compassion which colors
and textures life with warmth and meaning.

III

The wicked experience within
their souls a loneliness of the heart.
For to be wicked is a form of
a person's being selfish which cuts
off other people, stemming the roots
which connect humans to each other.
For connection is a way of life;
and without connection to others
we find we wither deep in the bones.

IV

This is why wicked people are called
'fools' or 'boors' because wickedness is
a form of stupidity cutting
deep into the soul of the wicked
which wickedness needs recovery
from that they may not have time to do.

V

Our Torah is a chart to being
a happy person who has goodness
on their side to the end of their days.

VI

In fact it was the goodness of God
that caused the Lord to create
the covenant of humanity.
God wishes happiness for people
who listen to God's dictates themselves
and hold them close to their hearts because
they see the rationality of
some of the laws and trust in the rest.

VII

For God we are an experiment
for we have the mind discerning laws
both natural and moral and yet
we are born fallible and finite.

Wifely Fidelity

I

*He has not eaten on the mountains or raised his eyes to the
fetishes of the House of Israel; he has not defiled another man's
wife; he has not wronged anyone; he has not seized a pledge or
taken anything by robbery; he has given his bread to the hungry
and clothed the naked he has refrained from oppressing the poor;
he has not exacted advance or accrued interest; he has obeyed My
rules and followed My laws; he shall not die for his father's sins.*
Ezekiel 18:14-18:17

II

The defiling of other men's wives
is considered sinful to Lord YHWH—
for a man's wife is a man's treasure,
we are told that "a virtuous wife
her worth is beyond rubies" and yet
the husband deserving praise "listens
to her voice" just as Abram listened
to Sarah regarding his two sons
that's Ishmael and Isaac and sent
away his concubine named Hagar
with Ishmael whom he loved also.

III

Each husband should see Sarah herself
in the wife he cleaves to his own heart.
For the wife's body it is more than
her husband's nakedness it's also
a holy vessel of Lord YHWH's—
just as though Kabbalistic theory
were true in regards women's bodies
and not the universe's fragments.

IV

That said the woman's body *is* still
her husband's nakedness and he hers.
As such the uncovering of it
is a crime against them both and God.
For fidelity is still holy;
it sanctifies both human marriage
and wedded bliss of Jews to YHWH.

The Murder of Children

That is [the son] has eaten on the mountains, has defiled
another man's wife, has wronged the poor and the needy, has
taken by robbery, has not returned a pledge, has raised his eye
fetishes, has committed abomination, has let at advance interest
or has accrued interest—shall he live? He shall not live!
Ezekiel 18:10-18:12

II

Like parents murdering their children—
for Gehenna is itself named for
the place where Canaanites took children
as sacrificial lambs to their gods—
those who do evil sacrifice to
the god of the self their own future.
Their children were their inheritance
and belonged to God before themselves;
God does not forgive committers of
the crime of infanticide itself.

III

For wickedness in this life will not
be punished in cruel gehenna's fires
the righteous won't be reborn again
to lives of the bliss of the devout.
Yet wicked people assume do not believe
that Justice will at last come for them.

IV

They assume that their deeds go unwatched;
worse, they will believe evil actions
go without consequences despite
the evidence shown contrarily.
The wicked flourish in their heads and
then find their actions punished by both
the lack of success brought by hard work
and gehinnom in the next life, too.

V

No, the truth is that lacking goodness
and then not returning to YHWH
will lead to ultimate death itself.
The sacrifice the wicked make will
be themselves on the altar they make
for themselves in their evil doing.

IV

The one who sacrifices his young will
go without leaving offspring himself
to take care of him in his old age.
For parents treasure their own children
and grandchildren in old age just as
the child who sees his sibling cut down
by parents will not treasure them for
they will think of their parents as those
who are less valuable to them than
the gods they worship themselves also.

V

For because unloved they will not love;
this is the fate of wickedness and
the person esteeming God knows it.
Yes a child unloved becomes a plant
which becomes uprooted like a weed
when in fact it's a precious white rose.

VI

This sacrifice of children could be
a metaphor of other crimes which
could involve sacrificing children
for the adult 'goods' that are evil.

VII

To neglect children is abuse which
includes the placing idols of self
like work and pleasure before children
is sinful on the parents own part.
This is true when there is no beating
of children itself, widely assumed
to be cruel these days to most people.

VIII

But in the days of ancient Canaan,
not even this was secure to them.
In ages past there were those taking
for granted children existed for
their parent's pleasures and not their own.
So infanticide of those babies
who were not wanted was so common
that to make sacrifices was not
exceptional save to the people
of Israel who understood that
the human person was made sacred.

IX

To Jewish people our God demands
that this not be the case with the Jews.
We regard children's exploitation
as wickedness's worst form.

X

We must not fall to this trap raising
our children, instead we should recall
how rabbinic law informs us that,
'if you must whip your child, do so with
shoe laces' so as not to hurt them.
Raise children as high priorities;
and they will be your riches to you.

The Lioness and Her Cubs

I

And you are to intone a dirge over the princes of Israel and say,
What a lioness was your mother
Among the lions!
Crouching among the great beasts,
She reared her cubs.
Ezekiel 19:1-19:2

II

Ah Lord! We were blessed by the strength of
our mother; for she was a lady
of valor in a lordly beast whom
is judged king of the jungle itself.
For indeed lionesses are queens
but kingly, too, as though they possess
"the heart and stomach of a king" as
Queen Elizabeth boasted as she
and England waited for King Philip
and his great Spanish Armada to
come attack England's great fleet off shore.

III

She raised up one of her cubs,
He became a great beast;
He learned to hunt prey—
He devoured men.
Ezekiel 19:3

IV

Yes, like his mother, Israel is
the mighty firstborn of Lord YHWH,
they draw strength from their motherland which
has nourished children who are touch as
the lioness's fur which covers
the muscles stretched taut on bones under
the frame that holds up the beast of prey.

V

Nations heeded [the call] against him;
He was caught in their snare.
They dragged him off with hooks
To the land of Egypt.
Ezekiel 19:4

VI

It was not lacking physical strength
Which caused the Israelites' fall from grace.
it was its moral laxity in
its behavior in comparison
with other nations in the region.
This was the northern kingdom's decline
in leadership while exiles fled to
the kingdom born as Israel's twin.

VII

When she saw herself frustrated,
Her hope defeated,
She took another of her cubs
And set him up as a great beast.
Ezekiel 19:5

VIII

Now Judah arose proudly to take
his brother's place in regards the land.
For Judah was like his twin brother
the son who bore their mother's namesake
a feminization of Jacob
called Israel, the name of the land,
with that of the ten northern tribes which
the Assyrians decimated.

IX

Now Judah was strong, with the symbol
of lions painted on his shield's front,
a warrior like David fighting
with his sling against Goliath who
had represented Philistine might.
This Judah, angels assumed, would take
on where the Israelites had left off.

X

He stalked among the lions,
He was a great beast;
He learned to hunt prey—
He devoured men.
Ezekiel 19:6

XI

So Judah became haughty.
He became arrogant to the Lord.
And Judah destroyed other nations
in the midst of the land of Judah.
He attacked nations as one
large, sleeping victim broken by swords
which overcome the unsuspecting—
and rip them apart into pieces.

XII

He ravished their widows,
Laid waste to their cities;
The land and all in it were appalled
At the sound of his roaring.
Ezekiel 19:7

XIII

Now Judah sinned to humankind first
and the Lord second as though those who
had suffered at the Jew's hands were now
to be called Kiddush Hashem themselves
and martyrs to a God of whom they
had no more knowledge than of Hindus.

XIV

This was thus especially heinous
on Judah's part when considering what
the Lord had forbidden to the Jews,
which is to say: murdering of non-Jews
just as the murder of Jews is called this.
It's only those who will burn children
who deserve punishment in Canaan.
For pagans despite being non-Jews
if Jewish people murdered them would
still constitute the Kiddush Hashem.

XV

Their sacrifice will anger YHWH.
Nations from the countries roundabout
Arrayed themselves against him.
They spread their net over him,
He was caught in their snare.
Ezekiel 19:8

XVI

Ah, these snares were not merely those of
bronze or base metals, pounded into
the hardened weapons of war itself.
No, they have also those included
of bombarding the Israel with
the sins of eating lobster or pork
and sins of molesting young virgins
or seducing those married women
who non-Jews could catch and then seduce.
This being the case, both heart and soul
were ensnared with the Jewish body.

VII

With hooks he was put in a cage,
They carried him off to Babylon
And confined him in a fortress,
So that never again should his roar
On the hills of Israel.
Ezekiel 19:9

VIII

Yet Mother Israel calls us back
to our great homeland constituting
a blossom in the very desert.

Quenching Fires

I

Your mother was like a vine in your blood,
Planted beside the streams
With luxuriant boughs and branches
Thanks to abundant waters.
Ezekiel 19:10

II

O Mother Israel who gave birth—
she was a queen with kingly bearing—
with nobility preparing for
the birth of Jewish salvation with
its calling forth of Judgment Day when
the thirst for justice will be filled—
to twin sons, Israel and Judah,
both nurtured on her, the land of God.

III

And she had a mighty rod
Fit for a ruler's scepter.
It towered highest among the leafy trees,
It was conspicuous by its height,
By the abundance of its boughs.
Ezekiel 19:11

IV

This scepter represented the might
that Israel held over nations
the Mediterranean like Rome.
It represents the physical force
of God but also morality;
for Israel shall possess goodness
and that will make it the Lord's stronghold.
God will bless Israel and the Jews.
They'll possess peace and prosperity
and they will possess it on their terms.

V

But plucked up in a fury,
She was hurled to the ground.
They broke apart and dried up;
And her mighty rod was consumed by fire.
Ezekiel 19:12

VI

When Israel did evil to God
the Lord sent punishment to her door;
she was then rooted out of the earth.
Pulled at the base, her roots came on out
like a weed covered in thorny brambles
contrasting with the bloom of a rose;
for it is nothing but a wild rose:
a gorgeous flower mistaken for
the weed that nobody wants to grow.

VII

Rose petals fell to the ground like tears
of blood for humanity's sinning.
Then like the incineration of
the Jews in Auschwitz the rose will roast
in gardens where the rose's soul lives
in darkest hours it will live on still.

VIII

Now she is planted in the desert
In ground that is arid and parched.
Ezekiel 19:13

IX

The land of Israel will become
as desolate as highways at night.
Yet the soul of the Jewish people
will reside with its mother, the land.
For millennia, their heart will breath
in the land promised them by their God.
At Treblinka and Auschwitz they call,
"O Israel, we'll come back to you
or die in attempting our return!"

X

Fire has issued from her twig-laden branch
And has consumed her boughs,
She is left without a mighty rod.
Ezekiel 19:14

XI

Yet despite losing mighty rods with
their ability protecting those
who own these weapons from those who don't
the burning of the Israelite's soul
is creative, not destructive, and
keeps Israel's live Spirit going.

XII

O fire of the soul, burning bush that
is not quenched, not by water or death,
you do not burn but relieve the soul.
You cool the Jewish spirit itself
till they can return to their homeland
and pray by the great wailing wall, too.

The Mocking of the Prophet

I

And I said, "Ah, Lord God! They say of me, he is just a riddle monger."
Ezekiel 21:5
The word of the Lord came to me: Further, O mortal, arraign, arraign
the city of bloodshed; declare to her all her abhorrent deeds!
Ezekiel 22:1-22:2

II

"O you who call me riddle-monger,"
spoke the Lord's prophet Ezekiel.
"I speak in YHWH's parables and
of senses overwealmed by YHWH
with colorful images made fresh.
Lord YHWH renders my deeds holy
so I may preach the righteousness which
is needed by the Jewish people;
I do not speak my own words but God's."

III

Then Ezekiel added to them,
"You shall be punished for your deeds which
are bloody handed towards children just as
the Canaanites you imitate in
the passing your own children over
the fire of their god Molech himself."
Yet scoffers said "If it be YHWH
who speaks, He should speak clearly to us
and not the riddles of this prophet."

IV

The prophet Ezekiel cursed them;
he little noticed the awe he got
from ordinary people who looked
at Ezekiel's vision to them
as recognizably a genius—
who despite those who scoffed as he spoke
would speak of waking dreams he lived through.
For waking dreams left those to whom they
were described to more reverent at
images because they were bizarre.

V

Yet scoffers existed who believed
that Ezekiel suffered madness,
"The prophet himself's possessed," they cried.
They parodied his visions to them,
"Poor Ezekiel had too much drink
and heard the buzzing like wasps within
his ears, the curtains of the Temple
then falling down on him to seem
to resemble all kinds of things that
were marvelous to Ezekiel.
In reality he must have been drunk."
The prophet Ezekiel would cry,
"You who lack piety should suffer!"

VI

And most of the Jews believed his words
and trembled at the Lord's wrath at them
while considering this bad treatment.
For they all regarded him as though
the prophet were a holy fool for
the Lord the prophet venerated.

The Abuse of Child

I

*Base men in your midst were intent on shedding blood; in you they
have eaten upon your midst [committed idolatry]. In you they have
uncovered their father's nakedness; in you they have ravished women
in their impurity. They have committed abhorrent acts with other men's
wives; in their depravity they have defiled their own daughters-in-law;
in you they have ravished their own sisters, daughters of their fathers.*
Ezekiel 22:9-11

II

The crime of incest was brought to us
by base men traveling in forests
of depravity who should be shunned.
These tribes have violated more than
the Jews including unfortunates
alike both Jew and non-Jew known best
in Egypt, such as Hatshepsut was
who married her own father, brother
and nephew within her own lifetime—
she was the only female Pharaoh.

III

The sin of incest involves a form
of idolatry, a form which is
a particularly depravity
of soul and body sacrificed not
to lust as people imagine but
to power over victims who are
small compared to their victimizers—
for the most common kind of incest
is that form involving the children
of their own father, uncle or priest.

IV

For it's the crime most unnatural
that people commit, unspeakable
and closeted by abusers and
yet also by the victims themselves.
For they don't want the stigma of it
or accusation of making it up.

V

It is a crime of secrecy and
yet to the Lord there are no secrets—
Lord YHWH wills an airing out of
the crimes which have most involved children
for it is the cry innocents which
need hearing and calls from the darkness.

VI

It idolizes power itself.
For power is what abusers want.
The normal tie for parent to child
is love, as it is to our Lord.
Abusers will so damage the children
by misusing the power they have.

Sins Against God

The word of the LORD came to me: O mortal, say to her: You are an uncleansed land, not to be washed with rain on the day of indignation. Her gang of prophets are like roaring lions in her midst rending prey. They devour human beings; they seize treasure and wealth, they have profaned what is sacred to Me, they have not taught the difference between the unclean and the clean, and they have closed their eyes to My Sabbaths.
Ezekiel 22:23-22:26

II

The wicked prophets prophesying
that good things will come without good work
will soon find themselves stunned when they
see Ezekiel's prophesies are
when fulfilled predicting their own death.
For they have led the people to think
that indifference to the Law is
a thing that's permitted to the Lord.
You have them saying, "The Jews may do
whatever they feel like they want to,"
when God's Law requires, "Jews shall be good."
"The Jews shall be good" is God's intent.
The Laws were given with that intent.

III

Her officials are live wolves rending prey in her midst; they shed blood and destroy lives to win ill gotten gain. And the people of the land have practice fraud and committed robbery; they have wronged the poor and needy, have defrauded the stranger without redress.
Ezekiel 22:27; 22:29

IV

These crimes are one which people commit
not towards God but towards others.
They result in a lack of the faith
but pour out of a person's heart to
then poison behavior to others.
A person is first sinning towards
Lord YHWH comes to sin next against
their fellow human being, it's said.
Lord YHWH does not step in until
the sins a people commits will harm
those outside of God who cares for us.

V

I have poured my indignation upon them; I will consume them with the fire of My fury. I will repay them for their conduct—declares the Lord GOD.
Ezekiel 22:31

VI

For sinners find their punishment for
the crimes they've committed in their works
and not for their false beliefs only.

Oholah and Oholibah

I

There were two women, daughters of one mother. They played the whore in Egypt; they played the whore in Egypt; they played the whore while still young. Their breasts were squeezed, and their virgin nipples were handled.
Ezekiel 23:1-23:3

II

Lord, it is hard to remain pure when
You live on Egyptian streets where men
will molest young girls without thinking.
These streets were covered with grime and filth;
the heat with which men approached women
was often unwanted to women.
It was as victims women lived there.
They loved the Lord but could not stay chaste.

III

Their names were: the elder one, Oholah; and her sister, Oholibah. They became Mine, and they bore sons and daughters. As for their names Ohalah is Samaria, and Oholibah is Jerusalem.
Ezekiel 23:4

IV

Now You, Lord, gave us new names which were
strange to our ears and strange to our hearts.
We loved You but still wondered ourselves,
"Where was our Lord when we were in tears
on Egyptian streets molested by
the men of the land along the Nile.
So it was that we played the harlot
to punish our Lord YHWH's absence.

V

Oholah whored while she was Mine, and she lusted after her lovers,
after the Assyrians, warriors clothed in blue, governors and prefects,
horseman mounted on steeds—all of them handsome young fellows.
Ezekiel 23:5

VI

"O Lovers," Oholah cried to them.
"You're beautiful yet forbidden to
the mother Oholah with children
who have God as their Father who is
the beloved of faithless children
and wives who have chased after lovers.
For the Lord is a spiritual God
and Oholah a carnal being.
She finds her lurid desires unmet—
she is a pagan at heart who will
not give up her lusts for her husband."

VII

She bestowed her favors upon them—among the pick of the Assyrians
and defiled herself with all their fetishes after which she lusted.
Ezekiel 23:7

VIII

"O fetishes of Assyria,"
cried Oholah, "You are my desire;
I pine for my Lord less than for You.
You see I am called impudent by
Lord YHWH, in his eyes I'm shameless.
And perhaps YHWH regarding us
is right for YHWH offers us love,
the open relationship we share.
As brazen towards Lord YHWH as if
a married woman left her house with
her outright naked body exposed."

IX

And the Lord wept for his first wife and
the elder sister of the two twins.
She did not give up the whoring she had begun with the Egyptians;
for they had lain with her youth, and they had handled her
virgin nipples and had poured out their lust upon her.
Ezekiel 23:8

X

"O Lord," spoke Oholah of lovers
"My sins were involuntary in
the land of Egypt where I first lived
as a slave girl to abusers who
were owners debauched by deeds against
their slaves who built the pyramids for
their afterlife and served their beds in
this life and so were exploited both
in this life and the next life as well.
I was a troubled slave girl You saved
but I was wretched and out of faith."

XI

There I delivered her into hands of her lovers, into the hands
of the Assyrians after whom she lusted. They exposed her
nakedness; they seized sons and daughters, and she herself
was put to the sword. And because of the punishment
inflicted upon her, she became a byword among women.
Ezekiel 23:9-23:10

XII

Ah! Oholah! You've angered the Lord,
more, you've crushed the Lord's heart from within,
and become lost to Your Lord YHWH!
Your jealous God is heartbroken and
yet some of your sons and your daughters
made good their escape southwards so that
in Judah they could renew their faith;
for despite fecklessness they loved God.
They cried out in pain, "O our Lord who forgives
please forgive us yet one more time now!"

XIII

Her sister Oholibah saw this; yet her lusting was more depraved
than her sister's, and whoring more debased. She lusted after the
Assyrians, governors and prefects, horsemen mounted on steeds—
all of them handsome young fellows. And I saw how she had defiled
herself. Both of them followed the same course, but she carried
her harlotries further. For she saw men sculptured upon the walls,
figures of Chaldeans drawn in vermillion, girded with belts round their
waists, and flowing turbans on their heads, all of them looking like
officers—a picture of Babylonians who native land was Chaldea.
Ezekiel 23:11-23:15

XIV

Lord YHWH saw that Oholibah
would shape images of lovers whom
she committed adulteries towards
Lord YHWH who had created her
in words of prayers better said to God.
The Lord cried bitter tears while saying,
"O strumpet whom I took from Egypt
I granted you love from deep within.
Why did you and your sister rebel?"
"Ah, but Lord, where were You when needed?
When You left us all only without
a friend in Pharaoh's Egypt itself
as an abused child with a deep pain
which is still buried in our own hearts."

XV

At the very sight of them she lusted after them, and she sent messengers for them in Chaldea. So the Babylonians came to her for lovemaking and defiled herself with them, and defiled herself with them until she turned from them in disgust. She flaunted her harlotries and exposed her nakedness...
Ezekiel 23:16-23:17

XVI

O Oholibah chases after
the sins which Oholah had pursued.
As the Lord had cried—unbeknownst to
the sister Oholah till too late—
and likewise Oholibah heard him
and said, "O Lord, the flesh is weak
and easily yields temptation with
the onslaught of the images
from Babylonian gods themselves.

XV

These graven stone images pull us
to contemplate them forgetting God
so as imagining there's instead
a material world which still lacks
a spiritual worth contained in it.

XVI

It tempts us because it is vivid;
a spiritual, unseeable God is
more demanding to human beings
who are still unable to read books—
or have no manuscript they can read.
It invokes stillnesss of the spirit
or chanting like the Orthodox pray.
The physical will beckon to us.

XVII

*... and I turned from them in disgust. She flaunted her harlotries and
exposed her nakedness as I had turned disgusted from her sister.*
Ezekiel 23:17-23:18

XVIII

Lord YHWH became coldness itself
to Oholibah, herself a whore.
God could not speak through the rage God felt.

XIX

*But she whored still more, remembering how in her youth
she had played the whore in the land of Egypt; she lusted for
concubinage with them, whose members were like those of
asses and whose organs were like those of stallions. Thus you
reverted to the wantonness of your youth, remembering your
youthful breasts, when the men of Egypt handled your nipples.*
Ezekiel 23:19-21

XX

"O YHWH, our sins against You had
once begun in the land of Egypt."
Thus cried the Israelites while sobbing,
"We loved You in our adolescence
and yet we suffered sexually as
though we were prostitutes men molest
in childhood while they're neglected
by parents or sold outright as slaves
while strangers molested us while You
were nowhere to be seen by us still.

XXI

"Our pagan nipples hurt while pinched by
our 'lovers' took cruel advantage of
our youth and Your cruel absence itself.

XXII

*Assuredly, Ohlibah, thus said the Lord God: I am going to rouse
against you the lovers from all around—they shall take away your
sons and daughters , and your remnant shall be devoured by fire.*
Ezekiel 23:22; 23:25

XXIII

Ah alas, Lord YHWH whom we love!
For deep down in our heart we do love
our Lord still even as we cry for
the crimes Lord YHWH punish us for!
We wish that we could forget our 'sins.'
We wish that we could forget the pain
of adolescence when molested by
the lovers who chewed on our nipples.

XXIV

*I will put an end to your wantonness and to your whoring in the land
of Egypt, you shall not long for them or remember Egypt any more.*
Ezekiel 23:27

XXV

"My people Israel," cried YHWH,
"Your lovers shall cause you pain no more!
For instead you shall be called holy!
And you shall be ones rewarded for
the love you have shown your Lord YHWH.
And you shall not cry for my absence."

XXVI

And Israel wept. Her tears ran down
her face and she said, "You came to me
in Egypt as I waited, hoping
that my Lord would come for me at last;
Yet as soon as I was safe, acted
out against my Lord in my revenge.

XXVII

"Please, O Lord, forgive our sins against
You and we will act according to
the will of the Lord whom we will love.
We will act obediently in
in regarding of the Law You gave
to the Jews who are chosen by You.
And doing so we will next hold to
the mitzvoth tenderly in our hearts."

XXVIII

And so the Jews cried to Lord YHWH,
   "If I [do] forget you, O Jerusalem,"
let our souls rot from within us and
with that in mind, the Jewish people
in Babylon would forgive their Lord,
and beg for pardon so they could go
and return to their Israelite homes.

Sleeping

I

*For thus said the Lord God: I am going to deliver you into
the hands of those from whom you turned in disgust.*
Ezekiel 23:28

II

O YHWH punishes the people
not just for lust but for hatred itself
for hatred is the worst of sins to God
and while it appears to its excite
the senses actually will cause them
to numb the use of reason itself
and people suffer more from this crime
than any other under the sun.

III

It creates the cruel Sleeping Uglies—
those princesses of hate immune
to those signs they are wrong in regards
to their own prejudices and asleep
to the signs of the righteousness of
those whom they persecute as sinners.
It's hatred that brings cruel death to us
and YHWH bids Jews they take no part
in this foul moldy human outgrowth.
It mars our humanity if we
share the guilt oppressors have towards
the Jewish people themselves through hate.

IV

They shall treat you with hate, and take away all you
have toiled for, and leave you naked and bare; your naked
whoredom, wantoness, and harlotry shall be exposed.
Ezekiel 23:29

V

Lord YHWH shall lay Judah stretched out
like lama fur stretched out across the loom—
its silky texture darned by the Lord—
patched with soft spun string on a needle
like Sleeping Beauty's needle when she
had pricked her index finger on it.

VI

So Israel is the Lord's Beauty
and Judah is one also of God;
but they are tainted with the traits of
a 'Sleeping Ugly' when they hate God
as once their ancestors did feuding
with their Lord over grudges past by
in Egypt regarding gods foreign
to the Jews who God has claimed in love.

VII

Yet her sleep shall be a great nightmare.
she'll experience the great hatred
that even at her worst she never
poured onto other peoples within
the country in which she lived and loved.

VIII

*These things shall be done to your harlotries with the
nations, for defiling yourself with the fetishes.*
Ezekiel 23:30

IX

O Lord! In her sleep Beauty drams of
the prick of bloodstained fingers draining
her until becoming light headed
she passes out on the bed nearby.
In fitful dreams she will imagine
The tortures of hell itself crying
out its guilt, hoping it's not too late
for redemption to the Lord YHWH.
O woozily she sleeps in hopes that
her beloved Lord will soon return.

X

*You walked in your sister's path; therefore I
will put her cup into your hand.*
Ezekiel 23:31

XI

O Beauty quaffs the drink of God's wrath
and yet she also quaffs God's mercy
Lord YHWH spared a remnant's children
who went south when the Assyrians
came invading the Northern Kingdom.

XII

Ah, with a kiss she will be redeemed;
and even those sons who are wicked
shall be ones reborn anew to be
ones given second chances by God.

The Martyrs to the Lord

I

*Then the Lord said to me: O mortal, arraign Oholah and
Oholibah, and charge them with their abominations. For they
have committed adultery, and blood is on their hands; truly
they have committed adultery with their fetishes, and have
even offered to them as food the children they bore to Me.*
Ezekiel 23:36-23:37

II

Lord YHWH's two wives were as wicked
as Jezebel was said to have been
Lord YHWH's children so that they could
make sacrifices of them in the act
adultery towards our Lord YHWH.

III

More, YHWH declared that his two wives
were unfaithful to promises made
in between these two and Lord YHWH
adulteries which consisted of
not keeping the Lord's covenant pure
but instead sacrificing their bodies
to gods they believed in with the Lord
with bloody acts which involve children—
these children belonging each to God
as the third parent conceiving them
as physical genes come from parents
but the soul's of the babies instead
are given on loan from Lord YHWH.

IV

They are not to be sacrificed to
the cause of infanticide for gods.
The children sacrificed to Molech
were martyrs for our faith by parents.

V

On the very day that they slaughtered their children to
their fetishes, they entered My Sanctuary to desecrate
it. That is what they did in My House.
Ezekiel 23:39

VI

O Oholibah; you have bloodied
the altar of God with your children
who are the children of God also.
For YHWH plaintively cries for these,
the infants the Lord counts as God's own.
O martyrs for Me, cries Lord YHWH,
ones brought down exposed before their time.

VII

Your souls are beloved and buried
not in the land of sheol but in heaven.
For children who die you are those called
the saints in heaven after their deaths.

The Tarantella

I

Moreover, they sent for men to come from afar, [men] to whom a messenger was sent; and they came. For them, [Oholibah] you bathed, painted your eyes, and donned your finery; and you sat on a grand couch with a set table in front of it—and it was My incense and My oil you laid upon it.
Ezekiel 23:40-23:41

II

O Oholibah whose breach of faith
in her adultery towards her God
with mascara that's colored like shells,
a pale blue robin's egg in its nest
the finely woven eyebrows plucked thin—
with lips red like a poisonous plant,
a mushroom without the white spots.

II

You brazen trollop ravishing to
the mortal men you pursue like mad.
O Oholibah if you only
would keep your finery at home with
Lord YHWH, locked up to be admired,
the Lord would forgive everything that
You had done, letting eyebrows grow in
but with a less thick coating of paint
on upper eyelids colored pale blue.

III

The poison-less lips would be colored
like the rose petals that you smell of
your naturally inborn beauty
to shine through from the inside to out.

IV

And the noise of a carefree multitude was there, of numerous
men brought drunk from the dessert; and they put bracelets
on their arms and splendid crowns upon their heads.
Ezekiel 23:43

V

"O Lovers of my Oholibah
who grasp this wanton woman by hips
like dancers tangoing in the night
while tambourine's beat across the hands
of the band accompanying them.
You are her destruction," says the Lord.

VI

"O Lord," says Oholibah, "I was
meant to dance, tangoing in the night."
"O tango woman!" cry the lovers.
"O tango woman with great broad hips!
We love to dance the tango with her!"
"O wicked woman!" cries Lord YHWH.
"O wicked woman," God yelps in pain,
"for I loved you with a love that's pure!
O I raised you as though a lamb was
what you were, a child dandled fondly
in my lap, not a strumpet dancer."

VII

"Ha ha!" cry those cruel tango lovers.
"Lord YHWH can't have Oholibah!
For she loves tangoing like we do!"

VIII

*Then I said, "To destruction with adultery! Look, they are
still going on with those same fornications of hers." And
they went to her as one goes to a prostitute; that is how
they went to Oholah and Oholibah, wanton women.*
Ezekiel 23:43-23:44

IX

Yes over God's cries dancing went on,
but then it became lurid with lust,
and Israel lay to be mounted
by lovers who then lay down as one
who's satiated with the sex act.
The pagan gods could provoke this slut
but could not satisfy her desires.
She practiced worship of all the kinds
of Babylonia and Canaan—
the Temple prostitution along
with children being sacrificed to
the deities of ivory and
of painted wood images carved by
the hands of pagans lusting for gods.

X

For indeed, she found herself tempted
but unfulfilled by many crimes which
she committed with pagan gods who
could not give fulfillment as they were
not really gods but no-gods-at-all.
Still, however, their wicked tempting
was more that our Lord YHWH could take.

XI

But righteous men shall punish them with the
punishments for adultery and for bloodshed, for they
are adulteresses and have blood on their hands.
Ezekiel 23:45

XII

Lord YHWH finally said to them,
"The just among the peoples who pray
to the wrong gods but are still righteous
won't punish Israel for her sins—
that is for today, for in the times
which are the distant future I shall
send worse men to be punished the Jews—
and they shall take the strumpet from beds
of disgusting gods and flog my wives.
But the Just will try to hide the Jews.

XII

They shall take her from tangoing and
with leather straps they'll put her in stocks
and flog her bottom in the manner
of the harsh Puritans years after
the Israelites lived in their own land—
but before nineteen forty nine when
the Jews would reclaim their state again.
And the slut shall be flogged, says the Lord.

XIII

For thus said the Lord GOD: Summon an assembly against them,
and make them an object of horror and plunder. Let the assembly
pelt them with stones and cut them down with their swords; let
them kill their sons and daughters, and burn down their homes.
Ezekiel 23:46-47

XIV

The Lord will set a judge above them;
his two wives will meet justice for deeds
they did with abandon with lovers
whom were once forbidden to the wives
with the two having married the Lord.

XV

They tore the Lord with jealousy and
the rage which transformed gentle love to
a determined wrath grimly upon
wives Oholah and Oholibah,
the sisters found in Egyptian lands.

XVI

I will put an end to wantoness in the land; and the women shall take warning not to imitate your wantonness. They shall punish you for your wantonness, and you shall suffer the penalty for your sinful idolatry. And you shall know that I am the Lord God.
Ezekiel 23:48-23:49

XVII

"Yes, others will be frightened off from
you because of your sins," says the Lord,
"They will cry, 'Avoid Oholibah
the woman and her crimes which she did.
The Jews who are her descendents will
read of her crimes will shudder in fear.
'O foolish Oholibah,' they'll cry.
But there will also be a sense which
they will say, 'Our Lord is good to us,
why would this strumpet ignore her Lord?'"

XVIII

"Yes, Oholibah's children will love;
they'll become Israel once again.
For disobedient teenagers come
to love their parents once more when they
are too old to go tangoing still."

The Allegory of the Stew

I

Further, speak an allegory to the rebellious breed
and say to them: Thus said the Lord GOD:
Put the cauldron [on the fire], put it on,
And then pour water into it.
Ezekiel 24:2-3

II

Like witches calling into the night
the kind which Shakespeare describes singing,
"O Double, Double, Toil and Trouble…"
fire is to be lit underneath of
the cauldron bequeathed by Lord YHWH.
This recipe is made to mirror
the predicament the Lord has with
the people who play the harlot
by sacrificing children to gods.

III

Yet it is strange that the Lord uses
the means of sorcerers to get through
his message to his people the Jews.
Strange, for King Saul was punished when he
sought out a witch in order to call
the prophet Samuel up to talk
from beyond the grave as a spirit
out of reach of the living themselves.

IV

Yet in the mulched meat the Lord's prophet
would prepare, the souls of small children,
would hover overhead and chant psalms.
This was thus clearly unholy save
that our Lord YHWH ordered the act.

V

Take the best of the flock.
Also pile the cuts under it;
Ezekiel 24:5:1-24:5:2

VI

O bleating lamb that cries out its pain
while sacrificed with a knife themselves
O little lamb with snow white fleece like
The nursery rhyme of a "Mary"
claimed that her gentle creature possessed.
O lamb, so gentle, kind and good;
lamb beloved of mother sheep with
whom it would nuzzle in the night when
the cries of jackals scared it greatly;
for indeed if a shepherd kills more
of their sheep than the predators who
bay at the moon do, they are trusted
by their flock of sheep whom they care for.

VII

The sheep trust; little lambs love
their butchers just as children will trust
their parents either wicked or good.
O surely to eat meat is therefore
an act of cruelty towards the sheep.

VIII

Collect pieces [of meat]
Every choice piece, thigh and shoulder;
Fill it with the best cuts—
Get it boiling briskly,
And cook that cuts into it.
Ezekiel 24:4; 24:5:3-24:5:4

IX

O savory cut of lamb chopped up,
so Ezekiel with the ghosts chants
while recalling the legend saying
that before Noah's flood swept the earth
no one, no matter how good or bad
ate meat of any kind, raw or cooked.

X

Cain himself was a vegetarian.
In later days the meat was salted
so the blood was drawn out of the meat.
In the case of the meat God ordered
to be cut into strips to be boiled,
the lamb was covered with thick layers
of salt which soaked up blood like a sponge.

XI

Assuredly, thus said the Lord God:
Woe to the city of blood—
A cauldron whose scum is in it,
Whose scum has not been cleaned out!
Empty it piece by piece;
No lot has fallen upon it.
Ezekiel 24:6

XII

This killing is a species of wrong
an injury which YHWH permits
and yet would bless if it were erased.
The pieces of boiled meat stewed and limp,
to connoisseurs of meat a waste of
the tender lamb which was once butchered
for the sake of this stewed dish served warm.

XIII

The meat will be peeled from the sign of
the killing of the innocent lamb.
Yet the leftover paste from the lamb
will possess the sin of its killing.

XIV

For the blood she shed is still her;
She set it upon a bare rock;
She did not pour it on the ground
To cover it with earth.
Ezekiel 24:7

XV

O blood of God's lamb sacrificed for
the food boiled in the cauldron itself;
this represents the blood of innocents who
are children meeting untimely death.

XVI

O death of the lambs, sent from the Lord,
The infants murdered in the fashion
of pagans slaughtering to their gods
the children to whom their wives give birth.
These children were not theirs to give to
the gods by "passing over the fires"
for children belong to our Lord first;
they require the love the Lord demands.
Like children animals are the Lord's
made vulnerable, requiring care
which the Lord demands of us for them.
For it's a mitzvah to spare their meat.

XVII

For the blood she shed is still in her;
She set her blood upon the bare rock;
She did not pour it out on the ground
To cover it with earth.
Ezekiel 24:7

XVIII

O the blood of the stewed meet remains
in the pot while in Israel she
should pour her sins to the ground and so
then begin anew with flour to eat
and vegetables for a new stew.
The blood is instead the lamb Abel's
poured onto the ground just as Abel
was slaughtered with his blood poured onto
the earth from his sliced open throat wound
with blood which gushes towards the ground.

XIX

Yet instead of the prophet pouring
on the thick liquid paste of brown goo,
it is small children murdered instead
of mere sheep bleating out in their pain.
It would be best to give the sheep up;
it is worst to give up the children.

XX

Assuredly, thus said the Lord GOD:
Woe to the city of blood!
I in turn will make a great blaze.
Ezekiel 24:9

XX

And Ezekiel took the stew and
placed it on a fire declaring what
the Lord had spoken, "Hear now for God
is speaking through me demanding words
be spoken to you, Israel, now!
The Lord is pouring his wrath on us!
Like this stew are children's entrails!
God punishes us likewise, and soon!
For we have slaughtered innocents and
the Lord will punish us for their deaths!"

XXI

Then Ezekiel priests cried the words
Pile on the logs,
Kindle the fire,
Cook the meat through,
And stew it completely,
And let the bones be charred.
Ezekiel 24:10

XXII

And the priests gathered to eat the lamb.
This angered Ezekiel and he
poured the stew onto the ground himself.

XXIII

Then he cried out to those who'd gathered,
Let it stand empty on the coals,
Until it becomes so hot
That the copper glows.
Then its cleanliness shall melt away in it,
And its rust will be consumed.
Ezekiel 24:11

XXIV

"The floor shall burn up the stew I fixed,"
said Ezekiel, "It's a symbol
of Israel's sins towards the Lord."
But multitudes came and ate the stew;
they believed it had magic powers.
And Ezekiel cursed their bad faith
in favor of the gluttony of
the boiling porridge soaking the ground.

XXV

Then Ezekiel cried out to them,
It has frustrated all effort,
It's thick scum will not leave it—
Into the fire with the scum!
Ezekiel 24:12

XXVI

And then fire which was to be under
the pot caught fire to some of the oil
in the hot porridge and the mob left
in terror at the wrath of the Lord.

Ezekiel: Lover of Two Wives

I

*The word of the Lord came to me: "O mortal, I am about to
take away the delight of your eyes from you through pestilence;
but you shall not lament or weep or let your tears flow."*
Ezekiel 24:15

II

But Ezekiel could not obey
Lord YHWH's command regarding her.
The prophet reached out in bed to hold
his wife's warm body tight next to him.
She awoke, "Husband? Ezekiel?"

III

"The Lord says we'll be separated,"
said the Lord's prophet Ezekiel.
"I see," said Ezekiel's wife to
the prophet gently holding her close.
"How will you live on without me here?"
asked Ezekiel's beloved wife.

IV

"The Lord says I must do so,"
said Ezekiel, "It is a test;
or so I am sure having received
no better explanation from God."
"It seems an awfully cruel test of
a God who should be kind to his priests,"
said Ezekiel's petulant wife.

V

"For you have devoted your life to
the Lord God, working in the Temple."
And Ezekiel trembled in fear
Had Ezekiel given God all
of the rooms within inner mansions?
Were there still hidden corners within?
Why would the Lord take away his wife?
But Ezekiel found that he was
more overpowered by love of spouse,
the best friend—save one—he'd known ever.

VI

When Ezekiel's wife died later—
in two months later after sobbing—
he remembered that David's first son
by Bathsheba died, so that David
cried while the child still lived in hopes that
God would spare the child, to change God's mind,
but after the child's death, David rose up
and would grieve no more over the child.

VII

So Ezekiel quietly cried when
he was one separated from his wife
and took all their time together as
though she were his one reason to be
a man still living; even as she
had caught an illness justifying
his staying home with his wife so that
at the hour of their parting he would
be near her so she would not fear death.

VIII

But the Lord spoke to Ezekiel.
Moan softly; observe no morning for the dead: Put on your
turban and put your sandals on your feet; do not cover over
your upper lip, and do not eat the bread of comforters.
Ezekiel 24:17

IX

For Ezekiel's beloved wife
meant more than his own life to him as
the woman he'd loved most of his life
and Ezekiel knew God's demand
for stoicism was for her sake.
God wanted Ezekiel to act
as bravely as a Samson in that
in dying she would find God's comfort.

X

She had been a good wife; she deserved
his strength to support her now in death.
Yet after her death Ezekiel
would meet God's demand of the prophet
for stoicism in the face of his grief.

XI

More, she had never questioned his place
in the role of the divine plan he'd
had revealed to him at six or eight.
Images he had described to her
were never questioned by this soul mate.
Those strange images were blinding;
she would write down some of them for him.

XII

*In the evening my wife died, and in the morning I did as I
had been commanded. And when I spoke to the people that
morning, the people asked me, "Will you not tell us what
these things portend for us, that you are acting so?"*
Ezekiel 24:18-24:19

XIII

For Ezekiel wore red that day,
a grand silk turban which shocked people
who knew of his great tenderness for
his wife for years while she was living.
"O fickle is man towards his wife,"
cried Jerusalem's women as they
saw Ezekiel without his wife.
"Why does he not mourn the wife he loved?"

XIV

*I answered them, "The word of the Lord has come to me: Tell
the House of Israel: Thus said the Lord GOD: I am going to
desecrate My Sanctuary, pride and glory, the delight of your eyes
and the desire of your heart; and sons and daughters you have
left behind shall fall by the sword. And Ezekiel shall become
a portent for you: You shall do just as he has done, when it
happens; and you shall know that I am the Lord GOD."'*
Ezekiel 24:20-24:22

XV

The citizens of Israel stood
in awe, for Israel would suffer
like Ezekiel, a tear struggling
to escape his eye but still falling.

XVI

*According, you shall do as I have done: you shall not cover
over your upper lips or eat the bread of comforters; and your
turbans shall remain on your heads, and your sandals upon your
feet. You shall not lament or weep, but you shall be heartsick
because of your iniquities and shall moan to one another.*
Ezekiel 24:22-24:24

XVII

And Israel moaned like the husband
of one bride who dies young and leaves him
alone while Ezekiel's wonderful wife
was eternally youthful to him.
Poor Ezekiel's life had ended;
This was the second time since the girl.

XVIII

*You, O mortal, take note: On the day that I take their stronghold
from them, their pride and joy, the delight of their eyes and the
longing of their hearts—their sons and daughters—on that day a
fugitive will come to you, to let you hear it with your own ears.*
Ezekiel 24:25-24:26

XIX

The prophet Ezekiel saw her;
a woman taken from him in youth;
no longer tender bodied as though
a mother doe who suckling her young.
She, instead, was made of aged leather.
She had not lost her tender eyes, though,
or her soft mane of horse's thick hair
now colored softened gray strings from what
the color artists call burnt umber.

XX

This woman came to Ezekiel
and knelt embraceing his feet within
her arms now that years separated
the two from youthful passion which still
kept them from their sleep deep in the night.

XXI

Now Ezekiel cried the words to
the shocked group viewing him from outside
the lovers' circle involving two—
the prophet and the lost slave he loved;
the woman torn from his grasp while young.

XXII

*On that day your month shall be opened to the fugitive, and you shall
speak and no longer be dumb. So you shall know I am the LORD.*
Ezekiel 24:27

XXIII

And Ezekiel bent to his love
embracing her with open arms with
the words, "I never thought you would come!"
but pious watchers took it to be
a sign of Ezekiel from God—
the fugitive in human form whom
he'd predicted would come to him first
and Israel when prophecies of
their exile were so fulfilled later.

XXIV

The woman stayed with Ezekiel
who never married again and yet
had one sole woman during the rest
of Ezekiel's life time—this one.

The Punishment of Tyre

I

They shall destroy the walls of Tyre
And demolish her towers;
And I will scrape her soil off her
And leave her a naked rock.
She shall be in the heart of the sea
A place for drying nets;
For I have spoken it
--declares the Lord.
Ezekiel 26:4-24:5

II

"O Lord!" Tyre's citizens cried to God,
"What have we done to deserve this fate?
Were we not friends of Solomon and
did we not help to build the Temple?
Why are You harsh with Hiram's children?
The children of King Solomon's friend?"

III

O Tyre! You who were wealthy once when
King Solomon paid his friend Hiram
Gold to build Solomon's great Temple.
Yet YHWH did not want a Temple;
it was built for the people only;
God would have preferred to go without
and Solomon was corrupted by
this buying, as he was by having
so many wives—particularly wives
from distant lands with foreign gods they
brought with them, reminding them of home.

IV

As slaves they ignored Solomon's God.
As with King David's relationship with
the woman Bathsheba, its women
who were King Solomon's sure downfall—
more, enslaving the Israelites with
his heavy taxes loaded onto
the Israelites' back like a donkey's.

V

Were Solomon's great projects blessings
to the Jews themselves—did God approve?
Did Hiram do the Jews a service?
And was it done for more than mere gold?

VI

Ah! Solomon sent precious funds to
Tyre, bankrupting his country to build
his palace as well as the Temple.
This debauchery of wealth led to
the Israelite's fall and yours with it.
For if the Israelites were sinful,
you were more so, in squeezing debtors
and encouraging them to borrow
more money than was affordable
to them when they had borrowed from you.

VII

Tyre squeezes needy people for cash—
that is Tyre's sin which consists of greed.

VIII

She shall become spoil for the nations,
And her daughter-towns in the country
Shall be put to the swords.
And they shall know that I am the Lord.
Ezekiel 26:6

Tyre's Children

I

For thus said the Lord GOD: I will bring from the north, against
Tyre, King Nebuchadnezzar of Babylon, a king of kings, with
horses, chariots and horsemen—a great mass of troops.
Your daughter-towns in the country
He shall be put to the sword;
He shall erect towers against you,
And cast up mounds against you.
Ezekiel 26:7-26:8

II

O Tyre's own daughter towns far from her
will meet her same fate at the hands of
King Nebuchadnezzar who invades
from the north Tyre and southern Judah.

III

These daughter towns have citizens who
have taken part in the crimes of Tyre, who lend gold
at unfair interest to others;
who aided Solomon in lending
to him at the back breaking cost which
caused Israel to groan as she had
in Egypt's bondage of them as slaves;
you share in the sins wealthy people
are known for, callousness and mere greed.

IV

How much gold does one person require?
The question rings true regarding Tyre.
For sins associated with wealth
Tyre shall be punished by the Lord God.

God Bless the Child

I

They shall intone a dirge over you as they wail,
And lament for you thus:
Who was like Tyre when she was silenced
In the midst of the sea?
When your wares were unloaded from the seas,
You satisfied many peoples;
With your great wealth and merchandise
You enriched the kings of the earth.
Ezekiel 27:32-27:33

II

O country of wealth! You are Tyre now!
You place your trust in money and think
a wealthy man blessed by the Lord and
the one impoverished as blighted
by the same Lord who rules the earth, too.
It is as though your optimism
is believing that when life is good
you should be miserly in regards
to your good fortune to poor people
and when times are bad you should blame them
for their allowing you to sink with
them into the deep muck which is Tyre's.

III

What you should know is that God wills that
no person be poor if he's willing
or unable to work for himself.
The Lord wants us to eradicate what
it is that causes poverty so
that all will become able to be happy.
Tyre is self-satisfied in her wealth;
she preys on those less fortunate than
she herself, blaming them for her woes.

IV

But when you were wrecked on the seas,
In the deep waters sank your merchandise
And all the crew aboard you.
All the inhabitants of the coastlands
Are appalled over you;
Their kings are aghast,
Their faces contorted.
Ezekiel 27:34-27:35

V

O wealth! You cannot guarantee that
the future will be taken care of
or that your possessor will be one
who's happy at heart with what they have.
They may lack inner resources to
be able survivors of woes that are
still ordinary to the average man.

VI

When Carnegie had acquired wealth he
gave most of it to other people;
yet the truth is that if he hadn't
he might have found it boredom to own
such great wealth without acquiring more.
Do wealthy people acquire money
so that they can keep themselves free from
the admittance that they have too much.
But what will happen when the money
Has disappeared, to those who had it?
What happens if the czar has escaped
with no cash to his name to his friends?

VII

The merchants among the peoples hissed at you;
You have become a horror,
And have ceased to be forever.
Ezekiel 27:36

IX

In a book read years ago I read
a person give a benediction,
"Thank God the bastard's dead," and return
to eating his meal, relieved of one
less thing to worry over now that
the wicked rich man met his maker.

X

A person's merits shines when the time
the Cesar palls while Cicero shines
but it is because of the second
that historians recognize with
cold contempt Cesar's and Rome's value.
For Cicero lived and died one who
had deserved a Rome better than his.
His memory, though, is one which is
as sanctified as Akiba's own.
He's counted as a righteous gentile.

Fear of the Egyptians

I

Thus said the LORD:
Those who support Egypt shall fall,
And her proud strength shall sink;
There they shall fall by the sword,
From Migdol to Syene
--declares the Lord GOD.
Ezekiel 30:6

II

O Lord the Egyptians once oppressed
Your people Israel as their slaves;
yet we say on their behalf: spare them!

III

For the crimes committed by Pharaoh
were some three millennia ago;
they called us adolescents rebel against
the Pharaoh regarded as a god
whom Egyptians would worship when dead—
in great tombs built by Hebrew slaves with
straw converted to edifices
of mud brick so that Pharaoh's life could
move continuing on in the grave
to remove the sting of death itself.

IV

Why pity Egypt? People might ask.
We pity them their fears, say we Jews,
for because we trust YHWH we know
we have not one thing to fear in death;
and despite their life's luxury cling
to it when they die, like children will cling
to blankets at night in the face of
the unknown darkness surrounding them.

V

O Lord to not despise the fears
that make the Egyptians fear their deaths;
we do not do so despite the fact
it makes them cruel in wanting their slaves
to mount great edifices for them
as homes to live in after their deaths.
This fearing death made Egyptians cruel—
for it was in their frightened fury
that they would chastise their slaves back then.

Egypt

I

They shall be the most desolate of desolate lands, and her cities shall
be the most ruined of cities, when I set fire to Egypt and all who
help her are broken. Thus they shall know that I am the LORD.
Ezekiel 30:7-8

II

O ancient Egypt, glorious once,
but invasions long since have destroyed
the marvels that were ancient Egypt
down to the Sphinx's having its nose
shot off by Napoleon's troops as
they used it for their target practice.

III

The scar mars the great sculpture's beauty;
this despite its great beauty glaring
out from the shining piles of gold sand.
The missing nose seems tragic because
it was such a feat creating it
and such a wasteful act to destroy
the beauty of an ancient sculpture.
Why would a person do such a thing?

IV

Yet the Lord decreed Egypt's fate was
To fall with invasions till it reached
The state where its first culture became
in pyramids and other buildings—
a fossil like a dinosaur's bones
if discovered while birds fly nearby.
The aforementioned birds are born as
the descendants of dinosaurs as
the modern Egyptian may have blood
that dates back to the pyramids, too.

V

The ancient civilization of
the Egyptian fades like an echo—
yet the Jews remain until this day.

War Tears the Earth

I

From the depths of Sheol the mightiest of warriors
speak to him and his allies; the uncircumcised, the slain
by the sword, have gone down and lie [there].
Ezekiel 32:21

II

O YHWH does it matter whether
a man who dies in circumcised or
fought in a "just war" when he falls to
the earth to caress the earth as though
she were his longed for mother at home—
for young men long for mothers at home
when vulnerable as the women
who understand them best in childhood.

III

"Mom," dying soldiers cry to the earth
friend both to sinners and to the good.
"O Mom do you cry for me at last?"
the soldier, circumcised or not, cries.
O Mother Earth cries for her babies,
"O darling sons on battlefields dead
as unnaturally as if murdered;
as often dead for a king's money
as for the honorable cause claimed.

IV

Assyria is there with all her company, their graves
round farthest recesses of the Pit.
Ezekiel 32:22

V

O Assyria, your fate is sad;
in sheol you cry for those soldiers
sent to war, youthful and strong, to die
and so to live lives incomplete as
the men are not much more than saplings.

VI

Their early demises are for what,
O Assyria, you were a cause who
was particularly known to be
a brutal one in exporting those
you conquered as a cultural death
a genocide God has spared the Jews.

VII

There masses round about her tomb, all of them slain, fallen by
the sword—they who struck terror in the land of the living—now
they bear their shame with those who have gone down to the Pit.
Ezekiel 32:24

VIII

Ah! Elam! Forgotten these days save
for Bible verses only record
this anger towards Elam itself
in a tale fundamentally of
a people outside yourself judging
a lost group as live Assyria—
which is still remembered in footnotes
in textbooks for those semester gigs
called Western Civilization I.

IX

They have made a bed with her among the slain, with
all her masses; their graves are round her.
Ezekiel 32:25

X

O soldiers in the battlefields where
your country has sent you out to fight:
when there's no body returning is
there still a soul that comes back home to God?
Does bravery have nothing to say?
O Earth you cry for young men fallen
who however their courage inspires
are lost to grieving parents at home.
O parents, grieving, pray for the day
when warfare bleeds the earth no longer.

The Colossal Wreck of Egypt

I

I will cause your multitude to fall
By the swords of warriors,
All the most ruthless of nations.
They shall ravage the splendor of Egypt
And all her masses shall be wiped out.
Ezekiel 32:12

II

O Egypt's citizens shall suffer
the fate of Jewish exiles abroad;
there shall be only a small remnant
of Pharaoh's people serving their cause—
or perhaps there shall be none at all.
For just as cities Hiroshima
and Nagasaki disappeared so
it's the case Egypt's persons are gone.
For it's the case that wicked people
shall not be reborn again to live.

III

I will make all her cattle vanish beside abundant waters;
The feet of man shall not muddy them anymore,
Nor shall the hoofs of cattle muddy them.
Ezekiel 32:13

IV

O Egypt becomes a great desert!
The Nile shall thin to a sea of Reeds
That a child may jump across on foot!
Dried! Victoria Falls dry to be
parched like a camel walking on roads
that join the Persian Gulf to the Sea.
Then water will have too much salt to
drink as poured from the Dead Sea itself.

V

This is a dirge, and it shall be intoned;
The women of the nations shall intone it,
They shall intone it over Egypt and her multitude
--declares the Lord GOD.
Ezekiel 32:16

VI

O Egypt! All that is left of you
is a great "Colossal Wreck"[13] written
on the walls of graves in words record
the boasts of distant, forgotten kings.

---

[13] Percy Shelley referred to Ramses' statue as a "Colassal Wreck" in his poems "Ozymandias." Like the Jews he knew Egypt's "greatness" was temporary.

VII

Will we leave imprints lasting as long,
we whose lives are more luxurious
then Ramses the Great himself because
we possess greater technology?
Or will we instead become extinct
the victims of our inventiveness?

Death of Edom

I

Edom is there [in sheol], her kings and all her chieftains, who, for all
their might, are laid among those who are slain by the sword; they
too lie with the uncircumcised and those who go down to the Pit.
Ezekiel 33:29

II

O Esau's children now lay murdered
in the land of the Pit called sheol.
O children buried in the dead's land;
will you rise again, you who deserved
life happily lived but were cut short?

III

Then Ezekiel spoke to Esau,
"O Esau, barbarous though you are,
you are blind Isaac's favorite son,
the grandson of his father Abram
and Jacob's own twin brother, as well—
whom you had forgiven for robbing
you of your blessing and your birthright
with a great wholehearted love proving
your worth to be blessed by Lord YHWH.
So Jacob's children mourn the loss of
poor Esau's children who lay slaughtered.
Give them a place in the world-to-come."

IV

The Lord with comforting words calls you,
"To see the children Esau saw die
lie murdered on their beloved earth
who is a mother to all soldiers,
is to see cruelty itself towards
alike both the young and the old."

V

In slaughter leading to Earth's shoulder
her sheltering embrace of them
the fallen heroes cry to YHWH,
"O Lord of compassion who looks on
as bodies lie strewn over the earth,
why don't You act in regards these sins—
for being uncircumcised ourselves
we regard ourselves as the heirs to
the promise Abraham was given.
Lord, do not forget your child, Esau."

VI

So God blessed Esau saying that he
"will have his place in the world-to-come."

Arguments of a Married Couple

I

*The word of the LORD came to me: O mortal, when the
House of Israel dwelt on their own soil, they defiled it
with their ways and their deeds; their ways were in my
sight like the uncleanliness of a monstrous woman.*
Ezekiel 36:16

II

When Ezekiel beloved heard
the harsh words regarding the nation
she protested to Ezekiel,
"Why do you use the female body
to describe Israel's worst sins which
you assure me have polluted her
far beyond what the Lord can admit?"

III

"Think of the uncleanliness which is
so associated with the crime
of her adultery fouls marriage,"
said Ezekiel to his first love.
"But Ezekiel," she asked of him,
"Am I pollution to you when
I have my monthly bleeding until
I'm old past childbearing years? Am I?"
"Why—no—" the prophet stammered to her.
"Is all of sex adultery, lord?"
said the first and last love of his life.

IV

Now Ezekiel spoke to his love,
in gentleness but without a clue
to what it means to be a woman,
"I do not see you as less than pure
but the blood nature produces when
a woman does not give birth is filth;
not *really* sin and yet messy;
it requires special disposal in
the dessert because it stains clothes.

V

"It is like leprosy for women.
For leprosy is not a sin and
yet lepers are those taken out of
the community for their own good."
"I am not worried regarding sex,"
said Ezekiel's first and last love.
"I speak of using menstruation
as if a symbol for what's unclean.
For surely this will disgrace women."
"I reverence you, beloved dove,"
said Ezekiel to his great love.

VI

"But father explained when I was young
what it means to act the role of priest;
the devout must speak as God wishes."
"But when we were young," she said to him,
"You resented his beating you and
then he sold me away far from you.
How can you reverence this man's words?"
Then Ezekiel began to cry,
"It is not just my father, my dove."
"Then what is it?" she asked the prophet.

VII

"I have lived my life visited by
the Lord of Israel since father
took you and I was lonely without
the woman I loved more than any.
To live the Law in gratitude with
you by my side is all that I want.
To live this Law that's inside me with
the beloved who'd disappeared is
all I ask of you, beloved friend."

VIII

A tear then trickled down her cheek and
the beloved whom loved him spoke up,
"Your God is my God, the Jews mine, too."
Then Ezekiel spoke as prophet—
but it was the Lord's message to her—

IX

"Now 'Ours is not to reason why,' is
the abeyance of soldiers as well
as Jewish people who I speak to.
An unjust death at stranger's rough hands
is not to be one questioned if I
am the one who sent it to you and
you will know I sent this fate to you
if you are asked to curse the Lord's name."

X

Then Ezekiel returned to her,
"Please believe for me the Lord is just.
I need you to be strong when I have
By myself received fiery visions.
The people depend on me leading
them in these turbulent days in which
the country Babylonia looms
both near and large to conquer our land."

XI

And indeed, Ezekiel was one
with her whom Babylonians took
to captivity and who led them.
His beloved friend stayed with him and
she believed in his vision abroad.

XII

"O Friend!" the prophet said in secret
"With you life is bliss; we are happy.
For leprosy is itself something
I could bare we were together with
you regardless of where we share it.
A home in Babylon we have love
and will wait for Lord YHWH to call
us back to Jerusalem someday.

Mourning Rites of a Kohen

I

*[A priest] shall not defile himself by entering the house
of a dead person. He shall defile himself only for
father or mother, brother or unmarried sister.*
Ezekiel 44:25
When Ezekiel explained these words
by saying, "My dove, I may not touch
the corpses of the dead save for those
of immediate relatives who
included parents, brothers, sisters."

II

"But Ezekiel," said his dear friend.
"What if of the two of us I die
first with your living onwards past me?
will my death go as unmourned as if
I were some animal left for dead?"
Then Ezekiel said to her that,
"I consider you my spouse, dear friend;
when you die I will put on the rites
of mourning so that we'll be bound
in death as together we lived as
a husband and his devoted wife."

III

Then he thought sorrowfully that he
wronged his poor first wife, perhaps, when dead
as he'd not mourned her death the way he
taught others to grieve a loved one's death.
For he had felt her death as dearly
as this more forthright woman with him.
When he looked up at his friend he smiled,
"I will mourn your death in tears, my dove,"
and Ezekiel's wife was grateful.

IV

It was not to be, however, as
the prophet Ezekiel who died before
his lifetime's beloved who loved him.
It happened after a long illness.
He arranged it so she mourned his death
like native Israelites did for those
who died as spouses, parents, children
or friends—and she inherited
all Ezekiel's wealth with servants
paid to make her last days as easy
as Ezekiel believed that she
had made his joyful—a gift from God.

V

O friendship exists between people
as unlikely as Ezekiel
and his two wives and surely they will
meet again in the world-to-come as
the separate selves made whole by love.
For Ezekiel led us well and
yet it was his wives who loved him best.
The Lost Testament of the Prophet Ezekiel

Dedicated to Lost Love

I

He had his scrolls in secret chambers,
and on one of them it was written,
"א
O Beloved, my heart desires you,
a sunbeam which comes where sleepers
lie under darkening clouds' tears
the drops that come while you shine through."
ב
You censor my work with your eyes,
O Beloved, Your love is mirrored in
the love I feel for my God who is
my Ishi but not Baali—
my Lord-who-is-not-my-Lord and
my Divine Husband up on high.
For women have needs like men—
and mine are unmet save for God.
You are woman, I am man;
we belong together, My love
God serves all my needs flawlessly
and yet can spirit feed the flesh?
ג
I know I am one bidden wait
for what the Lord will take care of.
For God sees even small things that
are hidden or best left so by
the human beings living in
the darkness waiting for the morn.

7

I pray that my beloved shall
return to me someday before I die;
my faith in the Lord relied on her love.
I am held up to the gorgeous sun
in remembrance of her whom I love."

II

The prophet Ezekiel stashed verse
in regards his long lost love, keeping
it in the Holy Temple's chamber
and when he was not praying he read
the poems he wrote for the woman
he pined for since her being taken
from him while guiltily he wondered
if this weren't treachery to his wife—
a wonderful young woman whom he
loved despite losing his true love lost
years before becoming high priest to
act replacing his father himself.

HOSEA

Hosea and Gomer

I

When the Lord first spoke to Hosea, the Lord said to Hosea, "Go,
get yourself a wife of whoredom; for the land will stray from following
the Lord." So he went and married Gomer daughter of Diblaim...
Hosea 1:2-1:3

II

When Hosea asked Gomer if she
would marry him the prostitute asked,
"Why are you interested in me,
You prophet to the Israelite God?
A holy prophet ignores harlots.
O prophet of God, what's your motive?
Have you been sent a lying spirit?
Have you been corrupted by YHWH?

III

"The Lord speaks through me," Hosea said,
as earnestly as though his life was
what was at stake in wedding Gomer.
"I'm bidden to love you as if you
were a fresh virgin's bloom in the spring
of life and not a woman used up by men.

IV

"And besides, I saw you once before
you became what you are now to men
and treasured you in my heart as one
who seemed more innocent than any;
I cannot believe that girl is lost."

V

A Charles Bovary would have balked
at marriage to this creature pregnant
with another's child already as
the prophet Hosea picked Gomer
to make her his own beloved wife—
for cowed by the fact she could live life
as respectable as her childhood,
the woman Gomer said, "I'd marry
about just anyone to have hope
in being a good woman once more."

V

So Gomer spat first and agreed.
She married Hosea the prophet
in public ceremony viewed by
the curious more than the devout.
He washed and combed her hair and brought her
silk garments, pears to wear as earrings
and gemstones for her fingers and toes.
She became beautiful in his sight;
and indeed, once cleaned she looked lovely.

VI

She forgot she had ever been one
who sold her body for mere money.
And Hosea held her near his heart.
Could Gomer remake herself to be
what the best virgins become as wives?
Can an old whore make her ways right when
there's a cloud of sin over her life,
that muddies her life's reputation.

Gomer's First Son

I

She conceived and bore him a son and the Lord instructed him, "Name him Jezreel, for I will soon punish the House of Jehu for the bloody deeds at Jezreel and put an end to the monarchy of Israel in the Valley of Jezreel.
Hosea 1:5-1:6

II

Now Gomer bled for Israel as
her husband spoke for his Lord YHWH.
It was as if his symbolic act
had granted her new life—as a Jew.
Although we're never pagan she had
been worse than pagan: she'd been a whore,
a woman selling herself for gold.

III

Not even courtesans were demeaned
to Gomer's degree, a street walker.
To have her husband remind Gomer
of her past as a wicked woman
seemed treacherous in spite of the fact
that Gomer honestly had acted
as Hosea's Lord claimed the Jews had.

IV

So Gomer cried for vanity's sake;
she'd forgotten how prostitution
had felt with 'lovers' plying her with
their dirty silver or gold pieces
in exchange for the favor of sex
in city alleys infested with
rats, disease, other uncleanliness—
our of the way haunts used in order
to protect the men's reputations.

V

Now Gomer wished to hide her own sins;
for she was embarrassed of her past
now that she lived a life which was deemed
a respectable one if hiding
her sins from others, keeping secrets
which on the surface would have stained her
to "honest" people including men
who'd purchased her "goods" in the nights' streets.
They played their society's whore with
their skulking, hidden ways in the night
while by day demonstrating virtue
in appearance to others like them.

VI

Ah! Wickedness! Why did poor Gomer
come to be exemplifying it
to people especially women?
So Gomer cringed in hearing both sins:
hers and that of the Israelites for
she felt a sisterhood with the Jews
just as her husband was like a God;
for because Gomer loved him she was
in awe of him as one who'd saved her.

VII

How could she explain to him that she
did not want her past sins exposed to all?
That Israel, too, might just resent God's wrath?
That this was despite her love, a love
that exists even where there's anger.
How could she explain her own message?

The Second Child

I

*She conceived again and bore a daughter; and He said
to him, "Name her Lo-ruhamah; for I will no longer
accept the House of Israel or pardon them."*
Hosea 1:6

II

Now again Gomer pondered her shame;
how Hosea made public her crimes
as she shrunk deep down within herself
she thought she'd escaped the fate
of ending her life in the street's filth.
She wanted to have her sins taken
and buried deep down within the earth.
She wanted Hosea to respect
her as though she had been a virgin
when they got married and not a whore.

III

She wanted secrecy in regards
to that past Hosea had revealed
his beloved wife possessed to all
as symbolic of Israel's sins:
the Divine Husband was so angry
at the adulteries with the gods
that he was ready for a divorce.
Yet if the Jews would return to God,
then like poor Gomer he would admit
them as God's beloved Bride once more.

IV

At Hosea's and Gomer's wedding
there had been a faint snickering from
the crowd which gathered to see the farce—
a wedding ceremony thrown for
a prophet to a prostitute who
was nameless save for her trade till then—
an anonymous street walker made up
in lovely clothes like a new bride.
The genuinely fresh virgin's tittered
to cause an especial blush to rise
on the poor sinner-become-a-bride.

V

At first it this made difficulty for
the other women to accept her.
Then Hosea had started preaching
and Gomer could not leave the house for
fear of her being groped by men outside
as a whore still and open season
to unmarried men especially—
young studs not ready to get themselves
wives "settling down" with "unspoiled" virgins.

VI

So it was Gomer resented him—
that is to say, the prophet lampooned
for marrying a streetwalker and
then "proving" Gomer's unworthiness.
For Gomer's reputation now spread
as Hosea's whore captured by him,
and she had become symbolic of
all sins of unfaithfulness to God.

VII

"O Lord," cried Gomer, "When will I be
one punished enough for the sins of
my past as a girl deflowered and
cast out of house and family home?
For it was only once that I sinned
by choice and much more that I needed
what money I could receive at all.
I was shocked Hosea would want me;
why can't the prophet love all of me?"

Escaping the Prophet's Love

I

After weaning Lo-ruhamah, she conceived and bore a
son. Then He said, "Name him Lo-ammi; for you are
not my people, and you will not be my God.
Hosea 1:8-1:9

II

Then Gomer made her escape plans from
the prophet Hosea to return
to the streets, plying them as a whore,
a merchant with her body itself.
For Gomer's wish for dignity was
one combined with her desire to be
judged to have her pride outside of stocks,
the punishment the Puritans used
she wanted to have the right to pride.

III

For in fact never proud of being
a hooker she was audacious once.
She assumed that was why he noticed
among the many of the street's whores.
For after all, she thought, I had spunk.
I had the pizzaz of an artist.
I added up the heat in regards
to inspiring the customer's to
those crimes their wives least suspected them.
For married men do have to please wives;
she does not exist for them only.
The pleasure princess is what I was.

IV

O! To be pinned to a mere prophet!
To be a prophet's beloved wife!
To be sure it had compensations.
When he was lonely with her he was
a gentleman who spoke as gently
as he spoke angrily to the crowds;
he never expected her love as
though he took it for granted himself.

V

He called her, "my lost lamb, mine only"
and admissions that he loved "her more
for how strange it all was when love came
the Lord should bid me love one of whom
I little suspected how much she
would come to matter to me myself.
For God bid me love you on your terms."

VI

Yet Gomer could not savor his love
so long as it was symbolized sin.
She could not believe herself sinful
although she'd sinned so many times she
accepted only goodness from him.
It was what people said of her that
"the prophet spoils that useless hooker."

VII

For only Hosea would believe
she was a redeemable wife as
she was and not as she ought to be.
If he loved her on her own terms than
she would be made a lovable wife.

VIII

How could poor Gomer receive his wrath
to other Israelites on these terms?
Yet she dared not tell him her own fears.
For Hosea was consumed with it,
with Israel's need regarding God;
and in crowds he would declare it so
and symbolize his cause with his wife—
and Gomer could not receive it as
it made a spectacle of their life—
both together and apart made one.

Gomer's Escape

I

Oh, call your brothers "My People,"
And your sisters "Lovingly Accepted!"
Hosea 2:3

II

A second passed and Gomer trembled.
"O Lord," she whispered chilled to the bone,
"My husband preaches for me at last;
What now? Should I stay Hosea's wife?
Why run from Hosea's side now that
I'm rehabilitated to him?
When I am beloved at last why
should I flee from my husband's Lord God?"

III

Then Gomer remembered in despair,
"How can I trust him now that I'm resolved?"
This resolve, formed just before he preached
now seemed to be too entrenched to move
yet fragile, even tenuous to
the wife of the great Hebrew prophet.
"Lord," Gomer cried out, "Lord forgive Gomer!"
and while the prophet Hosea preached
the impending good times for the Jews
and eulogizing them like Gomer
the best wife a man could have in spite
of all the Lord had predicted of
his prostitute-wife whom he adored.

IV

He did not eulogize their merits;
but emphasized their eventual gift—
that millions of Jews flourish worldwide.
That said they gathered as if honey
was being offered them as she-bears;
and perhaps the Lord's consolation
did involve some words "You make me proud."

VI

Yet, perhaps, he still imagined that
poor Gomer's children would be counted
among the numberless mass of Jews.
He sounded like a boy in first love.
The woman Gomer fled from his home.

VII

At sundown Hosea found his house
an abandoned shack near the dirt roads;
he carried his dear mission with him
and when the prophet Hosea saw
his beloved wife, Gomer, was gone
he cried and crying himself to sleep
he took it as a sign of God's wrath.

Hosea and the Children

I

When Hosea came returning home
to find it abandoned by Gomer
he sobbed till realizing his children
were still at home in his home with her,
"My children," murmured Hosea as
he found them lonely under blankets
in compartments he'd prepared for them
in the weeks before marrying her.

II

He found his children in tears crying,
"Where is our mama? Where's our mama?"
A rush of anger swelled in his gut
although kind to his lost wife's children,
they heard him denouncing their mother
and Israel the next day outside
in the great marketplace where people
came to shop, "Mother Israel sins!"
he cries to the merchants, "God wills her death!
O prophet, denounce Israel now!"

III

Rebuke your mother, rebuke her—
For she is not my wife
And I am not her husband—
And let her put away her harlotry from her face
And adultery between her breasts.
Hosea 2:4

IV

His proclamations became bolder,
his anger within his chest swelled up.
Else will I strip her naked
And leave her as on the day she was born:
And I will make her like a wilderness,
Render her like a desert land,
And let her die of thirst.
Hosea 2:5

V

Some merchants booed the prophet outright;
some others cackled, laughing at him
like crows and jackdaws taunting him
the ladies called him "imbecilic"
and "boorish" and pimps vulgarly asked
if they could "sell him another wife"
while Gomer watched him from quite afar—
for Gomer heard his threats of revenge.
They seemed so futile—as though he longed
to forgive Gomer and yet could not—
it hurt too much that she had left him.

VII

His love ached for his beloved wife
and he swore he would punish Gomer
if ever she came back to him on her knees—
he would find himself relenting in
the very streets with merchants laughing.
The sad truth was that he longed for her
and could not be as dignified as
he knew as a man he ought to be.

It was as if he could not give up.
He longed to hold his wife in his arms.

VIII

I will also disown her children;
For they are now a harlot's brood...
Hosea 2:6

IX

The children shook with fear at those words.
Would they be abandoned yet again?
But at the end of the day their father
Led them home, Gomer watching all four—
the father and three children—walk on
to their house in peace as though happy.
So Gomer followed jealously from
a distance believing her children
loved Hosea more then their mother.
He fixed their meals and after they ate
tucked them in for their bedtime as they
let out small sobs and cries of "Mama!"

X

So Gomer visited past 'lovers,'
her customers and received her pay
for services she received for gold.
She pursued these men relentlessly
and indeed vengefully as though she
had already lost Hosea and
her children's love now must now survive
by marketing her body for spite—
now punishing those little children
for petulantly crying "Mama!"

to rousing her urgency and guilt at
her having wounded children's heartstrings
in her dreams during fitful sleep when
not enriching her pocket with those
mere pennies men would pay her for sex.

XI

Her reputation grew as a whore.
She knew her children suffered because
her husband's memories of his wife—
and indeed, she spied on him often—
her husband's memories of his wife
through association with these three
he was forced to raise all by himself
and without the help of poor Gomer.
For the girl even looked like Gomer;
the oldest boy still remembered her.

XII

In that their mother has played the harlot,
She that conceived them has acted shamelessly—
Because she thought,
"I will go after my lovers,
Who supply my bread and water,
My wool and my linen,
My oil and my drink."
Hosea 2:7

XIII

"When will our Mama come back," they cried,
in pitiful wails Hosea heard
and finding himself lonely turned to
his Lord called YHWH, meditating.
He claimed his God felt similar pain
and meanwhile prayed with Gomer's children
for Gomer's return to him and them.

The Bitter Herbs and the Honey

I

Assuredly
I will hedge up her roads with thorns
And raise walls against her,
And she shall not find her paths.
Hosea 2:8

II

On vacant streets in the cold of night
the wife of Hosea would ponder
the truth that his words held about
the result of her selling herself
to strangers and cold acquaintances—
the acquaintances wreaking more pain
than all-out strangers inflicted on
the mournful Hosea's wife Gomer;
for they knew Gomer and scorned Gomer
as though her wickednesses surpassed
their wrongs in buying Gomer's body.

II

These regulars were wealthy or poor,
alike but regarded her badly.

III

Pursue her lovers as she will
She shall not overtake them;
And seek them as she may,
She shall never find them.
Hosea 2:9:1-2:9:4

IV

For alas Gomer's looks were now gone
and nothing is as pitiful as
an ugly whore who clamors for work,
who begs and steals but to no avail.
For people believe her to be worse
than money-driven to foul trade:
they see a nymphomaniac who
is driven onwards towards a lust
both unsightly and just like madness.

V

Yet some men encourage them when they
are young and lovely as a spring day.
As Gomer's trade had never involved
much money in her transactions it
was not a very lucrative one.
Now Gomer was left lonely
and men would repulse her when approached.

VI

Then she will say
"I will go and return
To my first husband,
For then I fared better than now."
And she did not consider this:
It was I who bestowed on her
The new grain and wine and oil;
I who lavished silver on her
And gold—which they used for Baal.
Hosea 2:9:5-2:9:8; 2:10

VII

Did Gomer never remember him?
Could Gomer remember no earrings
no necklaces, no finger-sized rings?
In the night's corridors watching him go
home in at sunset with their children—
this after preaching against the land—
and against his wife Gomer herself.
Could Hosea still forgive Gomer?

VIII

As she watched him while preaching by day
and preaching against her she doubted.
Her doubts were much like Israel's doubts;
could the Lord forgive the Jews after
they'd worshipped besides the Lord?
"O Lord," she cried in despair to God,
"Could You still forgive everything now?"

IX

Assuredly,
I will take back my new grain in time
And My new wine in its season,
And I will snatch away My wool and My linen
That serve to cover her nakedness.
Hosea 2:11

X

O naked before Israel's God!
this is truth of poor Gomer's state, now.
For penniless in ancient times she
had, as a woman, only one thing
to sell men and that was her body.
She lost her looks; that was not the point.

XI

As an old decayed fossil of sin
she possessed nothing valuable which
could be sold; that was the point, at last.
An ugly whore could find for herself
a customer when young and saucy
but elderly whores looked like they were,
as dirty and old women, icky.

XII

Now will I uncover her shame
In the very sight of her lovers
And none shall save her from Me.
Hosea 2:12

XIII

And, indeed, her shame lay bare to all;
for Gomer lived in the dark alleys
of Samaria's cities without
nice clothes or food or clean water.
Oh that she had stayed with her husband!
But she could not turn back to him now!
She couldn't let her spine be broken;
she couldn't bend down herself to have
a will as broken in as chattel's.

XIV

For Gomer believed she must be strong—
she stood by her rights against her God.
She could not go back home to her spouse.
For even her own children meant less
than her pure desire to have freedom
at any cost to whoever was
hurt by her decision to live life
on her own terms and not on others.

XV

Her husband loved her dearly as life;
still, she could only live her life free.
Wild, crazy and free, she loved the moon
on Friday nights which mark the Shabbat.

VII

And I will end all her rejoicing:
Her festivals, new moons, and sabaths—
All her festive seasons.
I will lay waste her vines and her fig trees,
Which she thinks are a fee
She received from her lovers;
I will turn them into brushwood,
And beasts of the field shall devour them.
Hosea 2:13-2:14

VIII

"O Hosea," she cried, "Why couldn't
you leave my faithlessness towards you as
an unmentioned fault because like God
you've forgiven past indiscretions?

Why announce them to multitudes of
our fellow Jews in Samaria?"
But her pride swelled up within her as
she starved in Samaria's backstreets.
She could not return to the prophet.

IX

For indeed, he had forgiven all
save he used her name prophesying that
the ways of the land were as sinful
as Gomer's profession was to God.
Now sand blew in his wife's face while she
would recall his words against her acts.
She could not bend to salacious words.

X

Thus I will punish her
For the days of the Baalim,
On which she brought them offerings;
When, decked with earings and jewels,
She would go after her lovers,
Forgetting Me
--Declares the Lord
Hosea 2:15

XI

These words were inserted by Gomer
in later times when Gomer came back.
She insisted on these words because
she had thought often that she'd return
but sin as flagrantly as before
but behind Hosea's back with 'loves'
that involved forbidden rites of those
foul Temples that her husband abhorred.

XII

She would dance behind his back and be
more hypocritically evil
than before she'd been openly so.
She would eat his food and sin greatly.

XIII

*Assuredly
I will speak coaxingly to her
And lead her through the wilderness
And speak to her tenderly.*
Hosea 2:16

XIV

Now Gomer, bathed in her tears, returned.
Although she had nursed her hurt pride with
a sullenness of a spoiled young girl,
an adolescent with newly formed breasts,
she could live lonely no more and found
she loved her prophet dearly despite
his strange ways and words wounding her pride.

XV

She knew no other man would have her;
she also knew she could love none else.
She begged him, "On the country's behalf
will you, my husband forgive Gomer?
Let me come back to you for all time."

XVI

And Hosea went out to declare,
I will give her vineyards from there,
And the Valley of Achor as a plowland of hope
There she shall respond as in the days of her youth,
When she came up from the land of Egypt.
Hosea 2:17

XVII

And Israel cheered; they now believed.
For it was love that overwhelmed her;
love overwhelmed the Israelites, too.

Ishi not Baali

I

And in that day
—declares the Lord—
You will call [Me] Ishi,
And no more will you call Me Baali
For I will remove the names of Baalim from her mouth,
And they shall nevermore be mentioned by name.
Hosea 2:18-2:19

II

The Lord is husband to the Jews as
the 'Ishi' is a derivative
of the word in the Hebrew for man
while 'Baal' or Lord refers also
to the god Canaanites use for storms.

III

There is deep significance in this;
the Baal is a Lord of Canaan.
To call God 'Ish' is to raise men to
the level angels possess with God.
It suggests intimacy with God.
It also suggests wives call husbands
their 'Ish' and not their 'Baal' after
the pagan god Jews should not yield to.

IV

This equalizes relationships
with humans to their beloved God
and women to their darling husbands.
So women with their spouses remain
free when they join to husbands in love
and free to leave their husbands if those
don't live up to their expectations.
For if a husband can leave his wife;
than surely a wife may leave as well.

V

Our God is more than Lord; God is Friend.
For YHWH was a friend to Abram.
And our God spoke to Moses as well.
God also spoke through Sarah saying,
"O Abram listen to her voice, too,"
in regards to his son by Hagar.

VI

And Miriam spoke for God after
the Egyptians drowned, leading women
in singing "The Song of the Sea," to
their own God known as YHWH to them.
For women love God as much as men.
So they will remember that Ishi
is the name for their Divine Husband.
"O Ishi, Ishi," their hearts will sing,
"To Miriam's God we send prayers."

The Breath of Return

I

And I will espouse you forever:
I will espouse you with righteousness and justice,
And with goodness and mercy,
And I will espouse you with faithfulness;
Then you shall be devoted to the LORD.
Hosea 2:21-2:22

II

Real return to faith is God's demand.
This return, repentance's essence
is necessary for the good as
for wicked people committing sins.
For human beings all do some wrongs.
The unrepentant soul does not forgive;
that is why God bids to all, "Return."

III

So Hosea spoke tenderly to
both Israel and his wife, Gomer
who'd abandoned him for her 'lovers,'
her paramours who paid her money,
and Hosea spoke to her in words,
"You are my beloved and I yours;
we together shall form one sole life—
one single drop of Divine Sunshine."

IV

Then continuing, "Oh dearest lover
you whom the Lord loves despite her sins—
for Israel loves her Lord YHWH—
you love God despite inconstancy—
yours, of course, as God watches his wife
while I as prophet loves his bride, too.

V

"For maiden Israel pours out faith
to God while refusing to obey
the mitzvoth God gave Jewish people—
for there are those who will be reborn
in the next life, the world-to-come as
those having been good in this lifetime."

VI

Then there are those who give lip service
to a high idealism which they
don't practice despite find speech to God.

VII

True Return is God's demand of us.
It is faith fulfilled with pure actions,
with mitzvoth done from the heart itself.
For knowing the Law is not enough
a person must breath into it life;
a soul's must breath the life of the Law
just as the Lord breathed into humans
God's very soul, his beloved breath.

Freedom of the Will

I

The LORD said to me further, "Go, befriend a woman
who, while befriended by a companion, consorts with
others, just as the LORD befriends the Israelites, but they
turn to other gods and love the cup of the grape."
Hosea 3:1

II

Once before Gomer came back for good
she went back briefly to her husband.
She repented; she resented words
which reminded her of her sinning.
For Gomer believed she'd been promised
a clean slate on her return back home.
She had been dragged back to her husband;
for somebody told Hosea of
her whereabouts in Samaria.

III

Then I hired her for fifteen shekels of silver, a homer of
barley, and a letech of bareley, and I stipulated with her, "In
return, you are to go a long time without either fornicating
or marrying; even I [shall not cohabit] with you."
Hosea 3:2-3:3

IV

Now Gomer herself felt a deep pain,
a humiliation in her heart
but also she felt relieved by words
that indicated to her that there
would be no cohabitation with
men regardless of variety.

V

For truthfully a prostitute will
not generally enjoy sex with
her customers, the degradation
of her job outweighing all besides.
Still, being a less-than-wife rankled;
athough he's kindly Hosea was
a zealous reformer of Gomer;
the prophet would wake her up early
and leave her with a servant to watch
as she would care for their three children.

VI

These three watched Gomer suspiciously—
as though she might leave anytime as
she had one so once before, they knew.
For Hosea had explained to them
years earlier how Gomer left them.
And Lo-ruhamah remembered it.

VII

Yet Gomer tried, for a while, to be
a good wife for her appearance sake—
her life on the street chastened Gomer—
who perhaps did not want to be free
when she thought of what freedom cost her.
But one night she got up from her bed
and started to leave the house again.
As she left Hosea found her out.

VIII

"O prophet," Gomer told her husband,
"I can't be happy with you this way."
Now Hosea breathed a sigh, "I can't
keep you here against your will; go on."
So Gomer left in the pale moon's light.
And Hosea cried himself to sleep;
he knew she could not be made to be
a good wife willing something else which
was contrary to goodness at heart.

The Source of Evil

I

[False] swearing, dishonesty, and murder,
And theft and adultery are rife;
Crime follows upon crime!
Hosea 4:2

II

Oh in the days of Hosea when
the wife of Hosea would listen
to Hosea preach her sins to all
he declaimed the sins of the people
for apart from gods apart from God
they acted sinfully to others.

III

Yet Gomer wondered, "Isn't this age
like every age in that regard?"
For every age is one taken
to be a unique time to those who
have participated in it with
its passions, violent or humane.
The stubbornness of humanity
burst forth like the blood mosquitoes' drink
when they are squashed by those they've bitten.

IV

Is there not theft or murder always?
the wife of Hosea had wondered.
When times are good aren't there still those
who aren't just, trustworthy or kindly?
And are these words true anywhere still?

V

It occurred to the prophet's wife that
what made her husband's words live always
might be that he spoke to ills plaguing
the human species since time began.
For even prostitution itself
was 'the world's oldest profession' to
the masses involved in the trade which
so degraded the women involved.

VI

Although the circumstances would change
the human heart's own darkened chambers
might forever be the same itself.
Yet YHWH bid that humanity
reach for the good as long as humans
would remain in their existence still—
till humanity becomes perfect
or loses everything in trying.

VII

For God sends out the messiah when
all human beings are good or bad—
and only God knows which it will be.
We know it is God's mercy only
which makes our humanity likely
to succeed in our troubled lifeline.
We know that our age continues on;
yet if we do not renew hope we
have nothing left to live by besides.

VIII

"O YHWH," Hosea's wife Gomer
would never use God's personal name,
"From whence does optimism spring forth?
It surely does not come from our lives;
does it come from You as a Being
whom only prophets—which I am not—
have seen and related to others?
I know both evil and pain only;
I never cleaved to the good myself.
Now I try righteousness and find that
I hear the echoes of the goodness
my husband speaks of, but mere echoes."

IX

"I have a parable of my own.
Two monkeys under a tree find fruit
and start to grab up fruit to carry
to grab fruit to eat later on when
they have both leisure and its safety.
Then when they are both ready to eat
the larger monkey takes his pick first
thus making the small monkey take what
is his not by right but might only."

X

"If the two monkeys were men they'd say,
'We'll divide the fruit in half' because
they'd know they could eat only so much.
This is why monkeys become human:
they learn the 'fairness' concept and yet
they are not angels because they still
act like apes often practically.

XI

Yet is our intelligence enough
to save us from our being monkeys
with a great capacity towards
war which the monkeys are not able
to carry out for lack of I.Q.?"

XII

*Does justice satisfy us when we
so often cruelly demand revenge?
When the right is not practiced itself?
Are human's capable of meeting
the Lord's clear demands of us today?*

XIII

So Gomer wondered, only sure of
the goodness of her YHWH because
she sensed God's permeating her world
with joy despite gloomy thinking.
Although we seem like the apes we are
still capable of meeting YHWH
in the soul's dark night, creating Day.
When physical worlds produce evil
the spiritual realm reaches forth to
the human on the other side, Here.

Prayers of the Mountain Peaks

I

They sacrifice on the mountaintops
And offer on the hills,
Under oaks, poplars and terebinths
Whose shade is so pleasant
That is why their daughters fornicate
And their daughters-in-law commit adultery!
Hosea 4:13

II

Among the idolaters the Jews
climbed up the mountaintops to worship
the Canaanite gods with their poplars
and then make secret sacrifices
to gods in unholy rites without
their having recorded these same rites
for posterity recording what
their sacrifices were or how made.

III

O secret societies steeped in cruel sin.
And yet they tell us, "Didn't Moses
climb up to the top of his mountain?
Don't you seen in our arcane rites more
than sacrifices, Moses himself?
For we search for the prophet Moses
in Israel's peaks having grown up
in valleys below our search for God?
You may think our rites blasphemous still
but we search for the truth among hills."

IV

And Gomer wept at this groups fresh crimes
for before Hosea her husband
she was like Canaan herself and she
had resembled the daughters whoring
and daughters-in-law whoring also.

V

For she had nestled a man gently
once as a girl and was thrown onto
the streets to fend for herself and gained
the knowledge suffering and woe bring.
It began sweet as honey with him
and yet the debauch following was
still anything but pleasurable.

VI

I will not punish their daughters for fornicating
Nor their daughters-in-law for committing adultery;
For they themselves turn aside with whores
And sacrifice with prostitutes,
And a people that is without sense must stumble.
Hosea 4:14

VII

"Ah Lord!" Said Gomer, Hosea's wife,
"You punished me! I suffered for sins
like those who pray on our peaks and hills.
These fellow sinners brandish their faith
as a prize glorious as the sun
should heretics be branded as such
when showing devotion to a cause

deemed holy in their own eyes at least
and with such selflessness in regards."

VIII

"I chased men who were married as well
as those who were still single so that
I could count silver and gold coinage
in the dark where I worked bedrooms,
in inns and alleys, wherever there
was anonymity made by place
or circumstance for a while he—
the customer, I mean—lay in the bed
drunk, rank with sweat and dirty besides."

IX

"To my own husband I was a whore;
but it seemed that these worshippers of
their beloved is sincere towards
Lord YHWH whom they long to find as
though God was not near in the mountains.

X

"The presence of God overflows all;
it pours from spiritual to the world
of matter shackled as it is to
that which dies in plane existence now.
The mountain dwellers long for spirit;
and I learn this from heretics now.

XI

"I shouldn't have been tainting my flesh
with the sweat of men because it kept
    me from the experience of love.
    For to be a whore is not to love
    a single man but to be sinned with
    a multitude of men in mere sex.
    I wish I could live my life over.

XII

"A ' Love for Sale' is no love in truth,"
    it violates a holy deed like
    a pile of dirt poured onto a meal—
    to eat an uncleaned potato with
    live earthworms living on top of it.

The Fidelity of Gomer

I

You have loved the harlot's fee
And the new wine shall betray her.
Hosea 9:1:5; 9:2:2

II

Now Gomer recalled returning to
her husband Hosea and being
a faithful wife from then on in spite
of his great suspicions in regards
to Gomer's wifely fidelity.

III

She tried to curb her inclination
to sin in the eyes of her husband
and—more—the eyes of the God who spoke
through Hosea the prophet to her.
For despite Hosea's own assurances
poor Gomer believed the words he spoke
to Israel were actually for
the prophet Hosea's wife, Gomer.

IV

For believing him though she did she
still wondered if he spoke to Gomer—
her personally apart from those
in Israel although they're sinning
were loved by YHWH, Hosea's God.

V

Ah, Jews had told the prophet the words,
"O prophet, we speak to God through you.
We speak to God as meekly as mice,
'O our God, we are devoted to
You,' why do you curse us in Your name?'"
O Gomer longed to plead with the Jews,
"We love our God; why is God angry?"
but even more, "What have I done wrong in
Your site my beloved, my husband?"

VI

Yet she could not speak; she knew
that Gomer was no Abraham with
these Sodomites who relied on her.
She felt for the Jews more than Sodom
yet she felt herself undeserving
to speak like Abraham for those whom
Lord YHWH chastised through his prophet.

VII

O to be a good woman to God
than she could chastise her dear husband,
"The people suffer too much right now."

The God of Gomer

I

From birth, from the womb, from conception
Ephraim's glory shall be
Like birds that fly away.
Hosea 9:11

II

Now Gomer said it to her husband,
"When will God forgive Israel for
The crimes of her youth against her Lord?";
for Gomer wished that Hosea could
at last grant forgiveness for her crimes.

III

"O Hosea bid our Lord forgive;
the only reason I came back was
for forgiveness from the man I wronged.
I long for the love I don't deserve.
O YHWH respond to your people
as we pour our hearts before your feet.

IV

"I wanted to have freedom from You;
now I want loving forgiveness more.
I want your warmth and affection now;
I want to be a shepherded lamb
of YHWH; hold me back no longer
come tp embrace Your wife as
she was a prostitute at one time
for despite sinfulness she loves you.

V

"Yes, at last Gomer loves her husband—
while Israel loves her Lord Husband—
with devotion she has embraced You.
Lord I cry out to You, to forgive.
O relentless God, become gentle."

VI

And the Lord softened Hosea's heart
in speaking to God's servant, Gomer,
"You're forgiven with Israel, too;
for God loves those who repent as much
as those who were good always because
God understands that changing is hard.
And Gomer, the Lord sees you have changed."

VII

For God loved Gomer with her husband.
And likewise Hosea had always
loved Gomer as though chastity was
the quality which defined Gomer;
for Hosea saw a fine woman
deep inside this Bride-for-sale to men.
This was the result of his knowledge:
for Hosea was acquainted with Gomer
in childhood before she had become
the harlot familiar with the streets.

The Motherhood of Gomer

I

Give them, O LORD—give them what?
Give them a womb that miscarries
And shriveled breasts!
Hosea 9:14

II

Now Gomer's breasts sagged with age
and she felt the guilt of the people
press downwards upon her bent shoulders.

III

"O Lord," said Gomer, "Forgive us all;
We have not always proven faithful
but we have always loved You within
our hearts as wayward children will love
the parents that they disobey, too.
Our love for the Lord consumes our heart
like that bush Moses found in flames in
the desert hills near the priest Jethro's."

IV

"To lose a child in childbirth if you
are a Jew is more painful than death
for Jewish people value children
as precious beyond silver and gold.
'Our children are our builders,' Jews say;
'Don't harm our newborn infants,' Jews add,
'For the tie between parent and child

is from Lord YHWH given to us
and children love their parents like God
(it's natural to love both of them)
with God as Divine Mother as well
as Divine Father to God's children."

V

"For when Jews suffer they lay their heads
on God's own shoulder to cry their tears
as little children sit in the laps
of mothers who will bandage them up
when they're cut from a sudden fall and
need tenderness and healing as well."

VI

For Gomer became a great mother;
she nurtured her three children with love
like Hosea who loving her with
a tenderness to the sick as she
had been a morally sick person.

VII

Now Gomer said this boldly to God;
the repentant whore finally was
a kindly mother, beloved wife,
and spoke on behalf of those like her.
In return the Lord granted children
a universal place in heaven.
This concession by God pleased Gomer;
and Hosea was grateful as well.

Children Among the Blessed

I

But the din of war shall arise in your own people,
And all your fortresses shall be ravaged
As Beth-arbel was ravaged by Shalman
On a day of battle,
When mothers and babes were dashed to death together.
Hosea 10:14

II

"O Lord," cried Gomer, "I pray for them:
the mothers and their children who love
their beloved who judged them faithless
so incurring the brunt of God's wrath."

III

"O Lord, these mothers adore their God;
these babes are incapable of sin.
Why injure these poor innocents who
are the least guilty of sin themselves.
O Lord, the mothers are the mothers
of Your own children whose souls You breathed
right into them through the nose at birth."

IV

"These little one are prized by mothers
who've little time to do much save for
nurse these small bundles crying to them,
"O Mama, mama," in cries which are
loud, indecipherable and shrill.

For 'Mama' is what they mean only;
their vocal chords can't even form words.
But they love 'Mama.' Do they know God?"

V

"For after all is it not one of
the Lord's ten commandments to honor
one's parents beyond the self because
to love your parents is to 'fear God,'
and little children love their parents
as unconditionally as if
a good dog devotedly loving
one who's its master caring for it."

VI

"A child will naturally love God.
'O YHWH,' cries the beloved child,
'You whom the tall trees clap their hands for!
You formed me in the womb for my life!'
Yet the child is mute in these words as
the child is not yet thinking out loud.
For heaven exists within the self
as well as with Lord YHWH Itself.
The child loves God; please spare this same child.'"

VII

And the Lord agreed children, who love,
were judged as believing Jews to God.
Although the commands given to them
are few, all children belong to God."
And God then prepared a place for those
who die in childhood as those who died
as martyred tzadikim in words of
the *Sh'ma* prayer given up to YHWH.

The Last Prayer of Gomer

I

Samaria must bear her guilt,
For she has defied her God.
They shall fall by the sword,
Their infants shall be dashed by death,
And their women with child ripped open.
Hosea 14:1

II

This is our tender spot, O YHWH,
cried Gomer for the Jewish people,
"We love our children dearly as life,
and Jews have been those martyred enough
to know the value of life cheaply taken
by those who conquer Israel with
their alien gods carried along,
and forced hard upon the Lord's alter
a rape of sorts on Jewish people
and the God that they believe in still.
Why destroy children of Your children
for despite our flaws we love our Lord."

III

Forgive all guilt
And accept what is good;
Instead of bulls we will pay
[The offering of] our lips.
Hosea 14:3:4-14:3:7

IV

The offerings of the lips only
are prayers granted Israel's God.
These words moved the heart of Lord YHWH.
God gave fresh words to Hosea when
the Israelites had agreed with her
the repentant wife Hosea loved,
I will hear their affliction,
Generously will I take them back in love;
For my anger has turned away from them.
Hosea 14:5

V

So it was Hosea the prophet
would impart these last words to Gomer.
And Gomer and the people were now
judged forgiven by Lord YHWH.

JOEL

The Mourning of the Maiden

I

Lament—like a maiden girt with sackcloth
For the husband of her youth.
Joel 1:8

II

A maiden who is not yet married
will mourn a lost spouse like a lost child;
for the spouse lost would have been father
the children she would have shared with him.

III

For after all: the wedded bliss that
they hoped for never came to be in
a lifetime the together shared.
The hazy, hoped for glory of love
is snuffed out like a lighted matchstick—
and dies with potential still unmet—
this is the tragedy for many.

IV

Yet we must have faith in their rebirth;
we must still believe they'll be returned.
When experiencing our losses
we must pour out our broken hearts to
God who will listen to our griefs with
the love of our own parents when we
were children ourselves asking them why
a pet or a friend of ours had died?

V

O friend of Abraham, hear us now,
don't cut down young men not yet married;
for women weep for spouses cut down.
Those who have suffered belong to God,
but those left behind are left mourning.

VI

The Lord will comfort those who have mourned;
for even non-Jews recognize this
while denying rights to those who gave
the truth to them that people must mourn
their losses to then recover them.

The Rejoicing of Israel

I

Gather the people
Bid the congregation purify themselves.
Bring together the old,
Gather the babes
And the sucklings at the breast;
Let the bridegroom come out of his chamber,
The bride from her canopied couch.
Joel 2:15

II

Bring together the Israelites to
pray to Lord YHWH for the mercy
which gave the divine kiss to Moses
when he died in the wilderness where
he was with God alone amongst sands
of Time and Physicality from
which he would cast his bodily shell
and join his Maker in the Heavens.

III

Here below, all of Israel come,
for love draws forth God's forgiveness of
sins committed by Jewish people;
if Jews bond for love of each other
then their Lord YHWH would next forgive
the Jews for any and all sins done
for God loves Jews for the fact they love
each other and God more than themselves.

IV

For unselfishness is a sign of
the true and sincere heart God demands.
Like David a man may have flaws if
his heart shows transformative love for
the God of Israel and the Jews,
the people God sewed within Egypt.

V

Between the portico and the altar,
Let the priests, the Lord's ministers, weep
And say:
"Oh, spare Your people, LORD!
Let not Your possession become a mockery,
To be taunted by nations!
Let not the peoples say,
"Where is their God?"
Joel 2:17

VI

And God hears these words, replying thus,
"To be joined as a people in love
for your God is all that I demand.
You shall be forgiven for your sins."
And the Jews rejoiced with Lord YHWH.
For YHWH though he's strict, loves the Jews.

The Joining of Flesh and Spirit

I

After that,
I will pour out My spirit on all flesh;
Your sons and daughters shall prophesy;
Your old men shall dream dreams,
And your young men shall see visions.
I will ever pour out My spirit
Upon male and female slaves in those days.
Joel 3:1-3:2

II

Both male and female shall than become
one in God's eyes and then there will be
priests who are women themselves praying
for the sake of the Jewish people
and joining the Jews shall be non-Jews,
those kept from the faith because of years
of persecution towards the Jews.

III

This promise overflows the heart of
the Jewish people throughout the earth.
O Lord, we pray for redemption from
You, longing as we do for You to
keep promises made to us while young.
The vision dreamed of by Jews shall be
the uniting of peoples to God.

IV

We pray to our Lord for all time that
the age old dream shall come true for all
and united all humanity
will stand up together as one group
'a little boy shall lead them' with the Jews.

V

The Divine Husband shall than possess
the Soul of Humanity Itself.
And that shall consummate the Jew's dream.

Children Sold into Slavery

I

I will gather all the nations
And bring them down to the Valley of Jehoshaphat.
There I will contend with them
Over My very own people, Israel,
Which they scattered among the nations.
For they divided My land among themselves
And cast lots over My people;
And they bartered a boy as a whore,
And sold a girl for wine, which they drank.
Joel 4:2-4:4

II

"My children," YHWH told the prophet
"Are sold for silver and gold as slaves
but shall be returned back to their home.
The children sold to become the slaves
of other nations serving the whims
of foreign chattel drivers will be
those returned to their parents at last
as humanity's servitude ends.

III

Lost to their parents ages ago
they shall be reunited at last;
the children embracing their parents
shall say, "We are Jews! We have returned
to the land promised to us by God!
At last we're recognized God's children!"

And parents will embrace those children—
the ten tribes themselves shall be returned
to Israel embracing Lord YHWH.

IV

O priestly nation beloved from
where Jews were scattered throughout the earth,
you shall be forgiven for your sins
and your Lord will at last say, "Well done!"

V

O YHWH grant us strength to grasp
your mitzvoth with arms open to You
embracing You like a bird in flight
embraces the sky through which he soars.

VI

Our striving is as imperfect as
the human race yet our love will last
till Judgment Day comes itself from God
for children martyred will be counted
like tzadikim[14] and tzadikoth[15] in
the favor of the Jewish people—
for though they're filled with sorrow they have
still remained true to Lord YHWH.

---

[14] Tzadikim—according to Jewish mysticism there are thirteen "righteous persons" (the translation of the word) on whom the world depends for its exists at any given time. There are many good people, of course, but only thirteen who merit the world's continued existence.

[15] Tzadikot—the female form of Tzadikim.

In Defense of Philistia

I

What is this you are doing to Me, O Tyre, Sidon, and all districts
of Philistia? Are you requiting Me for something for My benefit?
Quick as a flash, I will pay you back;... I will deliver your sons and
daughters into the hands of the people of Judah, and they will sell
them into captivity to a distant nation—for the Lord has spoken.
Joel 4:4; 4:8

II

O Lord, please forgive the Jews our sins
but also those who've persecuted
the Jews as we have forgiven them
as greater criminals have slaughtered
our innocents more than Tyre's people
or even Philistia itself.

III

The menstrual blood's stain on a piece of
cloth which has almost disappeared and
yet it is remembered by some of
the Jewish promise has been made for
them only in place of the Jews while
the Philistines tried to steal the land
but had no interest in killing
or exterminating the people
of Judaism beyond that goal.

IV

God forgive Philistia with us;
Your beloved ones trust Your goodness,
which overflows the Jewish people
and thus can extend even towards
their animals, "A righteous man knows
the needs of his beast" in sharp contrast
to Philistia whom we defend.
For surely Philistia matters
as much as the sheep that we raise for
their wool in the fields, giving up meat.

AMOS

Martyrdom

I

Thus said the LORD:
For three transgressions of the Ammonites
For four, I will not revoke it [the decree of punishment]:
In order to enlarge their own territory.
Amos 1:13

II

God's wrath is upon Ammon because
the children Israel bore her Lord
were slaughtered by the Ammonites with
the pregnant women sliced wide open
to leave both woman and the child dead.

III

These women cried, their lives cut short, with
the same shrill screams of Auschwitz itself,
"Why, O Lord, have You forsaken us?"
And the Lord's answers seemed harsh or vague.

IV

"O Lord," they cried, "Why have You left us,
thus abandoning us to those who
are enemies to Your poor children?"
Those remaining would abstain from sex
till Ammon was through with its cruelties.
These women had been fortunate in
they were not pregnant when the soldiers
of Ammon invaded their country.

V

These atrocities were crimes against
God's chosen people grieved for their loss,
"Why would the Ammonite choose those who
were defenseless, most innocent and
of the least military import to kill?
Yet these same women said to their men
"Spare Ammon's women from the same fate
that Ammon visited on women."

VI

For Ammon's women are like ours were;
They're defenseless, most innocent and
of these least military import to kill.
Do not take an eye for our eye lost.
We ask that instead you show mercy."

VII

So Israel spared Ammon's women
and the Lord sent his blessing down to
the Jewish women who had spoken
as well as those who had been murdered.

VIII

For martyrs for God are blessed because
of their own sufferings, but those who have
saved others from their destruction are
the Oskar Schindler the Lord honors
among Lord YHWH's people themselves.

The Courtesan

I

Father and son go to the same girl,
and therefore profane My holy name.
Amos 2:7:4-5

II

This girl was just like Hosea's wife
as unmarried but a courtesan and
not a street walker who walked the roads
at night in search of customers who
would pay her paltry sums for her soul.

III

This courtesan was thoroughly bad;
but she lived comfortably instead.
Still, she had Gomer's sickness: her pride.
She had no desire to be a wife
and in those days there was no way save
by prostitution or by marriage
for women to be given money.

IV

Now this girl was a courtesan who
would invite lovers to her place who
would pay her bills for expenses she
would insist needed payment for her
in lieu of outright money for her body.
The customers who went to this girl—
there open secret was known to all
and Amos happened to live nearby.

V

This high-class prostitute was colored
like half the pale-faced crescent moon up
in the great starlit night which shines on
the sands near the Dead Sea's salt waters.
This girl was born on the Dead Sea, too;
its toxicity was in her blood;
while beautiful to look at she reeked
of sinful flattery from which she
gained many an old man's wealth so that
the streets of Tekoa were filled with
the same old men's poor orphans with those
who until then were beggars to them.

VI

She wore silks with gold encased gemstones.
She also owned a graven likeness
of the false Queen of Heaven which was
then dedicated to the goddess.
This goddess lounged nude across from those
who owned great wealth and received favors
from this whore obsessed with life and youth;
like legendary vampires she would
have sacrificed all if she could have
than remained beautiful and youthful
but especially wealthy beyond
the grave with her life continuing.

VII

This woman received an old man as
a lover for his great wealth meanwhile
she also seduced the man's own son
aged sixteen for his virility.

VIII

When Amos heard he was shocked and spoke
harsh words to condemn this great insult
to the Lord; father and son with her
a wench whose particular flagrance
was known to all in Tekoah when
the prophet Amos condemned her sins.

Tomorrow

I

Proclaim in the fortress of Ashdod
And in the fortresses of the land of Egypt!
Say:
Gather on the hill of Samaria
And witness the outrages within her
And the oppression in her midst.
Amos 3:8-3:9

II

O Lord You look at the bad in us
but ignore the good; we have good traits
such as our deeply felt love of You.
Our devotion to You has survived
the hardships of the millennia
both within Israel and without.
Search our heart and You will find us kind;
search out our dealings to find us fair;
search out our prayers and find in us
a holiness which translates Your peace
for our peace is our greeting as well
as our way of our bidding adieu.
For love and peace are one both the same
and both flow from You, O Lord YHWH.

III

For tomorrow will lose its sweetness
the further it is deferred until
we sink deep into the grave itself.
God we can't live for tomorrow with
no hopes for good things today itself.

IV

For aspirations and hopes are what
we're made up of in this life besides
the world-to-come that's promised to us.
For without hopes our life will become
a drudgery filled with grief only.
So take us, Lord, as we are today;
we are not made of such rarified stuff
that we can't live with thoughts of today.

Abandonment of Israel

I

Fallen, not to rise again,
Is Maiden Israel;
Abandoned on her soil
With none to lift her up.
Amos 5:2

II

Lord, You have condemned us too quickly
for You have spoken saying that You
would never give up the Jews themselves
"In those days," You said of the future,
"I will make a [great] covenant for
us with the beasts of the fields," but more
"the birds of the air and [then also]
the creeping things of the ground" these things
as witnesses in the place other gods took
in contracts of the nearest itself.

III

You promised the Jews that they'll receive
an "everlasting covenant" with
the Jewish people themselves as we
have finally come to love our God.
Who will pray to You, YHWH, if You
throw the Jews from You as a people?

IV

For the Jews have prayed to You for as
long as there have been Jewish people
and the Jews' suffering has surpassed
the nations persecuting
the Jews as keepers of faith with God.
Lord, there have been more Jewish people
who've sanctified Your name as martyrs
then there are living Jews now today.

V

Lord, act, for we are a small people
and greatly in need of our Lord's help.
Our proof of our Lord's existence is
our very survival when there has
been unmitigated hate towards
Jews expelled from their holy places.

The Love We Crave

I

And so, hear the word of the Lord. You say I must not prophesy
about the House of Israel or preach of Isaac; but this, I swear
, is what the Lord said: Your wife shall play the harlot in the
town, your land be divided up with measuring shall die on
uncleam soil; for Israel shall be exiled from its soil."
Amos 7:16-7:17

II

O do not prophesy to the Jews
these harsh words are hard to bare for us.
We long for rapturous warmth from You,
Lord YHWH's passion when You are pleased
in Your vast overflowing love which
embraces all of humanity.

III

The unfolding heart of God makes up
our desire far from analysis
of the cool head of philosophy
but nearer to the human heartstrings.

IV

For understanding of Lord YHWH
flows through the heart, from Gods to ours
like emanations from the spirit
to the earth's material being.
It may prove impossible to prove
to skeptics that there is a God through reason
but through the heart flows God's words to us.

V

Through doing mitzvoth we move closer
to our God, whose flame consumes without
our being consumed like the bush found
by Moses in the wilderness which
is passionate yet kindly throughout.

VI

This loving being demands our faith
The spirit's chastity as well
as chastity of the flesh which
will translates as its corollary.
For religion is marriage to God;
the faithfulness we crave fulfills
more than a lecher pretends to be
a satisfied man after using
too many others casually for
sex only to than forget their souls.

VII

God demands our hearts abstain from sin;
More! God loves us in purity when
we sacrifice our hearts to the Lord.
Do not speak, prophet, of God being
a strict God; it is God's love we crave.

Broken Bones

I

"And the singing women of the palace shall howl on that day—
--declares the Lord God:
So many corpses
Left lying everywhere!
Hush!"
Amos 8:3

II

O bones which cover the ground itself
like a great Persian carpet stretched out
your coloring is beautifully red
the effect would be startling on one.

III

On the ground, however, you have cursed
the viewers tears of sadness for you
are blood soaked, beaten, and broke beyond
what Jerusalem feels she deserved.
Yet compared to the charred bones left of
both Treblinka and Auschwitz itself
you are a joyous sight which shines bright
in human's blood soaked history with
its carnage and its battles leaving
the tears of widows and their orphans.

IV

O Lord this devastation is great;
why don't You act and intervene for
the sake of those You shoes to call Yours?
Why is it ever more wars plague
the Jewish people despite the fact
of the great loyalty they've shown You?
Why will You not prove You love the Jews?

V

O bleeding bones we bury you with
tears towards the earth preparing us
for worse times coming in the future—
just before redemption comes for us.

JONAH

Jonah's Whale

Ho! Ho! Ho! I am Jonah's great whale.
You wonder how I appeared herein
in a book of the Torah's women
but I am not just whale but woman
a female whale who rides the high waves.
In my life I've birthed many young calves—
but these calves have caused me less pain than
the prophet Jonah in my belly.

II

Now I was called by YHWH so that
I'd swallow this great prophet of wrath
for being derelict as prophet—
for Jonah hated Nineveh with
its history of its crimes against
the Jewish people whom he loved as
he loved his own life and his own god—
but Jonah's love was tainted to God.

III

So Jonah's reconciliation
with YHWH as necessary
as Nineveh's—for Jonah's anger
was the thing separating him from
his being righteous before YHWH.
For even within Israel he
was known for irascibility.
So YHWH wanted me to help with
the educating of the prophet.
Not that God gave me a choice in this.

IV

And when Lord YHWH commands a beast
it has no choice but obedience.
The unmerciful Jonah blamed men
Who needed food and drink to survive
and seemed less devout because of it.

V

Yes, Jonah lacked the common touch with
his insistence of purity in
the Jewish people's ritual practice.
He was the kind of prophet whose prayers
were said while others finished his work
For him as a child respectfully—
as Jonah inspired fear in the hearts
of his peers even as a young age.

VI

So YHWH sent me to meet Jonah
when he gave him an odious task—
to save a sinful, foreign city.
For YHWH knew the prophet would fail
to come through for the Ninevites when
the Jewish YHWH demanded it.

VII

God knew the stubborn pride of Jonah
and Jonah made his escape from God.
Then I and a storm entered his life.
For YHWH cried, "Go, whale, to Jonah!"
and so I went with YHWH driving
me against desires propelling me.

VIII

I groaned to YHWH, "O God, hear me;
Let Jonah go on to his own ruin
and find another prophet to serve
You in the cause of Nineveh as
a people created by You, Lord."

IX

Yet YHWH would not relent in this;
a storm went following the prophet
in the ship escaping LORD YHWH
and I was following that great storm.
The sailors aboard Jonah's small ship
Would eventually discover him.
And afterwards they threw him into
the sea where I lay waiting for him.

X

I opened my mouth wide to let in
Not the krill which is a whale's diet
but Jonah himself—a whole human—
and so he entered my large belly,
that part of the whale where krill are held
till they are digested as my food.

XI

And both he and I suffered greatly—
it was as though I had a rock tied up
in my throat causing swallowing to
be made as painful for me myself
as the threat of his digestion was
a painful threat to Jonah himself.

XII

And Jonah cried to me, "O great fish
let me out of your belly so both
you and I can breathe freely again."
I answered, "Without permission from
your LORD I cannot let go of you.
I wish I could but God took my will;
For it hurts me to hold you inside—
Yet physically I am controlled
if temporarily by YHWH.

XIII

So Jonah realized the need to talk
to YHWH and not to me—the whale—
He said:
In my trouble I called the LORD,
And He answered me;
From the belly of Sheol I cried out,
And You heard my voice.
They who cling to empty folly
Forsake their own welfare,
But I, with loud thanksgiving,
Will sacrifice to You;
What I have vowed I will perform
Deliverance is the LORD's!
Jonah 2:3; 2:9-2:10

XIV

Lord YHWH caused me to spit him out!
This relieved us both: Jonah and me.
And so the prophet Jonah traveled
to meet his destiny as prophet
in Nineveh—a reluctant one
not like the prophet Moses plagued by
doubts of his ability to lead
but strangled by his arrogance till
at Nineveh he learned to be meek.

XV

When he went back to Israel he
was never guided by pride again.
By Jonah's death he saw good in men—
and women—and the natural world.

XVI

For YHWH would tell Jonah these words,
"And should not I care about Nineveh, that great city, in which there
are more than a hundred and twenty thousand persons who do not
yet know their right hand from their left, and many beasts as well."
Jonah 4:11

XVII

With these words YHWH thus included
the animal world itself as part
and parcel of God's creation which
is important to the Lord YHWH—
including I, the prophet's great whale!

MICAH

The Transgressions of Samaria

I

All this is for the transgressions of Jacob,
And for the sins of the House of Israel.
What is the transgression of Jacob
But Samaria,
And what the shrines of Judah
But Jerusalem?
Micah 1:5

II

O Lord, how can You not see our love?
For we have waited upon You, Lord,
in our hearts we've embraced You YHWH,
like a child on his dying Father
we wait on You our undying God—
for Abraham rests with You, O Lord—
we trust in You or reunion with
our ancestors from ages ago.

III

The Samaritan places from which
we pray are devoted to prayers
said by those who can't travel to them
from Israel to Jerusalem.
We do not understand the sin here.

So I will turn Samaria
Into a ruin in the open country,
Into ground for planting vineyards;
For I will tumble her stones into the valley
And lay her foundations bare.
Micah 1:6

V

Ah! Lord You are harsh with Your children;
we plead on behalf of the land which
is the bride of God, Israel, who
will initiate God's reign on earth.
We love our land next to You only;
we love her because she is Your gift
and also Judaism's mother.
Don't destroy our open country
or uproot vineyards we live upon.
Do not strip us like tree of their bark,
till exposed skin can't survive because
the tree's held together by its 'skin.'

All her sculptured images shall be smashed,
And all her harlot's wealth be burned,
And I will make a waste heap of her idols,
For they were amassed from fees for harlotry,
And they shall become harlots' fees again.
Micah 1:7

VII

Ah, Lord we shall smash our own sculptures
for we will prove to You that You rule
us totally and not just partly
in our hearts and our synagogues, too.

VIII

Yes we shall take and smash the Baal;
El the Bull shall go also with him;
so, too, will Asherah and Anat,
the mother goddess and her daughter.
Athough they're potent symbols, to us
mean nothing compared to Lord YHWH.

IX

The God which is what existed first.
Your name's "I will be what I will be,"
the self-defining God in each will choose
in each new generations what God is
and how God relates to us as well.
This is the Bible's secret meaning;
that God will exist with us now as
God has in the pasted existed, too.
For the Lord's spirit suffuses life.

Faith Stripped Naked

I

Because of this I will lament and wail;
I will go stripped and naked!
I will lament as sadly as the jackals,
As mournfully as the ostriches.
For her wound is incurable,
It has reached Judah,
It has speared to the gate of my people,
To Jerusalem.
Micah 1:8-1:9

II

"I, Micah, walk stripped naked for God,"
the prophet Micah declared himself,
"I am like David when he conquered
the city Jerusalem with the great Arc.
Saul's daughter condemned David because
he 'displayed his flesh indecently,'
yet it's his model that I have copied
in displaying Lord YHWH's anger."
So Micah became what in Russia
is called a 'fool for God,' the madmen
who love their God in aberrant ways.

III

For just as David danced half naked
in front of the Arc dedicated
to YHWH from the time of Moses
so Micah displayed himself for God
by acting outside Israel's norm.

IV

O holy fool stripped naked for God!
For Judaism honors its fools
as madness becomes inspiration.
In Micah's nudity is displayed
the fool God demands in God's prophet.

Birth

I

Now why do you utter such cries?
Is there no king in you,
Have your advisors perished,
That you have been seized by writhing
Like a woman in travail?
Micah 4:9-4:10:2

II

We cry, O Lord, for mistreatment at
Your hands as tyrannical as if
You were an abusive spouse Yourself.
Yet our own writhing creates a birth;
You Yourself allude to this "travail,"
the pain of giving birth to an age
with grandparents and parents, there, too,
and then our spouses with our children;
one reunion in heaven itself.

III

There will be more, of course: long dead friends
and children who died when they were young.
Food will be eaten; besides people
a person's faithful pets will be there.
It will be one great banquet glowing
with happiness and mirthfulness, too.
In this age the Jew's sufferings shall
be redeemed so that Jewish people
will forget how they suffered when they
lived in a 'veil of tears' in this life.

IV

Although this life is full of joys as
well as its sadnesses, life for Jews
so often filled with martyrdom's cup
of bitterness is like the Dead Sea,
too salty to drink without God's help.
So Jewish survival is helped by our Lord.

V

Indeed, many nations
Have assembled against you
Who think, "Let our eye
Obscenely gaze on Zion."
Micah 4:11

VI

But little do the nations suspect
Your plans, O Lord, for both us and them.
You shall come to Your beloved's aid,
just when it appears that our foes are
an invincible army fighting
as one in spirit towards the Jews.
We wait for this brief moment in time;
we exult as we fear for our lives.

VII

But they [the nations] do not know
The design of the Lord,
They do not divine His intent
He has gathered them to threshing floor.
Micah 4:12

VIII

The Lord shall conquer all on this day,
and those who are the conquered shall be
the enemies of the Jews themselves
but the fight shall be carried out by
the Israelite men themselves at war.

IX

Up and thresh, Fair Zion!
For I will give you horns of iron
And provide you with hoofs of bronze,
And you will crush the many peoples.
You will devote their riches to the Lord,
Their wealth to the Lord of the earth.
Micah 4:13

X

And Israel shall rise in triumph;
the Lord of Israel will rise them
up onto a great plateau in love;
and many nations shall then convert
but voluntarily not through force.

XI

O Israel shall finally be
a people glorified with their God
the great king of the nations on earth.

XII

For Israel is completed through
Lord YHWH acting as yeast in bread
and humankind is fed through the bread.

In the Name of Miriam

I

"My people!
What wrong have done you?
What wrong have I caused you?
Testify against Me.
In fact,
I brought you up from the house of bondage,
And I sent before you
Moses, Aaron, and Miriam."
Micah 6:3-6:4

II

We beg to know how we could deserve
such dreadful suffering at *Your* hands.
The night of Auschwitz haunts our nightmares
those dark dreams filling the heads of Jews
when the stars overhead are blocked out
by city smog where Jews now live now.
Our souls cry out to those lost to us
at Treblinka and Buchanwald with
our cleaving not just our Lord YHWH
but to them as well in their ashes.

III

For all death diminishes the world
most especially untimely death,
the death that's unnatural, man-made.
We remember the tale of Eden
when God had created the idyll
which is yet destined to be the end
of the blessed born to humankind with
its beginning portrayed innocence which
is remembered with nostalgia still.

IV

This bliss will reach out for the devout
in ages past and future as though
it is a taste of what waits for the blessed.
In the name of the prophetess we
beg for an explanation from You.

V

We long for the Lord's redemption from
the evils we have suffered through time;
but we want to know 'why' we suffered
still more when suffering seems so vast.

VI

Ah, Lord, give us our desire and we
will repent all of our sins that day!
For it is bewildered and hurt that
we feel, not angry at our lost Lord.

Who Can Direct Her?

I

Hark! The Lord
Summons the city:
For who can direct her
... but you?
Micah 6:9:2-6:10:1

II

Who can direct Lady Jerusalem
but her Lord with whom she finds comfort?
You, O Lord, mold us like a potter
with a clay pot smoothed out in Your hands,
for we wish to be caressed into
the gentle roundness found in statures
of the Earth Venuses in Europe.
This Venus is a mother figure
So it is thought that mothers like pots
will carry life in the hot desert;
for water is life itself to drink.

III

For after all, the Jewish People
bare the seed for the salvation of
the world which persecutes them itself.
The Lord gives Judaism the seed
from which the flower of faith bursts forth.

The Deaths of Infants

I

You have been eating without getting her fill,
And there is a gnawing at your vitals;
You have been conceiving young,
And what you bore I would deliver to the sword.
Micah 6:14

II

The pain of birth when the child has died
is beyond measure to the mother
as the child gives up its ghost to God
but leaves the mother's contractions which
have resembled a watermelon
that goes through a small lemon-size hole.

III

O God you've made birth suffering to
the physically weaker gender.
For men have suffered, but the birth pangs
of womankind have dogged at their heels
as survivor would rely on births
in larger numbers because most died.
It was a lucky person who lived
till their adulthood and we insist
that these young mothers mourned each stillborn
as attested to in the graveyards
where children's bodies lie in the earth.

IV

O Lord this is a punishment which
is terrible to consider and
we love these infants who died too soon.
Lord, we cling to You so that You will
give back our children who have died young;
for little children return to God.
Give us our infants back when we die;
for their loss is a great test of faith.

V

The picture of the child who died young
lies on the mantle of the house as
a testament to the love given
to them by the old lady who keeps
the picture until eighty years old.
But after this same lady has died;
she will meet the child she lost while young.

God Remembers Those Who Give to Bums

I

Woe is me!
Micah 7:1:1

II

"O Lord," said Samaria, "You have
drenched the land in the blood of martyrs
who died while little children themselves!
O Lord, though this is the fate of more
of the world's children than those who live—
or was this way in distant times past—
we can't accept a single one's death.

III

Yet this is not Your fault only, our God.
We refuse to say that we've not failed
to do more for those who need whether
those who are starving because of food
or sufferers of diseases which
like plague or AIDs kills its millions.

III

Half of the world still starves while the other
stands guilty if it will not act so
that it is complicit in their deaths.
Yet perhaps the key is in what's said:
for perhaps God made people so that
they could help others in times of need.

IV

By giving others from our hearts we
will redeem humanity for God.
In this sole respect homeless people
must be ones honored as if they were
the hidden tzaddikim who have searched
not for food but for merit itself.
To give is a great blessing from God.
God remembers those who give to bums.

V

This is what God made humanity
in order to have us do for him:
to remember if you save one soul
you may save a world—and you don't know
just whom that one soul may be or when
they will come out of hiding to find
you in your apathy to involve
you in your task God granted to you.

Alone

I

Trust no friend,
Rely on no intimate;
Be guarded in speech
With her who lies in your bosom.
Micah 7:5

II

O Lord why tear us from our brethren
whom we love in this temporal world?
For to love another soul deeply
is to live, blossoming in this life.
The purpose of life is love itself—
to love and be loved, both with our Lord,
but also with his creation, too.

III

God bids us enjoy our life's loves—
both Platonic and intimate loves—
so that we will find fulfillment in
the pleasure of our affections which
will outlast our deaths themselves at last.

III

For even the Greeks knew that friendship
will outlast all things including time.
For immortality's based on love.
Don't deny to Your servants this love.
How can we become separated
from friends as beloved as our lives.

IV

For son spurns father,
Daughter rises up against your mother,
Daughter-in-law against mother-in-law
A man's own household
Are his enemies.
Micah 7:6

V

O Lord, this is too much to bare as
our family is divided with
the group split down the middle itself
with right and left both warring against
each other over the land itself.

VI

O precious harmony in between
the family which loves each other!
This filial love is what Jews want
in exchange for the love of their God,
a tenderness of the Jews' spirits.
O Lord why did you bring us chaos?

VII

Yet I will look to the Lord,
I will wait for the God who saves me,
My God will hear me.
Micah 7:7

VIII

Yet despite our pain we speak as one,
"As long as the Lord rests in our hearts
we'll have no loneliness in spirit."

NAHUM

Untitled

I

He [God] commands his burly men;
They stumble as they advance,
They hasten up to her wall,
Where wheeled shelters are set up.
Nahum 2:6

II

O Lord, You who climb up the walls of
the city Jerusalem itself
and pursue her as though she were
a hunted wife tracked by a husband
as jealous as a dog which defends
bared teeth like the teeth table saws have.
You, whose lust for us is like the night
of a man with his virgin bride whom
he calls his partner whether sick or healthy.

III

O Lord why not speak tenderly to
your people, the Bride of Lord YHWH.
You ravish her like a mere harlot;
You treat her like the scum of the earth.
How, O Lord, can You be so cruel to
your people despite their love for You?
How can Your cherished wife play the role
of victim towards the God she loves?
O Lord do not send armies to her.
Send us peace with Your love and Your grace.

ZEPHANIAH

Untitled

I

Is this the gay city [Nineveh]
That dwelt secure,
That thought in her heart,
"I am there is none but me"?
Alas, she is become a waste,
A lair of wild beasts!
Everyone who passes by her
Hisses and gestures by her.
Zephaniah 2:15

II

O Nineveh, who ignored the Lord—
did you come to be one who ignored
the rights of other people as well?
For to say "there is none but me" is
to imply isolation outside
of God, it's to make yourself into
an idol for those yourself.

III

You say "I am God" to other people.
It is to be self-centered towards
those outside yourself claiming for you
"I am God; you are merely mortal,"
for even Eastern religions have
so denied selfishness to be good
that they call it the evil which trumps
all evil: the worst thing to be called
in Japan is summed up in "selfish"
a "selfish" person being the one
who puts the good of himself before
the good of others, practicing God—
while admitting they may call what we
call our God something besides their "God."

IV

But Nineveh would not see God in
Those people they had conquered and killed.
They would not recognize these people
as having feelings, thoughts, rights, because
they only love their arrogance with
no consideration of their crimes.
This is why she is punished by God.

Untitled

I

O Nineveh here your deeds are named.
She has been disobedient
Has learned no lesson;
She has not trusted in the Lord,
Has not drawn near to her God.
Zephaniah 3:2

II

Ah Lord! Says Nineveh, our leaders
have taken us in directions which
are just and promote virtue abroad
the military virtues are what
we believe grant us power so they
are what we promote in our conquests;
for severity is what we use
to dominate those conquered by us.

III

We, razing off our enemies heads
at the gates the cities conquered
by us in the names of those gods whom
we worship, have thus acted justly,
in the names of the power and greed
we've acquired by our mighty conquests.

IV

The official within her
Are roaring lions;
Her judges are wolves of the steppe
They leave no bone until morning.
Zephaniah 3:3

V

The merchants are full and bring plenty
while keeping profit for the king's bank.
This is how Assyria will take
its money to be managed so as
to enrich Assyria's wealthy
while its poor become vultures for bread.

VI

Our priests have assured us that
Her prophets are reckless,
Faith fellows;
Her priests profane what is holy,
They give perverse rulers.
Zephaniah 3:4

ZECHARIAH

Untitled

I

Away, escape O Zion, you who dwell in Fair Babylon!
Zechariah 2:11

II

O Zion, stand tall: Babylon's looks
are skin deep. Underneath them there lurks
the evil of a diseased spirit
and such a spirit's success can't last;
the earth's scum sinks to down the bottom
of the great ocean far from the coast.

III

What disguises this ugliness is
the glory of large armies along
with piles of money collected by
those armies themselves from the people.
There is no goodness lying in this.
O Zion do not weep; God will come.
It will not be wealth that brings the Lord;
it will not be your army, either.

Untitled

I

Shout for joy, Fair Zion!
For lo, I come; and I will dwell in your midst—declares the Lord.
Zechariah 2:14
Your beauty, says the Lord, lies within.

II

[An]… angel who talked with me came forward and said, "Now look up and note the object approaching I asked, "What is it?" And he said, "This tub that is approaching—this," said he, "is their eye in all the land." And behold, a disk of lead was lifted, revealing a woman inside the tub. "That," he said, "is Wickedness"; and, thrusting her down into the tub, he pressed the leaden weight into its mouth.
Zechariah 4:5-4:8

III

The woman, Wickedness, was a nag
like a horse with her black teeth decayed
mud covered fur and yellow eyes, too.

IV

This creature's grimy appearance was
matched with the kind of lust cats have when
they are in heat, but for things which are
more unsavory—the thrill Aztecs
got when they sacrificed to their gods
with human hearts, while reassuring
both themselves and the victims that those
who were then sacrificed to the gods

would join these gods in paradise and
whose female personification
is opposite of regal Virtue's,
who resembles her only in that
she's portrayed as a goddess as well.

V

O goddesses at war in the heart
With admirable instincts fighting
the despicable urges within.
O wickedness with witch's brooms made
of wood and straw for riding at night—
on Hallows Eve for non-Jews who still
have insisted on believing in
the magical thought of a past age
when most of humankind was itself
still largely illiterate itself.

VI

*I looked up again and saw two women come soaring with the
wind in their wings—they have wings like a stork—and carry
off the tub between earth and sky. Where are they taking
the tub?" I asked the angel who talked with me. And he
answered, "To build a shrine for it in the land of... Babylonia;
[a stand] shall be set down there upon the stand."*
Zechariah 5:9-5:11

VII

O Wickedness builds up for itself
a castle decadent and splendid
in Babylonia with remains
from what the Lord has left it with when
its ability to thrive is gone.

Are There no Prophets?

I

Look, this is the message that the Lord proclaimed through
the earlier prophets, when Jerusalem and the prophets, when
Jerusalem and the towns about her were peopled and tranquil,
when the Negeb and the Shephelah were peopled.
Zechariah 7:7

II

O Lord, are there no prophets today?
No female Miriams nor Debrahs
with Moseses and Isaiahs as
where are the pious female prophets
who make the Jewish Spirit complete?
Why are the women left out today?
Where's Miriam in today's shul now?
those described as blessed within the scrolls?

III

O holy fools for their Lord YHWH!
Would that they speak to us once again!
Once Moses spoke that "Would that all be
such as these" regarding two living
as Israelites who were called prophets.

IV

In spite of unorthodoxy in
their teachings Moses called them holy.
So, too, the Jewish philosopher
in often within the faith's left wing:
for Maimonides *Guide For the Perplexed*
and is the voice of modern prophets
hailed, the poets of the faithful themselves.
Yet this work was his classic defense
of Judaism and Monotheism.

III

Then Spinoza turned against his roots.
These unorthodox thinkers
could have been modeled on its prophets.
Their idiosyncrasies were those
of the faith they were born to as Jews;
they bore Lord YHWH within their heart.

IV

Born to a race of prophets they spoke
alike from their heads and hearts for God;
for both lived and died believing in
a God they discovered for themselves—
just as the prophets recovered God
and discovered what they claimed had been
a forgotten yet ancient folkway
with its God at its creedal center.

V

O YHWH, send us prophets today
so Jews can be once again reborn.

Untitled

I

And the word of the Lord to Zechariah continued... Do not defraud the widow, the orphan, the stranger, and the poor; and do not plot evil against each other.
Zechariah 7:8; 7:10

II

O Lord, these souls are given to us
in trust so that if we love the Lord
we must love them in the place of God.
For when we see Lord YHWH's likeness:
it's what shines through to us in people
who are now unfortunate themselves.

III

If suffering is the poor's burden,
than luckier souls have a duty
to ease the pain they experience.
This is the case till suffering ends—
while duty demands our small part be
done towards redeeming our world with
the compassion which extends to those
with less wealth than the givers possess.

IV

For just as when the tabernacle
cost money Israel had gathered in coins,
with each soul as one single shekel,
so the world's salvation should remain
the goal of Jewish people today
so as to bring the messiah on
the Day of Judgment, wooing the Lord
to bring the age old dream to our earth.

V

On that day, God's name shall be One, yet,
we also know that on that day we
will all be good or all be bad with
none of the people on earth shall be
in between—those who're Jews or non-Jews.

VI

We are those tested regarding what
we're capable of morally and
we will get rewarded or punished
in accordance with our deeds in life.

VII

O Lord, grant us that we are worthy
to be blessed with our prophet Moses,
that 'You called him a righteous servant.'
We long to be judged worthy of You;
for righteousness is what we have craved.

The Lord's Love is Impassioned

I

*Thus said the Lord of Hosts: I am jealous for
Zion, I am fiercely jealous for her.*
Zechariah 8:2

II

O Lord, we feel Your love burn for us
the unconsuming fire of the bush
where Moses in the wilderness found
the God of Abraham, the slaves' God.
Like the great unconsummated flame
where Moses met God for the first time
we have found ourselves too close to You.

III

Your possession of Your bride, the Soul,
of humankind, is feverish with
a husband's desire for his first wife—
for a good husband for his dear spouse
will transcend sexuality itself—
just as the Lord is revealed as though
the physical world's boundaries prove
that they are malleable to Spirit.

IV

O gentle, fiery Spirit called now!
O Being beneath existence Who
　　loves all but egoistically—
if such a word can be used so that
it connotes something positive which
will admit deep love in its response,
a possessive and strong-willed passion
which demands surrender in others
　　but one exalting the meek over
　　the hubris of the mighty on earth.

V

O Jealous Husband Who is our God
for whom we are His beloved spouse!
　　Your love is intensely felt by us.
The love sex pales before Your love,
　　that godly passion of the devout
which we get a mere taste on Shabbat.

VI

In song we glorify our God on
　　those Saturdays just before going
back home to study or sleep at night
　　in the old Yiddish tradition with
　　the afternoon rest of the Sabbath.

VII

*Thus said the Lord: I have returned to Zion, and I will dwell
in Jerusalem. Jerusalem will be called the City of Faithfulness,
　and the mount of the Lord of Hosts the Holy Mount.*
Zechariah 8:3

O Grandmothers

I

Thus said the Lord of Hosts: there shall be old men and women in the squares of Jerusalem, each with staff in hand because of their great age. And the squares of the city shall be crowded with boys and girls playing in the squares.
Zechariah 8:4-8:5

II

The aged have a place in the heart
of children and vice versa because
it is the person who is old who
tells the tales by which they live their lives
when his adulthood remembered those
who when they were young were too frail to
work as the ones whose old age tired them.

III

At the same time they produced children's
first taste of death with grandparents dead.
"O Grandma telling wonder tales to
your beloved child at ten years,"
cries the child in love with her Grandma.

IV

"Your death is my first childhood loss and
I always recall you as others
work, fixing breakfast or then going
out during market days to sells goods.
While others work the grandparents will
tell the tales their own grandparents told
and accumulate many Talmuds
worth of tales kept for generations
in families as treasured relics.
These relics will link antiquity
to eternity in space which is
both infinite in infinite time."

V

"The Jewish sages taught that these tales
had begun with the Mosaic laws
and were passed down till written upon
the parchment derived of soft sheepskin.
This lore was handed generation
to generation, a whole intact,
yet never written down in theory."

VI

The lore pours God's grace to his children
the humankind when unable to
look heavenward to comprehend God.
The universe was created with
the Torah used as its map and guide.
The map of our great universe is
so mirrored in each tiny Midrash
and pious fairytale told a Jew.

Misused Wealth

I

Tyr has amassed itself a fortress;
She has amassed silver like dust,
And gold like the mud on the street.
Zechariah 9:3

II

O wealth of Tyr! The city which loaned gold
to Israel's King Solomon to
build Jerusalem's Temple beside
King Solomon's great Palace nearby.
These massive structures owe to Hiram
their existence in Israel with
King Hiram (Solomon's friend) acting
as the one bankrolling the building—
of Palaces and Temple built to
act in their glorifying YHWH.

III

Yet Tyr would remain pagan themselves;
there was no conversion to God's ways.
For indeed, it was not the Lord who
had wanted there to be a Temple;
its purpose was for human beings
not Divine Need if such a thing Be.

IV

O Lord the Laws You gave us You gave
us for our sake as human beings;
they glorify You when they are kept.
But my Lord will impoverish her;
He will defeat her forces at sea,
And she herself shall be consumed by her.
Zechariah 9:4

V

For public works like Temples are not
good enough to gain salvation as
a person must be honest, just, chaste
and kind but it helps to have a heart
with mirth and laughter along with these.

The Lord's Victory

I

Rejoice greatly, Fair Zion;
Raise a shout, Fair Jerusalem!
Lo, your king is coming to you.
He is victorious, triumphant,
Yet humble, riding on an ass.
Zechariah 9:9

II

O Lord! Your messenger speaks for You.
He will come entering the city
of Jerusalem on a donkey.
O son of David, fresh from battle,
the day of Jerusalem shall come.
On that day Victory shall come to
greet the Jews at last at the end of time
and then the devout will sing to God,

III

"All of these ages we have waited
with anticipation and with dread
for the Lord reconciliation
with humankind as Judgment is held
on human beings living on earth
the blessed will be those resurrected
the irredeemably bad shall lie
for eternity in the dust of
that emptiness which pervading space
is unsoiled matter from which life was
dreamed of in the past ages before
the Big Bang itself exploded out."

IV

This creation was for those humans
on our earth to be born for waiting
the thousand millennia in which
the spiritual realm contracted and
gave birth to physicality which
would house the evolution of us—
as Jews and non-Jews both to Lord YHWH.

Untitled

I

The LORD their God shall prosper them
On that day;
[He shall pasture] His people like sheep.
[They shall be] like crown jewels glittering on His soil.
How lovely, how beautiful they shall be,
Producing young men like new grain,
Young women like new wine!
Zechariah 9:16-9:17

II

The beauty of the Jew shall become
a proverbial expression as
'the man of sorrow' becomes the man
whose beauty shines from within outwards.
"O Beloved Child," You seem to cry,
"Among the many Jews, young and strong,
I will pour into you my essence;
like a cup you shall be filled with God."

III

Lord, once we are filled with You within
we shall be beautiful in our deeds.
We shall then radiate Your goodness.
Or so we hope in what we risk as
the egotism of a rich miser;
for we run the risk of our lording
our riches—You're our riches over
those people ignorant of Your ways
and keeping You to ourselves only—
in both harsh treatment of our converts
and indifference to those outside
of the faith who have suffered greatly.

IV

This beauty transforms the Jews themselves
from being ordinary outside
to beautiful deep within our souls.

The Compassion of the Lord

I

*In that day I will annihilate all the nations that came up
against Jerusalem. But I will fill the House of David with a
spirit of pity and compassion; and they will lament to Me
about those who are slain, wailing over them as a favorite
son and showing bitter grief as over a first born.*
Zechariah 12:9-12:11

II

O Lord! the prophet Zechariah
has spoken truly regarding us!
We've mourned the loss of enemies who
we fought as ferociously at war
as though we were the lions hunting
down beasts of prey in Africa's heat.
We fight whom we love; for we love all,
though we love family first friends next
and other Jews next before strangers;
for to love forms a relationship.

III

We can love or fail to love when we
first meet each other in the street and
yet only those in relationship
can love each other—despite this, though—
an enemy who suffers a wound
will enter into relationship
with the man who could capture or kill
the casualty who lies on the ground.

IV

To carry wounded soldiers from us—
this is love of the active kind which
the Lord bids that his children should love
in this way human as a whole group.

Forgive the Horse and his Riders

I

The land shall wail, each family by itself: the family of the House
of David by themselves, and their womenfolk by themselves;
the family of the House of Nathan by themselves and their
women by themselves; the family of the Shimeites by themselves
and their women by themselves; and all the other families,
every family by itself, and their women by themselves.
Zechariah 12:12-12:14

II

Yes, women particularly sang
like Miriam at the Sea of Reeds
but with a different cause by far—
they sang to their Lord, "O Lord forgive
the horse and rider in the sea crossed
by the Jews on the way to Canaan.

III

"Give Pharaoh's soldiers another chance
to be good and so return to God—
as returning to our Lord amounts
to splinters of the Divine joining
God in the everlasting glory—
and outlasting the universe from
whence these small splinters become free souls."

Parents of the False Prophets

I

In that day, too—declares the Lord of Hosts—I will erase the very names of from the land; they shall not be uttered anymore. And I will also make the "prophets" and the unclean spirits vanish from the land. If anyone "prophecies" thereafter, his own father and mother... will say to him, "You shall die, for you have lied in the name of the LORD."... and his own father and mother will put him to death.
Zechariah 13:2-13:3

II

O brutal Lord Who places the love
of parents beneath that of YHWH—
Although our God is Father to us
it seem so unnatural to stone
a person who was one's own infant
the nestling bundle at the breast of
one's mother or the small child dandled
on the knee of it's father with love.

III

The Lord, we know, is as fond of us
but parentage's bond lays claims that
are holy and the parents honor
their infants with their hoary old men:
they're the prize displayed naked at birth
and fondly they're embraced by parents.
Can even murder cut down parental love?

IV

Are undeserving children able
to still be replaced like teeth and gums
which have so rotted without the care
of modern dentistry's own advice?
Although they're diseased what they are not
is replaceable to their parents.

MALACHI

Malachi's Great Love

I

Because the Lord is a witness between you and the wife
of your youth with whom you have broken faith, though
she is your partner and covenanted spouse.
Malachi 3:14

II

"O Lord," cried Malachi to his God,
"I left a woman once long ago
to hear of her years later, married.
I pondered how the act was wicked
but more I wondered, jealousy why
I left the beautiful maid now gone
and married to a second man who
would probably not be told about
our engagement a few years after
I left while promising her silence
to all save my Lord in the heavens."

III

"She was the first to see You gift to
Your servant Malachi—yet we could
not remain together; our fights drove
our lasting bodies but kept us from
a lasting which could relationship
lead to a real-life marriage that was happy.
She became shrewish and I sullen.
Yet it was when our blissful longing
were one day released that we realized
it was time to part—without children."

The Love of Man and Woman, Human and God

I

*Did not the One make [all,] so that all the life breath is His? And
what does that One seek but godly folk? So be careful of your life-
breath, and let no one break faith with the wife of one's youth.*
Malachi 3:15

II

The human being's life breath is both
that human's essence united with
Lord YHWH of All humanity,
our God's love such that it flows downwards
to flowers decked out in their petals
in golds and red with emerald leaves.

III

But human beings become one flesh
in marriage to one another, too.
This relationship mirrors that of
God to God's bride, the Jewish people
who stand in for all humanity.
The Divine Bridegroom enshrines his wife.
That said, the husband places his wife
on a great pedestal he constructs.

Prologue: Eve Gives Birth to the Golem
Eve entangled with this world's Chaos birthed
a monster with whom she could overthrow
both her man and her rival Lilith, too.
For though the Chaos destabilizes
God's created world the world formed from it—
which energizes but then disobeys
the Divine Lawgiver who gave Life
and made Light in the darkness of First Night.
Yet Woman felt left out and fought the Man
and Lilith, the Man's nightmare who reached out
to strangle Eve as Adam's second wife
on Cain's cruel altar where he slaughtered one
who was his brother, Abel, despite poor Eve's pleas.
Yet Eve, raped by the Chaos, birthed Golem,
the ancestor of Prague's great pogroms where
the legend foretells Europe's Holocaust
and remained whispered in the darkness then.
The Golem supposedly would save the Jews,
from non-Jews murdering their infants on
the bayonets around guarded camps.
Yet the light in the darkness—it was God.
The sacrifices of the victims' lips
rose to the Heavens for their messiah.
Yet the good loved the Jews though there was hate,
the hate of the great monster made of clay which
was nothing but an inhuman man.
These multiple births monstrous and strange
as anything that came in ages past
came to the Germans, Russians, Chinese, too—
in ideologies that other times
would consider mad, bad, and dangerous.
Yet Golems don't die peacefully in bed.
They raise hell when they can when others sleep
and by the light of day cling shadowlike

to walls where no one notices them.
The murderous men doing Hitler's work—
or Stalin's—or Mao Tse-Tung's—hide till night
when civilization has crashed to earth.
And Eve—Eve cries for humankind at night—
for though she birthed the Golem in huge pain
the labor was that which she regretted
as humankind was firstborn to poor Eve.
She witnessed Europe's twilight hours in grief
when murderers stalked the streets openly
and Russian soil was soaked red with blood—
of Russia, Ukraine, Poland, Hungary—
the entire Eastern Block kept in chains—
while the cruel disease within China took
the blood of millions in their unmarked graves.
The war drums beat and humankind
drank from the Cup of Death and strewn along
the rubble there were corpses unburied.
O Amos said to fear when Justice reigns
for saints gone mad with evil ideas
are all that monsters sometimes need to be
and what comes before a fall sometimes is
a grandiose scheme—made "for humankind."
A builder of dreams needs to know not to
go destroying with no plan, so that when
the cathedral of civilization
is gone, the wounds he leaves bleed life away
in ashes Europe's plague was worthy of.
The wounds gape open of the patient who
has surgeons who are irresponsible.
O monsters of Eve—What Hath She Wraught Now?

CPSIA information can be obtained
at www.ICGtesting.com
Printed in the USA
LVHW080719070422
715582LV00016B/215/J